Body Psychotherapy

In the past the practice of body psychotherapy has been taken less seriously in professional circles than more traditional psychotherapeutic approaches.

Body Psychotherapy redresses the balance, offering insights into a spectrum of approaches within body-orientated psychotherapy. A range of experienced contributors introduce new areas of development and emerging theory and clinical material, covering:

- The history of body psychotherapy
- Theoretical perspectives on body psychotherapy, including post-Reichian and development of integrative methodologies
- Body psychotherapy in practice, including applications for trauma and regression
- The future for body psychotherapy

This book shows how body psychotherapy can be healing, reparative and rewarding. It will make essential reading for postgraduates and professionals, whether they are already involved in this field, or wish to learn more about incorporating it into their own practice.

Tree Staunton is a UKCP registered Body Psychotherapist who worked for some years as a trainer, group leader and supervisor at the Chiron Centre for Body Psychotherapy, West London and now works as an independent consultant. She has previous experience working in the National Health Service as an Occupational Therapist and holds a BA degree in Conflict Resolution and Group Studies.

Contributors: Rose Cameron, Roz Carroll, Bernd Eiden, Margaret Landale, Babette Rothschild, Andrew Samuels, Nick Totton, Philippa Vick, Roger J. Woolger.

Advancing Theory in Therapy. Series Editor: Keith Tudor.

Advancing Theory in Therapy
Series Editor: Keith Tudor

Most books covering individual therapeutic approaches are aimed at the trainee/student market. This series, however, is concerned with *advanced* and *advancing* theory, offering the reader comparative and comparable coverage of a number of therapeutic approaches.

Aimed at professionals and postgraduates, *Advancing Theory in Therapy* will cover an impressive range of theories. With full reference to case studies throughout, each title will

- present cutting-edge research findings
- locate each theory and its application within its cultural context
- develop a critical view of theory and practice

Titles in series

Body Psychotherapy
Edited by Tree Staunton

Transactional Analysis: A Relational Perspective
Helena Hargaden and Charlotte Sills

Body Psychotherapy

Edited by Tree Staunton

BRUNNER-ROUTLEDGE
ALERE FLAMMAM
Taylor & Francis Group

First published 2002 by Brunner-Routledge
27 Church Road, Hove, East Sussex BN3 2FA

Simultaneously published in the USA and Canada
by Taylor & Francis Inc
29 West 35th Street, New York, NY 10001

Brunner-Routledge is an imprint of the Taylor & Francis Group

© 2002 Edited by Tree Staunton

Typeset in Times by RefineCatch Limited, Bungay, Suffolk
Printed and bound in Great Britain by
Biddles Ltd, Guildford and King's Lynn
Cover design by Sandra Heath

British Library Cataloguing-in-Publication Data
A catalogue record for this book is available from the British Library

Library of Congress Cataloging-in-Publication Data
Body psychotherapy / edited by Tree Staunton.
     p. cm.—(Advancing theory in therapy)
     Includes bibliographical references and index.
     ISBN 1-58391-115-4—ISBN 1-58391-116-2 (pbk.)
     1. Mind and body therapies. 2. Mind and body.
     3. Psychotherapy. I. Staunton, Tree, 1955– . II. Series.
  RC489.M53 B636 2002
  616.89'14—dc21   2001043873

ISBN 1-58391-115-4 (hbk)
ISBN 1-58391-116-2 (pbk)

Contents

Series preface

This series focuses on advanced and advancing theory in psychotherapy. Its aims are: to present theory and practice within a specific theoretical orientation or approach at an advanced, postgraduate level; to advance theory by presenting and evaluating new ideas and their relation to the approach; to locate the orientation and its applications within cultural contexts both historically in terms of the origins of the approach, and contemporarily in terms of current debates about philosophy, theory, society and therapy; and, finally, to present and develop a critical view of theory and practice, especially in the context of debates about power, organisation and the increasing professionalism of therapy.

I am delighted that one of the first two books to be published in this series represents current thinking in the diverse practice of body psychotherapy, especially as 'the body' has so often been viewed as a poor and at times embarrassing relation to the psyche – and, indeed, in the body of psychotherapeutic literature. Just as Wilhelm Reich was rejected both by the psychoanalytic establishment and left-wing political parties (and has the dubious distinction of having his books burned both in Nazi Germany and the United States of America), so too body psychotherapy is often noticeable by its absence from the bookshelves and from consideration on many training courses in psychotherapy, counselling, counselling psychology and related fields. The German philosopher Friedrich Nietzsche argued that philosophy must begin from a proper understanding of the body. If the *zeitgeist* of integration in psychotherapy is to mean anything, so too must psychotherapy begin from knowledge and comprehension of the body – the body personal and the body politic. This volume, ably brought together and edited by Tree Staunton, is a significant contribution to advancing theory in this field.

Keith Tudor

List of contributors

Rose Cameron, lives in Manchester, where she trained as a person-centred counsellor and supervisor, and also undertook formal training as a healer.

Roz Carroll is a body psychotherapist, massage trainer and supervisor at the Chiron Centre for Body Psychotherapy.

Bernd Eiden is a training member and managing director at the Chiron Centre for Body Psychotherapy, West London. He runs an individual psychotherapy practice and is registered with UKCP (United Kingdom Council for Psychotherapy).

Margaret Landale is an Integrative Psychotherapist, supervisor and trainer. She works in private practice in Oxfordshire and teaches at the Chiron Centre for Body Psychotherapy, West London.

Babette Rothschild is a psychotherapist and body psychotherapist, trainer and author now based in Los Angeles.

Tree Staunton is a group consultant, body psychotherapist and supervisor; she has worked as a trainer, group leader and supervisor at the Chiron Centre for Body Psychotherapy, West London for the last twelve years.

Nick Totton, as well as being trained in Reichian therapy, is a prospective group member of the Independent Practitioners Network, and is a member of the European Association for Body Psychotherapy.

Philippa Vick lives in central London and Bath; she has a private psychotherapy practice and teaches at the Centre for Transpersonal Psychology.

Roger J. Woolger is a British-born psychotherapist who currently lives in upstate New York and Brazil.

Acknowledgements

I am grateful to the Chiron Centre for their support and back-up in the process of compiling this book. Also to Andrew Samuels for his willingness and generosity in writing the Foreword.

I would like to acknowledge Cambridge University Press and Laurence Pollinger Ltd and the estate of Frieda Lawrence Ravagli for their help in sourcing as well as their permission to use the extract by DH Lawrence from *Reflections on the Death of a Porcupine and Other Essays.* I would also like to acknowledge The C.S. Lewis Company for permission to reprint extracts from *The Four Loves* by C.S. Lewis © C.S. Lewis Pte Ltd 1960 and also Harcourt Inc. (United States).

Thanks go to Su Jordan for her artistic impressions of the character structures in Chapter 2 (contact: susannabandit@hotmail.com).

I am indebted to all those friends and colleagues who gave their time in reading drafts and supporting me in this project – in particular Alex Wildwood, Suzette Clough, Shoshi Asheri, and Ros Lynes for her gifted hands in massage.

My gratitude also to Kenneth Newman for his indomitable and tenacious analytic – but more importantly relational – skills.

And of course to all those teachers, clients, supervisees and participants in the unfolding process of learning, of which this book is a part.

Finally, to acknowledge Keith Tudor, who has held the vision for the series.

Foreword

This book should make it possible for those psychotherapists whose training did not involve much (or any) focus on the theory and practice of body psychotherapy to think about adding a bodily perspective to their existing ways of doing things. And, it goes without saying, body psychotherapists will find the book an enormously useful resource – stimulating, comprehensive and responsible.

The various authors present body psychotherapy as a movement with more underlying coherence than is generally recognised. This does not imply a set of universally-agreed principles, but there is a consensually-agreed history of the movement's roots in the works of Reich, Freud and Jung. It also means that partisanship is tempered by a commonly-held set of assumptions. Hence it should become possible to conceive of a pluralistic approach to body psychotherapy – one in which the field is defined by differences of opinion within it. You are 'in' the field of body psychotherapy if you understand what the arguments between the body psychotherapists are about.

Many of the writers in this collection are clearly well aware of prejudices against body psychotherapy held by other types of psychotherapists and, most likely, in society at large. The question of whether or not body psychotherapy inappropriately raises the sexual tensions between therapist and client, the risk of possible acting out, the need to maintain a bodily perspective without actually touching traumatised clients, the way in which verbal and non-verbal interventions can (and even should) be mixed – these issues are thoroughly explored. The impression is of a field that is sensitively self-reflexive; while it does not claim too much, it is sufficiently endowed with healthy narcissism to reject the various accusations (or projections?) that have dogged it in the past.

In particular, I have been struck by the authors' attempts to find a workable balance between the literality of the fleshly body and the body as a metaphor for the whole self (or even, to use the Jungian convention, the whole Self) of the subject. The tension between the literal and metaphorical dimensions of our understanding of life, present in all psychotherapy, is explored here in a particularly suggestive and profound way.

It is clear that the body is both an end and a means to an end, both a thing-in-itself and a means of understanding the riddles of our existence. I was interested by the fact that, whereas some of the writers seem to consider the various parts of the body (limbs, organs) as offering a particular hermeneutic, other writers consider the body 'an sich' (the literal body rather than the body as metaphor), the holistic body.

The field of psychotherapy is entering a new era in which its relationships with neuroanatomy and neurobiology are going to receive much more attention than before. The danger of this is that practitioners who have not yet actually experienced body psychotherapy may idealise the body, attributing to it more than it can bear. Because the experienced body psychotherapists writing here do not idealise the body (though they love and respect it), the book could serve, paradoxically, as a kind of corrective to any excessive zeal on the part of those psychotherapists who might be thinking about the body and its connection to the psyche for the first time.

Finally, I want to draw the reader's attention to one further point. The body can be seen as timeless, universal, and possessing an essentialistic and elemental wisdom – a perspective I do not agree with personally, though some of the writers in this volume seem to. But I was struck by the way in which the essentialistic perspective was brought into balance with a more culturally sensitive perspective in which the body – impossibly counterintuitive though it may seem – is also a socially and culturally constructed entity. I wish books on other topics such as gender could walk that particular methodological tightrope as impressively.

I know from my own experience that body psychotherapy is anything but a blunt therapeutic instrument. Most verbal psychotherapists do not realise this. Their fantasy is that working with the body has to proceed along rather clumsy generalising lines, whereas those who work with words and the unconscious can make more finely-tuned discriminations and reach more precise understandings of the clinical material with which they are presented. Not true! This book will go a long way towards dispelling this myth and, as I said at the outset, could provide the impetus for non-body psychotherapists to start thinking seriously about getting some further training (either full training or intensive study and supervision) in the body psychotherapy of their choice.

Andrew Samuels
Professor of Analytical Psychology
University of Essex

Introduction

Tree Staunton

> Our body and mind are not two, and not one. If you think your body and mind are two, that is wrong; if you think that they are one, that is also wrong. Our body and mind are both two *and* one.
>
> Shunryu Suzuki, *Zen Mind, Beginner's Mind*

In the past body psychotherapy has been taken less seriously in professional circles than more traditional psychotherapeutic approaches. It has been associated with 'alternative' body *therapies* – primal therapy, rebirthing, Rolfing, shiatsu, Alexander, and Feldenkrais – and seen as a 'fringe' therapy. Freud's 'touch taboo' and Reich's expulsion from analytic circles for breaking this taboo contributed to it being placed outside mainstream psychotherapy, and this has meant that body psychotherapists have not contributed as much as they might to professional dialogue.

It is probably true to say that somatics are in ascendancy in the field of psychotherapy today, yet there remains a gap in relevant literature. Perhaps it is a function of the non-verbal territory that we are exploring: words don't always come easily. It is also a discipline cultivated in our methodology that words do not come too *soon*, truncating or bypassing a deeper process; the body holds pre-verbal memories and experiences which may be lost in the translation. The time has come for this translation to be made, and our American counterparts have engaged more readily than we in Europe: 'somatic psychology' (Johnson and Grand 1998: 8) and 'somatic psychodynamics' (Johnson and Grand 1998: 171) offer new and exciting developments in the field of psychotherapy, health and social psychology; feminism has emphasised the political importance of body-identity and 'body politics'; 'social somatics' (Johnson and Grand 1998: 182) explores 'societal shapings' and bodily introjects of group and cultural origins; there are important advantages of somatic work with shock and trauma, as illustrated in Chapter 5 of this book; the work with 'subtle energy' could become central to the scientific thinking of tomorrow, and in the UK there are breakthroughs in the application of subtle energy work with medical conditions.[1]

This book is intended as an introduction for interested professionals, offering insights into a spectrum of approaches within body-oriented psychotherapy. For those practitioners already in the field it attempts to elucidate some of the current dialogues and different applications of Body Psychotherapy today.

The many different approaches within the field of psychotherapy represent philosophical world views, beliefs and values and a favouring of different psychological positions. Research by Dr Andrew Arthur (Arthur 1998; 2000) suggests the speculation that 'psychological traits influence orientation choice and lead to a "fit" between psychotherapist and model that might be pre-determined' (Arthur 2000). Perhaps it is not coincidental that we end up as a client or a therapist within a particular approach. It 'speaks' to us or it 'feels' right, it 'touches' us or 'fits our picture' or gestalt. There is a deeper meaning to our orientation. So why choose a body-oriented approach to psychotherapy?

Some of our richest and most precious moments are held in our body memory: a smell, a touch, a look that stirs a longing, evokes a reawakening, bringing us back to something essential . . . the sense of a relationship or of a whole time period in our lives can be encapsulated in an image or a sensation. Yet, too, the experience of painful and traumatic memories is deeply held in the body; connection with embodied experience gives a direct access to the unconscious, opening us to the immediacy of our subjective world.

As therapists when we work with the body we are working with our own bodily reality in the room with the client, and we have a rich source of information which we may be able to access for use in the therapy. We listen *with* our bodies, and we listen *to* the client's body. We may ask ourselves what is at the *heart* of our experience with a particular client . . . how does the experience *sit* with us . . . what is the *flavour* or *texture* of an encounter . . . is it soft or hard, heavy or light? What impulse is stirred in us . . . is it to fight, or to nurture, to push or to pull? We bring our embodied imagination to the encounter.

The body may be brought to psychotherapy as 'the patient', the carrier of dis-ease, the aspect of the self that requires or demands attention. We find that the person looking for a therapist who works with the body may perceive their 'problem' in relation to a bodily experience or lack of it. They are asking to be touched; they need this touch in order to begin to experience themselves as embodied, yet touch can also be threatening.

Body psychotherapy is popularly known as a regressive, cathartic form of psychotherapy, and some of the presentations in this book might reinforce this impression. However, as Grand (1998: 172) points out

> The shaping of bodily experience and the bodily structuring of emotion, feeling, and efficacy continue throughout the life span, outside the family of origin.
>
> Johnson and Grand 1998: 172

The ageing process is an unavoidable opportunity to come to terms with our bodily reality. The rigidities of the mind and the energy blocks in the body concretise over time, closing the gap between idealised image and flesh and blood reality. Yet only when our bodies age, become less supple, more lived-in and in some ways more worn-out, does the soul-substance begin to take shape in our physical form. Perhaps when the literal body is less dense, the etheric shines through.

> Feelings and emotions, hormones, bodies and consciousness all change form and speak in many tongues. Shapes crystalize and liquify. No-one is fixed in concrete; rather some processes are ice or bone-like and others are more fluid.
>
> Keleman 1985: 57

There can be an essentially *progressive* aspect to body psychotherapy: a reaching towards, an invitation to explore new possibilities, new movements, sensations and feeling states – a spontaneous engagement in the present. How seldom in our daily lives do we move without forethought or intention, with no idea where it will lead or what it will become. Sometimes, rather than trying to retrace past experiences which have blocked movement, we offer a space to trace new pathways and reconnect to forgotten ones.

> If we are to move past the defensive ego, we must explore the body movement that defines us, and push more into the potential, our liberated and individuated body.
>
> Conger 1988: 199

When we work with a body-oriented approach, we are interested in deepening the *experience* and the *awareness* of the contact. Understanding follows on from the experiential knowledge. Being with someone's body is a whole different experience from engaging with their mind; as some of the case material presented in this book shows, it can be healing, reparative and renewing for the client to be accompanied through an experience, initially without a need for conscious processing. There is an experience of regaining a connection to oneself, commonly felt in this way of working, illustrated here by Stein's statement that

> Ego consciousness functions largely as the observing mind's eye, which tends to increase the distance between subject and object. Body consciousness, on the other hand, draws one into an immediate and direct contact with another person or with an object.
>
> Stein 1984: 12

Not many psychotherapists would dispute the truth of the body's involvement in the process.

> . . . the therapeutic passage is a very physical process. Often what is most essential is experienced first in the body; [It is . . .] a visceral process, rooted in emotional experience, with thinking and intellectual activity only secondary.
>
> Mann 1997: 182

In the last decade one aspect of the work which has become central to the study and development of the psychotherapeutic process across the whole field is the subject of countertransference: the therapist's feeling responses to the client are now generally seen as an essential contribution to the work. Nevertheless, psychoanalytic psychotherapies tend to attribute their non-verbal, body-based countertransferential responses to the borderline client, describing them as 'bizarre and intense phenomena' experienced with 'patients with primitive personalities and/or severe traumas' (Alexandris and Vaslamatzis 1993: 136).

Since the process of Body Psychotherapy involves bringing thoughts, feelings and memories to conscious awareness via body sensations and experiences, it follows that the practitioner values the somatic countertransference as an essential tool in all client work. Accordingly, the trained clinician in this field learns to ongoingly distinguish their own somatic process (*personal* countertransference) from their somatic process in relation to the client (*relational* countertransference).

Whilst many practitioners today may be interested in involving the body in their practice, they may lack the confidence or experiential knowledge to do so. This book goes some way towards illustrating how the body can be introduced into the clinical setting. It is demonstrated throughout the book that the fundamental premise in body psychotherapy is that our *core beliefs* are *embodied*, and that until we begin to experience the pain held in them *directly through our bodies* they will continue to run our lives, even if we mentally understand them.

The chapters take the reader through a spectrum of approaches involving the body, beginning with the more 'analytic' perspective through to a 'psychospiritual' one, from concrete to amorphous, literal to symbolic. In Chapter 1 Nick Totton emphasises the psychoanalytic roots of Body Psychotherapy, and shows how this informs his practice; Reich's understanding of orgonomics offers an underlying theoretical framework for many psychotherapists who work with the body. In Chapter 2, Bernd Eiden presents some of the historical development from Freud onwards, and demonstrates the usefulness of understanding character structure as a diagnostic tool to focus on core issues. Reichian character theory is frequently objected to on the grounds that it is classifying and objectifying, reducing people to 'types' or presenting too much of a 'medical model' for psychotherapy today. But to be understood fully, it cannot be interpreted literally; the character types represent 'snapshots' of positions, all of which we inhabit at various times. Thus, Reich's 'genital character' is not a person or type of person who has had the good fortune to emerge from childhood unscathed, and therefore lives a charmed life; rather, it is a glimpse *beyond* character structure, available to us all at any moment in time. It is a relationship to one's body-mind which transcends the restrictions of the body-ego.

Chapter 3 discusses the implications of Reichian and post-Reichian approaches to working with sexuality, including the issues of boundaries and touch when working with sexuality in the therapeutic relationship. In Chapter 4, Roz Carroll discusses the 'attentional and intentional use of touch' in biodynamic massage, which is an integral part of some Body Psychotherapy trainings. In Chapter 5 Babette Rothschild presents her own development of bodywork: a 'non-touch' approach for working with the body in shock and trauma.

Chapter 6 discusses the value of what Margaret Landale terms '*innate imaging* as a form of free association with distinct physical properties', demonstrating the use of imagery as a bridge between the mind and the body. This way of working with imagery reveals embodied memory, reflecting the developmental stages. Implicit in her discussion is an Object relations approach, giving us the view that, rather than being an extension or mirror of the psyche, the body is 'representative' of it in a number of different ways.

Chapter 7 shifts perspective: Philippa Vick offers a transpersonal view that gives meaning, a purpose, a sense that this *is* the life living itself – not that life is something that will happen after the core issue is dealt with or gotten beyond. To have this perspective, whatever the core issue, already places the person in a wider frame; there is distance, an observing ego – the 'I', no matter how damaged or non-existent in the developmental frame, can become the Self, the witness to the struggling ego in the transpersonal view. This feels fundamental: it gives back dignity, self-respect, hope, autonomy, relation to life and a sense of being held within a wider context.

Whilst character structures are observable physical structures, they can also be understood as *subtle body* structures, such that one can feel at one time energetically fragmented as in the schizoid structure, or at another time empty as in the oral and so on. In the context of body psychotherapy, these subtle dimensions can be worked with integratively, as a psychotherapeutic interpersonal process. Rose Cameron reflects in Chapter 8 on the inclusion of the subtle body in psychotherapeutic work.

Chapter 9 takes this subtle body work further into the area of past life therapy, where Roger Woolger argues persuasively for working with the embodied soul. Finally, in Chapter 10 Nick Totton pulls together the various strands of body psychotherapy theory and practice within the wider context of the therapeutic community, society and politics, positing possible future developments.

With the increasing professionalisation of psychotherapy, it becomes vital that we refuse attempts to impose rigid theoretical structures on the essentially experiential process which lies at the heart of the work: the blood, sweat and tears which form the medium of an unquantifiable exchange within the therapy room. We must keep our fingers on the pulse.

I am thankful to all the contributors for giving voice to their experience.

Note

1 Author and psychotherapist Elizabeth Wilde McCormick has been working therapeutically with heart patients since 1978. She writes: 'When we move the focus of our energy and attention to the heart and chest area, we have to slow down. We become truly aware of our breathing, and this can tell us a lot about how we feel. From this place we can become very specific about the nature of our tension and stress and how we carry it. Then we are in a position to use imagination, through visualisation or spot imaging, to help us to be open to hearing from the heart's intelligence about the healing it needs.'
Elizabeth Wilde McCormick and Dr Leisa Freeman, *Your Heart and You*. Piatkus Books 2001.

References

Alexandris, A. and Vaslamatzis, G. *Countertransference: Theory, Technique, Teaching*. London: Karnac Books 1993

Arthur, A. R. 'An investigation into the personality traits and cognitive-epistemological styles cognitive-behavioral and psychoanalytic psychotherapists'. Unpublished doctoral dissertation, City University, London 1998

Arthur, A. R. 'The personality and cognitive-epistemological traits of cognitive-behavioral and psychoanalytic psychotherapists'. Accepted for publication, *British Journal of Medical Psychology* 2000, 73: 243–258

Conger, J. P. *Jung and Reich: The Body as Shadow*. Berkeley, CA: North Atlantic Books 1988

Johnson, D. H. and Grand, I. (Eds) *The Body in Psychotherapy, Inquiries in Somatic Psychology*. Berkeley, CA: North Atlantic Books 1998

Keleman, S. *Emotional Anatomy*. Berkeley, CA: Center Press 1985

Mann, D. *Psychotherapy: An Erotic Relationship*. London and New York: Routledge 1997

Reich, W. *The Function of the Orgasm*. New York: Farrar, Straus & Giroux 1973

Stein, R. *The Betrayal of the Soul in Psychotherapy*. Woodstock, CN: Spring Publications Inc. 1984

Suzuki, S. *Zen Mind, Beginner's Mind*. New York and Tokyo: Weatherhill 1984

Chapter 1

Foreign bodies: recovering the history of body psychotherapy

Nick Totton

> The Freudian 'unconscious' is present and concretely comprehensible in the form of vegetative organ sensations and impulses.
>
> Reich 1973: 63

Introduction

Body psychotherapy is today widely understood as a form of humanistic psychotherapy or, for the traditionalists, 'growth work'. If it has in recent times taken on some psychodynamic elements, this is best seen as part of a tendency in contemporary humanistic therapy to adopt a psychodynamic colouration; these elements are often grafted on to a still basically humanistic structure. In this chapter, however, I intend to show that body psychotherapy, through its originator Wilhelm Reich, is in fact founded in psychoanalytic concepts and techniques, and becomes unintelligible without them. This fact is of more than historic interest: the recovery of body therapy's analytic context enables a practice which is sensitive to crucial issues of power and safety.

I am not aiming to reduce body psychotherapy to a subform of analytic work. In fact, in a sense my account implies that what currently presents itself as analytic therapy is a massive deviation from Freud's original insights, and that the Reichian 'heresy' is truer to those insights than analytic orthodoxy. There is something inherently tedious, though, about 'more authentic than thou' arguments. More realistically, the Reichian body psychotherapy tradition may represent a 'third way', which we could visualise as the third apex of a triangle with the humanistic and psychodynamic traditions as its other two angles. Like many of its own clients, however, body psychotherapy has been handicapped in developing its potential through a lack of understanding of its own history. Much contemporary post-Reichian therapy does indeed present itself as an autonomous 'third way', with its own language and categories of experience; but there are many gaps and incoherences in this presentation,[1] which I would suggest are ultimately the consequence of lopping off the work's psychoanalytic roots.

In arguing for the importance of the historical link between body psychotherapy and psychoanalysis, I am in many ways retracing my own history as a psychotherapist. My original training was in a thoroughly humanistic form of post-Reichian therapy (West 1984; Totton and Edmondson 1988), combining the style of aggressive bodywork which Reich developed in his late years (Baker 1980) with approaches drawn from Radix (Kelley 1974), co-counselling (Heron 1977; Jackins 1973), and other forms of growth work. My fellow trainees and I took on board the 1970s human potential movement's deep distaste for, and equally deep ignorance of, Freudian analysis. It was only very gradually, and over a period of years, that I reconnected with my own earlier interest in Freud's ideas, and saw that Reich's work emerged directly out of Freud's.

This also involved the rediscovery of my own intellectuality – my commitment to *thinking*. The frequent polarisation between psychodynamic and humanistic approaches has manifested itself partly as a characterological opposition between 'thinking' on the one hand, and 'feeling' and 'acting' on the other. This is unfortunate in many ways, not least because effective clinical practice involves the combination of all three activities (along with many more). If as practitioners we have a resistance to thinking, or to feeling, or to acting, then we need to challenge and develop ourselves rather than to seek out a therapeutic niche which supports us in our avoidance. Reichian character theory helps us to understand and explore these issues; but this aspect of Reich's work has itself been downplayed and de-emphasised in much contemporary body psychotherapy.

This chapter, then, will begin with history: briefly summarising the place of the body in Freud's theory, Reich's relationship with psychoanalysis, and the changes in psychoanalytic theory and practice which accompanied Reich's exclusion from the International Psychoanalytic Association. I will go on to discuss Reich's post-analytic development, and his subsequent reinvention as a founder of the human potential movement. Out of this historical survey, certain themes emerge as crucial for an understanding of body psychotherapy: these include 'body energy', 'hysteria', 'regression', 'character' and 'transference'. A careful study of these themes in relation to body psychotherapy shows us, I believe, how this form of work cuts close to the bone of the human condition, illuminating the profound difficulty of our existence as bodies in society. To examine them is to develop an account of the unique contribution that body psychotherapy can make to the field of psychotherapy in general. I shall end with a description of my own current way of working as a body psychotherapist.

Freud: 'a strange therapy'

> Yesterday Mrs K again sent for me because of cramplike pains in her chest; generally it has been because of headaches. In her case I have invented a strange therapy of my own: I search for sensitive areas, press on them, and thus provoke fits of shaking that free her.
>
> Freud to Fliess, 13 March 1895; in Masson 1985: 120

This is Freud writing to his friend Wilhelm Fliess, at a moment before psychoanalysis as such even existed, describing a form of work which seems to prefigure key elements of body psychotherapy. Nothing more is heard of this, and Freud's own practice moves further and further away from an initial active engagement with the bodies of his clients. In 1932, Freud's colleague, Sandor Ferenczi, complained that in the early days Freud used to spend 'if necessary . . . hours lying on the floor next to a person in a hysterical crisis' (Ferenczi 1988: 93). Similarly, in *Studies on Hysteria* we read of Freud 'pinching', 'pressing' and 'kneading' a patient's legs (Freud and Breuer 1895: 204–205), relieving stomach pain by stroking the patient and massaging her whole body twice a day (1895: 106–110), and, famously, pressing patients' heads with his hands to help them remember (1895: 173–174). There is little trace of such procedures in Freud's later analytic practice, and even less trace in that of most contemporary analysts.

As a theoretical system, though, psychoanalysis is intrinsically body-centred. I have argued elsewhere (Totton 1998) that it is a theory of how bodily impulses – the 'drives'[2] – are taken up and transformed through their psychic representation, and of the difficulties that arise from the confrontation of our bodily drives with countervailing forces, both internal and external. 'The source of a drive,' Freud says, 'is a process of excitation occurring in an *organ* and the immediate aim of the drive lies in the removal of this *organic stimulation*' (Freud 1905: 83, my italics). This remains his consistent position, even when his own focus of interest moves away from the drives. The bodily drives are the foundation on which Freud erects the whole superstructure of ego-psychology.

Freud traces in detail how the entire psychic apparatus is a development of bodily sensations and impulses. He states unequivocally that the ego 'is first and foremost a bodily ego' (Freud 1923: 364), and explains that this means it is 'ultimately derived from bodily sensations, chiefly from those springing from the surface of the body' (*ibid.*: 364 fn.). The ego, in other words, is a psychological version of the *skin* – a protective organ that gives shape and definition to the whole. (As we shall see, Reich makes one small but crucial development of this image, seeing the ego as embodied not in the skin but in the voluntary musculature.) Freud's later tracing out of the complex identifications through which the ego is structured in no way contradicts this insight; such identifications appear as imprints upon the body, 'incarnated', from a Reichian viewpoint, as specific patterns of muscular tension.

For psychoanalysis, neurosis and other psychological problems arise out of the inherent contradiction between the desires of the body – manifested in the drives – and the requirements of civilisation. 'Present-day civilisation makes it plain that . . . it does not like sexuality as a source of pleasure in its own right, and is only prepared to tolerate it because there is so far no substitute for it as a means of propagating the human race' (Freud 1930: 294). These requirements are mediated to the individual child through their family, and 'bound' into the structure of the individual ego which, as we have seen, means the structure of the individual body; the medium of this repression is the policing of bodily acts like feeding and excretion. According to Freud, this individual repression builds on a deep-rooted human difficulty in tolerating pleasure and spontaneity, a difficulty which psychoanalysis sees as possibly innate. Reich, however, insists that our fear of pleasure, however profound, is not innate but *implanted*.

This, then, is a compressed sketch of how psychoanalysis in all its conceptual complexity is founded on a *bodily* understanding of the human situation (for more detail, see Totton 1998). In the early period of analytic work, this bodily element was not simply theoretical. We have already seen Freud himself interacting with his analysands' bodies. Sandor Ferenczi, perhaps Freud's most prominent colleague, found himself towards the end of his career re-engaging with the physical body in ways which in some senses dismayed him: supporting and encouraging his patients into altered states where they apparently relived and abreacted forgotten traumatic experiences (Totton 1998: 64–68). These encounters with the power of the body eventually led Ferenczi to break with Freudian orthodoxy, arguing that the despotic power of the practitioner to define and control the therapeutic situation was actually retraumatising.

Reich: the somatic unconscious

> The psychic process reveals itself as the result of the conflict between drive demand and the external frustration of this demand. Only secondarily does an internal conflict between desire and self-denial result from this initial opposition. . . . There are *social*, more correctly, economic interests that cause such suppressions and repressions . . .
>
> Reich 1972: 287

In his development of body-centred psychoanalytic technique, Wilhelm Reich regarded himself not as a rebel against Freud but as carrying forward Freud's central project: to reconcile 'mind' and 'body' within the individual patient. Throughout the 1920s Reich was an increasingly important analytic figure, taking a leading role in the development of clinical technique and of group supervision as a training element. This led to a consolidation of analytic theory, which in turn produced his developing focus on the body. Even though his body-centredness was extremely unpopular in some quarters, it was primarily for his political position as an active Communist, rather than for his theoretical views or clinical practice, that Reich was excluded from the analytic movement (Sharaf 1983: 175–191). It is also true, however, that in the period during and immediately after Reich's exclusion, institutional psychoanalysis cleansed itself of many of its more radical and body-centred themes. 'Slowly but surely' as Reich describes it, 'psychoanalysis was cleansed of all Freud's achievements' (Reich 1973: 125); in particular, sexuality became a psychological phenomenon divorced from the body: 'sexuality became something shadowy; the 'libido' concept was deprived of every trace of sexual content and became a figure of speech' (*ibid.*: 124). The psychoanalytic mainstream and Reich himself began to move in directly opposite directions.

Reich's body-centred technique arises from an investigation of the real meaning of psychoanalytic concepts like repression. 'Until now,' he points out,

> analytic psychology has merely concerned itself with *what* the child suppresses and what the motives are which cause him to learn to control his emotions. It did not enquire into the *way* in which children habitually fight against impulses.
>
> Reich 1972: 300

Reich shifts the emphasis to *how* the child represses. He concludes that, just as libido and desire are for psychoanalysis ultimately bodily, biological phenomena, so repression – the force that opposes desire – is also a bodily phenomenon, located in the habitual rigidity of the musculature.

> Muscular rigidity, wherever it occurs, is not a 'result', and 'expression', or a 'concomitant' of the mechanism of repression. In the final analysis . . . somatic rigidity represents the most essential part of the process of repression.
>
> Reich 1973: 300

On this basis, Reich began to work both on his clients' character attitudes and on their muscular rigidity.

> Practical experience soon teaches us that it is just as inadmissible to exclude one form of work as it is to exclude the other. With one patient, work on the muscular attitude will predominate from the beginning, while with another, work on the character attitude will be emphasised. We also encounter a third type of patient with whom the work on the

character and the work on the musculature proceed simultaneously and partly alternatingly.

Reich 1972: 329–330

Reich's initial style of bodywork was slow, painstaking, and uninvasive: a close equivalent to analytic free association, patiently and repeatedly encouraging clients just to breathe and let go to any spontaneous bodily phenomena – trembling, jerking, facial expressions, sounds, or whatever manifested itself.[3] Often what manifested were thoughts, imagery, memories, and reactions to the therapist. To use a more contemporary language, Reich follows and supports his clients' process as it successively occupies different channels of experience, including bodily sensation and motor impulse, verbal and visual material, and the channel of relationship – the basic character attitude as it manifests towards the therapist.

Reich's work implicitly develops Ferenczi's insight that the therapeutic relationship is critical in body-centred work. Many of Reich's advances were made as part of his project (as leader of the Vienna Technical Seminar for young analysts from 1924 to 1930, and subsequently in a similar role in Berlin) of developing precise clinical tools for psychoanalysis, and in particular grasping the role and nature of resistance as a therapeutic phenomenon. We shall discuss below Reich's work on character as the link between resistance and repression.

After his exclusion from psychoanalysis in the 1930s, Reich developed his independent approach to psychotherapy and the study of life and nature, which eventually crystallised as Orgonomy. It would be fair to say that in his later years Reich steadily lost interest in psychotherapy; or at least, that psychotherapy as such became subsumed into a massive investigation of the cosmos and the place of human beings within it. In the context of his sense of a profound planetary emergency, what would now be described as an ecological crisis, Reich developed more and more heroic and invasive forms of therapeutic work, aiming to work always faster and more drastically to 'unblock' the energy of individuals sufficiently for them to function effectively and take part in his project of liberation. Ultimately, Reich lost faith in the possibility of straightening the bent tree of the adult body-mind, and concluded that the only effective work was to improve the way in which children were raised.

Orgonomy, of course, still maintains its independent existence as a fundamentalist 'church of Reich'. Some of Reich's work on character, resistance and clinical technique has been subsumed into psychoanalysis. But he has also, somewhat against the tenor of his own thinking, become a major influence on humanistic psychology and the human potential movement. This has happened largely through the mediation of Alexander Lowen and Bioenergetics (1975), and to a lesser extent through other figures such as Charles Kelley (1974) and David Boadella (1987). It has been a two-way process of influence, with Reich's body-centredness and positive valuation of sexuality[4] influencing humanistic therapy, and the latter's optimistic positivism and anti-intellectual slant also colouring many forms of post-Reichian therapy.

As anyone reading Reich's major works can quickly discover, although an extremely concrete thinker he was anything but anti-intellectual. And while he was essentially optimistic in his belief – against the grain of most Freudian thinking – that human beings are at their core loving and creative, he also saw both the urgency and the difficulty of accounting for what is destructive and deathly in human behaviour. In other words, Reich is a critical thinker in a much deeper sense than most of those he has influenced; and his work also carries within it some of the most complex and difficult elements of psychoanalysis; in particular, the challenge of understanding what *appears* to be an innate problem structured into human existence, an intrinsic hostility to pleasure and surrender. It is this which, Reich argues, produces – as well as repressive and destructive social formations – such bitter resistance to therapeutic change. Humanistic and body-oriented therapy tend to replace this problem either with a simplistic opposition between individual (good) and society (bad), or with nothing at all.

Body energy

> It would be wrong to speak of the 'transfer' of physiological concepts to the psychic sphere, for what we have in mind is not an analogy but a real identity: the unity of psychic and somatic function.
>
> Reich 1972: 340

As I have already suggested, Reich has a thoroughly concrete understanding of Freud's concept of libido – sexual energy – and of his assertion that it is the blocking of libidinal satisfaction which creates neurosis. He translates Freud's somewhat vague notion of dammed-up 'psychic energy' into a very precise concept of blocked *muscular* energy.

> All our patients report that they went through periods in childhood in which, by means of certain practices in vegetative behaviour (holding the breath, tensing the abdominal muscular pressure, etc.), they learned to suppress their impulses of hate, anxiety, and love. . . . *It is precisely the physiological process of repression* that deserves our keenest attention . . . It can be said that *every muscular rigidity contains the history and meaning of its origin.*
>
> Reich 1973: 300, original italics

Where Reich breaks with Freud in his treatment of body energy is that he *speaks from the side of the body*. In Freud's view, mental processes both do and should control bodily ones, deciding whether or not to permit energetic and emotional discharge (e.g. Freud 1915: 152–153). Reich argues that this mental domination of the body is the root of neurosis, and that the 'binding of vegetative energy' must be 'directly attacked' (Reich 1972: 315) leading to discharge. Emotional discharge, in his view, is not a result of the recovery of traumatic memory; rather, the other way around: *the concentration of a vegetative excitation and its breakthrough reproduce the remembrance* (*ibid.*: 315, original italics).

The notion of bound energy is very important here: although he is in dispute with some of Freud's positions, Reich is giving concrete meaning to Freud's 'economic model' – to the concept of the ego as *binding psychic energy*, which in the id or unconscious is unbound (Freud 1920, 1950). Reich anchors the concept of bound and unbound energy to the state of the musculature, and indeed of the autonomic nervous system: chronic tension of the voluntary musculature is the concrete form in which 'mind' (ego) seeks to dominate 'body' (id), by 'tying up' desiring impulses (Reich 1972: 286–295). In fact, the split between 'mind' and 'body' is an illusory and alienated one; it is derived from this state of chronic muscle tension, which leads to a developing identification between 'spastic ego' and the processes of thinking – processes which are actually as bodily as digestion (see Totton 1998, Ch. 7; Winnicott 1949).

Hysteria

> When the psychic system fails, the organism begins to think.
>
> Ferenczi 1988: 6

Ferenczi and Reich agree in stressing the crucial role in body-centred work of the complex phenomenon known in psychoanalysis as 'hysteria': a phenomenon characterised for psychoanalysis by, among other things, a process of 'conversion' whereby conflictual material is expressed directly in the body. Both men found that, through a therapeutic focus on the body and its impulses,

> Hysterical physical symptoms would suddenly make their appearance . . . paresthesias and spasms, definitely localised, violent emotional movements, like miniature hysterical attacks, sudden alterations of the state of consciousness, slight vertigo and clouding of consciousness often with subsequent amnesia for what had taken place.
>
> Ferenczi 1929: 285

These experiences are very similar to what Freud had long before described as the 'hysterical attack' (Freud and Breuer 1895: 64–68; Freud 1909); not only the bodily symptoms, but also the integral connection with *memory*. Hysterical attacks, as characterised by Freud, produce memories of the traumatic events which have created chronic hysterical symptoms (Freud and Breuer 1895: 66); these symptoms, in fact, are themselves symbolic representations of memories. Freud originally made the dramatic claim (repeated since by many trauma and abuse theorists) that the restoration of memory, with emotional discharge, removed the hysterical symptom.

> Each individual hysterical symptom immediately and permanently disappeared when we had succeeded in bringing clearly to light the memory of the event by which it was provoked and in arousing its accompanying affect, and when the patient had described the event in the greatest possible detail and had put the affect into words.
>
> Freud and Breuer 1895: 57

Unfortunately, like so many other therapeutic innovations, this 'cathartic technique' turned out to be far less reliable and effective than it initially appeared. Its motor force was revealed as an intensive positive transference towards the practitioner, which could not easily be mobilised. In a brilliant reversal, Freud pointed out that *negative* transference was itself a recapitulation of past traumatic experience (the therapist being identified with the source of the trauma), and thus offered a different and more easily accessed therapeutic route. Working with the transference, rather than with the body itself and its memories, became the core of the analytic process.

Extraordinarily, though, Ferenczi – one of the leading figures in psychoanalysis and in the development of transference analysis (Ferenczi and Rank 1986) – eventually returned to Freud's early use of bodily discharge as a core method of treatment, inducing what amounted to therapeutic hysterical attacks, '*trances*, in which fragments of the past were relived . . . one was forced to compare them with the Breuer-Freud *catharsis*' (Ferenczi 1930: 298, original italics). Ferenczi was ambivalent about this development:

> I must confess that at first this was a disagreeable surprise, almost a shock, to me. Was it really worthwhile to make that enormous detour of analysis of associations and resistances, to unravel the maze of the elements of ego-psychology, and even to traverse the whole metapsychology in order to arrive at the good old 'friendly attitude' to the patient and the method of catharsis, long believed to be discarded?
>
> Ferenczi 1929: 286

In part, this emergence of 'neocatharsis' is to do with the fact that Ferenczi was working with people who would now be described as suffering from profoundly traumatic abuse, and whom he portrays in terms strikingly similar to contemporary models of dissociation. But Ferenczi generalises from his traumatised patients to the normal situation of children in our culture, seeing a universal abuse in the 'projection of our own passions or passionate tendencies onto children' (Ferenczi 1988: 155). He insists in a letter to Freud that the original analytic theory was the correct one:

> In *all* cases where I penetrated deeply enough, I found uncovered the *traumatic-hysterical* basis of the illness ... Where the patient and I succeeded in this, the therapeutic effect was far more significant ... Psychoanalysis deals far too one-sidedly with ... ego-psychology – while neglecting *the organic-hysterical basis of the analysis*. This results from overestimating the role of fantasy, and underestimating that of traumatic reality ...
>
> Ferenczi 1988: xii, second and third italics mine

Reich agrees with Ferenczi that hysteria is a fundamental condition, a traumatised 'layer' which must be reached in any analysis. In a summary of the 'typical phases' of successful character-analytic work, Reich moves through ego interpretation to 'breakthrough of the deepest layers of strongly affect-charged material: *reactivation of the infant hysteria*' (Reich 1972: 292, my italics). In his developed work, the approach to this fundamental 'infant hysteria' – Ferenczi's 'organic-hysterical basis of the analysis' – is through releasing the tension of the voluntary musculature, and the feelings and memories 'contained' in the muscles (which can be the anchor point for far more mysterious somatic phenomena). Again it needs stressing that Reich and Ferenczi are not referring only to extreme situations of traumatic sexual abuse, but to a universal childhood trauma held in the body.

The foreign body

> We must presume ... that the psychical trauma – or more precisely the memory of the trauma – acts like a foreign body which long after its entry must continue to be regarded as an agent that is still at work ...
>
> Freud and Breuer 1895: 56

The focus on hysteria, then, is also a focus on the past: it ushers in the theme of *regression* which is so omnipresent in bodywork. To work with the body, it seems, is to work with the past in a particularly intense and 'here-and-now' way. As Reich says, 'every muscular rigidity contains the history and meaning of its origin' (1972: 300). Hysteria is a many-faceted concept and phenomenon; we can think of it as an experience of *crisis*, which threatens the individual's survival so deeply that it creates a permanent bodymind disturbance, a 'broken record' quality of perpetual warding-off combined with a perpetual impulse towards completion; in other words, a crisis that never goes away.

Freud repeatedly makes the link between hysteria and a core experience of attack, an external trauma that leads to defensive freezing. He characterises this as a 'foreign body', like a splinter, or perhaps a parasite, which enters and attacks the child's bodymind so that their psychic structure has to adapt and shape itself around it. This adaptation, it seems, leads to the experience of *one's own bodily excitation* as a repetition of the attack, a second 'foreign body' that threatens the artificial defensive stasis precipitated by the original trauma, and which has to be dealt with by desperate measures. Hence Freud even argues that strong emotions are 'universal, typical and innate hysterical attacks' (Freud 1926: 290) which take over the body in the same way as external trauma and undermine the bodymind's defensive stasis.

Although Reich does not explicitly use this concept of the 'foreign body', it is behind his whole conceptualisation of repression, aggression and resistance. Freud eventually summed up his thinking about these issues in his theory of the 'death instinct' (Freud 1923): he suggested that human beings have an innate drive towards death which is parallel to, and equally powerful as, the libidinal drive towards pleasure. In Reich's view, this is a misconception: the supposed 'death drive' misidentifies a deep-rooted resistance to surrender and spontaneity, the hysterical freezing in the interests of survival that results from external trauma.

> The patient's fear of death could always be traced back to a fear of catastrophes and this fear, in turn, could be traced back to genital anxiety ... *fear of death and dying is identical with unconscious orgasm anxiety, and the alleged death drive, the longing for disintegration, for nothingness, is the unconscious longing for the orgastic resolution of tension.*
>
> 1973: 155, original italics

Traumatic experience leads us to experience *our own body* as 'foreign', in its spontaneous impulses to surrender and flow: if it feels vital to suppress feeling and emotional expression, then this can only be achieved by alienating ourselves from our own bodies.

> As heroically as they [clients] once wrestled with the 'devil' in themselves, i.e., sexual pleasure, they now senselessly defend themselves against the cherished capacity for pleasure.
>
> Reich 1973: 336

The eminent psychoanalyst Jean Laplanche puts forward a reinterpretation of the death drive which is extremely close to Reich's position.

> My basic idea is then as follows: the death-drive is not a discovery but a reaffirmation, a deepening of the original and fundamental affirmation of psychoanalysis: sexuality; *it is nothing other than the extreme of sexuality, in its least civilized aspect, working according to the principle of free energy and the primary process.*
>
> Laplanche 1981: 85, my italics

Or as Reich puts it, death represents *orgasm*:

> The striving after non-existence, nirvana, death, is identical with the striving after orgastic release.
>
> Reich 1972: 336

Character

> A person's character conserves and at the same time wards off the function of certain childhood situations.
>
> Reich 1973: 305

Reich and Ferenczi – like the early Freud – see the full re-enactment of early traumatic experience as a *healing* crisis, a way in which the freezing and tightening (equally bodily and psychological) can melt back into a free flow of spontaneity. Conversely, character structure is the permanent enactment of the traumatic crisis: character traits embody both the original desire, and its repression through fear of outside attack. If 'the psychic structure is at the same time a biophysiological structure' (Reich 1973: 301), then it follows that bodily structure will vary with psychic structure; and this indeed is Reich's theory of character: character is the *embodiment* of trauma and defense. Character, thus, is a 'conversion phenomenon', a bodily expression of psychological conflict; all character is hysterical, the fundamental 'infant hysteria' that we have already mentioned.

In hysteria, as we have seen, object-relations are sufficiently traumatic that the ego is forced to turn against the impulses of the organism, seeking to change the nature of the body through complex processes of biofeedback, muscular spasm and what Ferenczi terms 'command automatisms', or bodily habits which internalise prohibitions or instructions (Ferenczi 1919: 89–104). As Ferenczi makes clear, this process is part – a larger or smaller part for different individuals – of every child's experience of growing up. This means that in its basic structure *all* character is hysteric and, as Reich says, will tend to manifest as hysteria when therapy reaches sufficient depth. At the same time, there is a *specifically* hysteric character position (known in post-Reichian circles as 'expressive-clinging', 'histrionic', 'rigid', 'crisis', etc.), which forms when these universal experiences of trauma and defense are focused around specific Oedipal issues of gender, power and erotic demand and prohibition.

Reichian character theory is both powerful and illuminating; it offers a model of individual difference that is both historical, bodily and politically inflected (character positions originate through our experience of power relations, in the policing of our bodily functions). However, it has tended to be downplayed or even ignored in many recent versions of body psychotherapy. This seems to result from a humanistic unease about 'pigeonholing' people, as if characterology involves tying the client to a Procrustean bed and stretching or removing the bits that don't fit. Certainly character theory can be misused if it is adapted to a medicalised therapeutic approach of diagnosis and treatment. But the theory itself is precisely a subtle account of *individuality in relationship*, and of the strategies and defenses used to preserve individual freedom – and the price paid in doing so. It is also noticeable that many of the post-Reichian approaches that do attend to character theory in fact tend to downplay or reinterpret the hysteric character position, *desexualising* it so as to avoid difficult issues of Oedipal trauma and gender identity (e.g. Lowen 1975; Kurtz 1990). The simplistic, naturalistic emphasis of the 1960s and 1970s on 'sexual liberation' was incompatible with such complex accounts.

Transference

> An abreaction of quantities of the trauma is not enough: the situation must be different from the actually traumatic one in order to make possible a different, favourable outcome. The most essential aspect of the altered repetition is the relinquishing of one's own rigid authority and the hostility hidden in it.
>
> Ferenczi 1988: 108

From what we have said about hysteria and the foreign body, there follows a specific body-psychotherapeutic formulation of the issue of transference. Transference is primarily the experiencing of the therapist as the embodiment of the 'foreign body': the invasive, abusive and/or seductive *external* force, and the subsequent threat from one's *own* bodily impulses. The therapist, like the 'foreign body', appears to offer both pleasure and death. By inviting, encouraging or – in the client's fantasy, and perhaps to some extent in reality – *compelling* one to yield to the spontaneity of the body, the therapist recapitulates and is identified with the early 'traumatic-hysterical' crisis and with the adults who took part in it, in whatever role.

The notion of 'cure' and 'putting right' in bodywork is a regressive one: a mutual transference fantasy, of great pathos but negative therapeutic value, which identifies the therapist as a magical rescuer and covers up the trauma again in the act of exposing it. This is just one of a group of fantasies to which body psychotherapy is uniquely prone. In our culture, intimate physical contact generally implies one or more of the following: a sexual relationship, an adult-child relationship, a child-child relationship, and a 'making better' relationship (doctor, nurse, dentist, etc.). If the therapist cannot bring awareness to these aspects, a mutual trance develops where both people fantasise about their relationship in one or more of the ways outlined, *without owning* those fantasies. The fantasies can be of great value in exploring core beliefs and patterns of relationship – but only if we can study them openly.

But doesn't this analytic approach to the transference render us liable to

Ferenczi's criticism: that the fundamental reason why regression and cathar-sis fail is the persecutory attitude of the therapist? Ferenczi resurrects what he calls 'the good old "friendly attitude" to the patient . . . long believed to be discarded' (Ferenczi 1930: 298); and shows how problematic the apparently straightforward issue of trust becomes when we are working with primal, traumatic material. But the problem is two-sided. Many bodyworkers believe that a simplistic 'friendly attitude' and an assumption of goodwill on both parts are sufficient to facilitate therapy – ignoring our inevitable implication, through the structure of the therapeutic encounter, in the client's traumatised fantasies.

Body psychotherapy has a particular problem around the fantasy of 'mak-ing better', because of its close association with techniques of skilled physical manipulation. No rigid boundary can be drawn between, for example, body psychotherapy and massage; Reich's own work overlaps between the two, and his successor in orgonomy, Elsworth Baker, offers specific physical techniques as part of his textbook on body psychotherapy (Baker 1980). This creates real and persistent difficulties with the countertransference position around bodywork: the therapist enjoys the sense of power and effectiveness offered by this identification as an expert who will cure the client, or employs a psychological 'white coat' to cover up more frightening feelings in themselves and their clients.[5] However, many practitioners of purely verbal therapy have a similar countertransference problem, often without seeing it as a problem; simply inviting the client to lie down, as in psychoanalysis, sets up some of the same fantasies.

Despite Freud's own opposition, psychoanalysis has always tended to see itself as a form of medical practice. The only battle which Freud lost in the International Psychoanalytic Association was over the restriction of analysis in America to medical doctors. Reich was a 'conservative' on this issue: he always supported restricting training to medics, one of the many ways in which he was not a humanistic therapist. Reich's reason for taking this pos-ition, however, was that, like many humanists, he situates the therapeutic encounter, with or without bodywork, as a transaction between *adults*; he never really addresses the regressive dimension of therapy, and often tends to approach neurosis, character structure, body armour, as 'foreign bodies' to be dismantled and stripped away by medical-style treatment.

Reich maintains this view despite the profound insight his own work gives into how character structure is bound up with the whole formation of the ego. One can sense two unintegrated aspects, almost two Reichs: one who sees himself as a super-medic of the mind, 'smashing' and 'dissolving' defenses and 'releasing' healthy genitality, and another who works patiently and care-fully to accept and understand defenses, and celebrate them as largely successful strategies for dealing with intolerable stress.

Later body psychotherapists have tended to agree with Reich that psycho-therapy is finally an adult-adult transaction, however primal the feelings that are aroused (see Rothschild 1994). This attitude originated in the tendency of humanistic therapy to see transference-countertransference feelings as 'unequal' and politically suspect. An accurate criticism of some patronising analytic attitudes towards the client led to a rejection of all relationships between client and practitioner that were not perfectly symmetrical in structure – either between two adults or between two 'children'. This leads to the curious fact that bodywork tends to be '*intra*-personal' rather than '*inter*-personal' in its model of therapy – in other words, it focuses on the process of the client rather than on the mutual process of client and therapist. This is explicitly the position of, for example, the Hakomi Method (Kurtz 1990); more recently Hakomi practitioners, like many other body psychotherapists from the humanistic tradition, have been looking to analytic theory for help on the therapeutic relationship (personal communications).

These two threads, then – the medical model, and the humanistic aversion to asymmetric relationships – came together to obscure understanding of transference and countertransference among body psychotherapists. Still in many forms of therapeutic bodywork little or no attention is paid to transference. Transference is actually likely to be 'hotter' in a bodywork context when the fact of there being two bodies in the room is explicit – not that feelings will be different, or stronger, but that they will be rather more in the here-and-now, more accessible to consciousness. Without explicit attention to transference, body psychotherapy can become an hysterical *folie a deux*, either simply replicating the trauma endlessly, or enacting a charismatic 'cure' which is only the other side of the coin from the trauma.

In bodywork, as in verbal work, there is a central question about where to put our attention: on unconscious desire, or on the 'transference resistance' which sums up and represents our defensive structure. In other words, do we support the 'deepest' impulse that we perceive in the client (generally, the ego's impulse to surrender in one way or another) or do we support the need to resist, to fight back, to understand the situation as an interpersonal one? This is exactly the question which Reich answered in *Character Analysis* (1945/1972), coming down decisively in favour of working 'from the outside inwards', interpreting the resistance rather than the 'id-impulses' – working through and honouring the effects of trauma and the experiencing of one's own body energy as alien.

Analytic body psychotherapy?

It should be clear from what has already been said that many of the difficulties in integrating bodywork into psychotherapy – and many of the transference issues it brings up – are essentially cultural problems around bodies and touch. Just as in the early days of psychoanalysis, body-centred therapy rubs (literally) on some of society's sorest spots: it brings to light all the ways in which body themes and experiences become traumatising aspects of individual history, through our culture's deep sickness in relation to sexuality. Child sexual abuse is the most obvious example of this; but it is crucial to take up Freud's insight that we are *all* traumatised though our adaptation to society's rules about sexuality, pleasure and body regulation as these are mediated through the family.

This wound is so deeply structured into our unconscious ego that it is illusory for any bodywork practitioner to believe themselves 'clear' or 'healthy'. This illusion was perhaps Reich's deepest error: his belief in an attainable 'genital character', and indeed that 'genitality' is a measure of detraumatisation rather than a *successful adaptation* to social norms (Totton 1998: 100–101). Whatever its faults, psychoanalysis has spent a century struggling for a balanced approach to this primary trauma, which creates the experience of a 'basic fault' (Balint 1968), an innate lack or unmeetable need. Although individual theorists may fall into a conservatism that is either pessimistic (like Freud) or normalising (like the ego psychologists), analysis as a whole strives for a radical balance around this issue, and hence around the related clinical questions of what we may hope for as a therapeutic outcome, and of how deeply the practitioner is implicated in the client's struggle with trauma. However helpful, loving and supportive, we as practitioners are also the foreign body, the alien, the Other who embodies society's demands; how can we incorporate this aspect into our work? How can we bear it?

Certainly bodywork is not inevitably a better or clearer form of therapy; with some clients it can be a rather poor choice. The simple fact of compliance – even of enthusiastic demand – in no way establishes that bodywork will be helpful in accessing core issues. For instance, sexual abuse survivors may consent to body psychotherapy as a means of *repeating*, rather than remembering and working through, the experience of abuse. 'Schizoid/ocular/boundary'[5] characters (whether or not abused) may be sufficiently out of contact with their own feelings and sensations that they just don't *know* that they find bodywork terrifying: they go along with the process while what they experience as their self is, in effect, floating up to the ceiling and observing from a safe distance. 'Masochistic/anal/holding' characters may demand pummelling and poking, seeking fantasised 'release' while actually absorbing the pressure into their defensive structure – and making the therapist sweat!

I want to end this chapter with a brief description of my current approach to working therapeutically with the body, an approach which arises out of everything I have said above. The integrative form of psychotherapy which I practice, Embodied-Relational Therapy, redefines bodywork in the Reichian tradition as centred on *breathing and relationship*. In fact, it explores the strange but fundamental question: *how can I breathe and relate to someone at the same time?*

As Reich showed, whenever we have difficult feelings in relation to someone, we restrict our breathing to suppress those feelings. Alternatively, to keep breathing we cut off relating, for example by turning away or closing our eyes. Trying to stay open both internally and externally at once is a way of immediately touching transference – and countertransference: this intense face-to-face relating combined with attention to the breath is highly demanding for the therapist as well as for the client.

In Reich's mature conception of therapy, breathing plays a role closely analogous to that of free association in analysis: a demand with which no one can fully comply, which 'represents an ideal which . . . can only be fulfilled after the analysis has ended' (Ferenczi 1927: 247). Or as Adam Phillips puts it, 'the patient is not cured by free-associating, he is cured *when he can free associate*' (Phillips 1995:102). More realistically, it is doubtful whether anyone can free associate; or rather whether, while free associating, anyone can remain 'themselves', in the sense of maintaining an experience of consistent, continuous and bounded identity.

In a very similar way, when one tries to allow the breath to happen freely *while attending to it consciously*, consciousness and spontaneity begin to interfere with each other: resistance emerges, corresponding to repression and embodied in the breath. Breathing is on the interface between voluntary and autonomic function: any attempt to 'control ourselves' – which is largely what repression is, Ferenczi's 'command automatisms' – emerges in the breath. This seems to be at least partly why many schools of meditation are centred on attention to the breath. It is through breath control that we create and maintain what I have called 'the spastic I' (Totton and Edmondson 1988) – the ego that is based in body *tension* rather than in body *awareness*.

The demands that interfere with each other are not ultimately *consciousness* and spontaneity, but *consistency* and spontaneity: the 'spastic I' learns to regard consciousness as a matter of self-consistency, a continuous self-commentary which saves appearances, and preserves us from the terrifying 'foreign body', the internal and external Other. Like free association, attention to breathing reveals the impossibility of maintaining both consistency and spontaneity. Said differently, it reveals that we cannot *deliberately* be consistent or spontaneous – because we can never be anything else. Looked at from this point of view, working with breath and relationship is a form of meditation, a spiritual practice.

This aspect goes back to the original insight of Freudian analysis. Reich describes drive theory as follows:

> Freud said: We cannot consciously grasp what drive is. What we experience are merely derivatives of drive: sexual ideas and affects. Drive itself lies deep in the biological core of the organism; it becomes manifest as an affective urge for gratification. . . . This was a profound thought: it was understood neither by those sympathetic to nor those inimical towards psychoanalysis. . . . This is how I interpreted Freud: it is altogether

logical that the drive itself cannot be conscious, for it is what rules and governs us. We are its object.

Reich 1973: 29–30

Breath work re-establishes our relationship with this unconscious biological core; it enables us to realise that, again in Reich's words, 'if Freud's theory of the unconscious was correct . . . one became an infinitesimal speck in the flux of one's own experiences' (Reich 1973: 39).

The central focus of embodied-relational bodywork, then, is on re-establishing a fuller, more spontaneous breath – not by efforting, but by gradually letting go of our need to protect ourselves from feeling by not breathing. Working systematically through all the levels of resistance to spontaneous breath – to 'being breathed' – therapist and client encounter all the familiar relationship issues that emerge through free association, or indeed any other sustained encouragement to let things happen spontaneously and without censorship.

This approach means that, even when bodywork is explicitly on the agenda, the client and I may never get that far: relationship feelings may become obvious before we do. For instance an unwillingness appears as the client starts to lie down, and we spend the session exploring that. If we do reach hands-on bodywork (which nowadays happens with a minority of my clients), then I follow the transference there too: in other words, I tend very much to work with the body issue or body area that carries the greatest *relationship* charge. I will focus on whatever part of their body wants to do something in relation to *me*: to hold me, push me away, hit me, turn away from me, fend me off – touch and be touched by me on whatever level.

Body psychotherapy conducted in this spirit, attending to breath, body impulse and relationship, seems to me to take up Freud's insight into the 'foreign body'. By offering oneself as Other in the heart of an individual's bodily process, the body psychotherapist can facilitate a new experience of the Otherness of that process, and a new loving relationship with the always already foreign body. In David Bowie's words, body psychotherapy is about 'Loving the Alien': the alien in one's own body,[7] and the alien body of the other person.

Notes

1 The most striking absence in much post-Reichian work is of any attention to the therapeutic relationship and issues of transference and counter transference: see my discussion below. Also important is a tendency – linked with the avoidance of relationship issues, and also discussed below – to see the work as essentially *curative*, a project of aligning the client as closely as possible with a normal or ideal human structure. Neither of these points, of course, applies across the board, but both can be traced back to elements in Reich's own approach.

2 'Drive' translates Freud's (and Reich's) German word '*Trieb*', which the *Standard Edition* renders incorrectly as 'instinct'. See Ornston (1992), 93–95.
3 In developing this style of work Reich must surely have been influenced by Ferenczi's 'relaxation technique' (Ferenczi 1930).
4 Unfortunately, both for Reich and for post-Reichians like Lowen and Keleman, this applies only to genital, heterosexual expressions of sexuality. See Totton (2000), 85.
5 The medical relationship itself is of course an intensely transferential one, including directly sexual transference ('playing doctors and nurses'). The 'white coat' only superficially sobers things up.
6 In the trios of character terms here, the first is the standard description, the second Reichian-analytic, and the third from Embodied-Relational Therapy, where like other post-Reichian approaches we have tried to find terms which are not inherently negative and pathologising.
7 So many clients refer at some point to the scene in the film 'Alien' where the creature forces its way out of its victim's chest.

References

Baker, E. F. *Man In The Trap: The Causes of Blocked Sexual Energy*. New York: Collier Books 1980 [1967]

Balint, M. *The Basic Fault*. London: Tavistock 1968

Boadella, D. *Lifestreams: An Introduction to Biosynthesis*. London: Routledge and Kegan Paul 1987

Ferenczi, S. 'The Phenomena of Hysterical Materialisation'. In Rickman, J. (Ed.) *Further Contributions to the Theory and Technique of Psychoanalysis*. New York: Brunner/Mazel 1994 [1919]

Ferenczi, S. 'The Problem of the Termination of the Analysis'. In *Selected Writings*. J. Barossa (Ed.). London: Penguin 1999 [1927]: 245–54

Ferenczi, S. 'The Principle of Relaxation and Neo-catharsis'. In *Selected Writings*. J. Barossa (Ed.). London: Penguin 1999 [1930]: 275–92

Ferenczi, S. *The Clinical Diary*. J. Dupont (Ed.). London: Harvard University Press 1988

Ferenczi, S. and Rank, O. *The Development of Psychoanalysis*. Chicago: Institute for Psychoanalysis 1986

Freud, S. *Three Essays on Sexuality*. In *Penguin Freud Library* Vol. 7. Harmondsworth: Penguin 1991 [1905]: 31–169

Freud, S. *Some General Remarks on Hysterical Attacks*. In *Penguin Freud Library* Vol. 10. Harmondsworth: Penguin 1979 [1909]: 95–102

Freud, S. *Repression*. In *Penguin Freud Library* Vol. 11. Harmondsworth: Penguin 1984 [1915]: 139–158

Freud, S. *Beyond the Pleasure Principle*. In *Penguin Freud Library* Vol. 11. Harmondsworth: Penguin 1984 [1920]: 269–338

Freud, S. *The Ego and the Id*. In *Penguin Freud Library* Vol. 11. Harmondsworth: Penguin 1984 [1923]: 339–407

Freud, S. *Inhibitions, Symptoms and Anxiety*. In *Penguin Freud Library* Vol. 10. Harmondsworth: Penguin 1979 [1926]: 229–333

Freud, S. *Civilisation and its Discontents*. In *Penguin Freud Library* Vol. 12. Harmondsworth: Penguin 1985 [1930]: 243–340

Freud, S. *Project for a Scientific Psychology*. In *Standard Edition of the Complete Psychological Works of Sigmund Freud* Vol. 1. London: Hogarth Press 1950 [1895]: 281–397

Freud, S. and Breuer, J. (1895) *Studies on Hysteria*. In *Penguin Freud Library* Vol. 3. Harmondsworth: Penguin 1974

Heron, J. *Catharsis in Human Development*. London: British Postgraduate Medical Federation 1977

Jackins, H. *The Human Situation*. Seattle: Rational Island Publishers 1973

Kelley, C. *Education in Feeling and Purpose*. Santa Monica, CA: The Radix Institute 1974

Kurtz, R. *Body-Centered Psychotherapy: The Hakomi Method*. Mendocino, CA: Life Rhythm 1990

Laplanche, J. 'Seduction, Persecution, Revelation'. *International Journal of Psychoanalysis* 1995; 76: 663–684

Lowen, A. *Bioenergetics*. Harmondsworth: Penguin 1975

Masson, J. (Ed.) *The Complete Letters of Sigmund Freud to Wilhelm Fliess*. Harvard, MA: Belknap 1985

Ornston, D. G. (Ed.) *Translating Freud*. London: Yale University Press 1992

Phillips, A. *Terrors and Experts*. London: Faber and Faber 1995

Reich, W. *Character Analysis*. New York: Touchstone 1972 [1945]

Reich, W. *The Function of the Orgasm*. London: Souvenir Press 1973 [1942]

Rothschild, B. 'Transference and Countertransference – A Commonsense Perspective'. *Energy and Character* 1994; 25 (2) [www.nwc.net/personal/ babette/arttransfer.htm]

Sharaf, M. *Fury on Earth: A Biography of Wilhelm Reich*. London: Hutchinson 1983

Totton, N. *The Water in the Glass: Body and Mind in Psychoanalysis*. London: Rebus Press 1998

Totton, N. *Psychotherapy and Politics*. London: Sage 2000

Totton, N. and Edmondson, E. *Reichian Growth Work: Melting the Blocks to Life and Love*. Bridport, Dorset: Prism Press 1988

West, W. *Melting Armour: Some Notes on Self-Help Reichian Therapy*. Durham: self-published 1984

Winnicott, D. W. (1949) 'Mind and its Relation to the Psyche-Soma'. In *Through Paediatrics to Psychoanalysis: Collected Papers*. London: Karnac 1992: 243–54

Chapter 2

Application of post-Reichian body psychotherapy: a Chiron perspective

Bernd Eiden

Introduction

The purpose of this chapter is to introduce the concept of character structure as originally conceived by Wilhelm Reich (1897–1957) and to demonstrate its use as a framework for the theoretical and clinical understanding as well as the practical application of working with the body in psychotherapy today. I will reflect further on developments in body psychotherapy since Reich, including those that led to the establishment of the Chiron Centre for Body Psychotherapy of which I am a founder and director. Finally I will offer some clinical reflections on working with the different character structures.

It has already been discussed how Reich developed his theory, continuing a basic understanding which Freud had as a medical doctor, of the connection between mind and body in any emotional disturbance. As Nick Totton points out, differences between Freud and Reich lay not only in the discussion around the use of touch, but in their fundamental belief about human nature, society and the need for repression. Whilst Freud accepted as human nature the fear of pleasure and spontaneity, and developed his work within an acceptance of the laws of repression which operated at that time, Reich fundamentally believed that character structure was *caused* by repressive forces in society and was not innate to the individual. It was essentially because he attacked these forces of repression that he was expelled from the psychoanalytic establishment.

Still today, work with the body in psychotherapy carries this 'outlaw' position in the wider field of psychotherapy. This perhaps partly explains the tendency for charismatic leaders to emerge – not always enhancing its reputation – to carry forward the work despite it being marginalised.

Reich's character analysis

Reich expanded on Freud's drive and libido theory and emphasised the energetic aspect: drive as an impulse, an energetic push from within to search for fulfilment of a frustration. He emphasised that emotional expression of a repressed and remembered situation, sometimes together with physical movement, needs to occur to enable change and healing. This was fundamental to the development of his vegetotherapy technique.

Reich's theory of the structure of the human personality was based on a view that human beings operate from an inner core – the primary level – which is *per se* spontaneous, positive and life enhancing, having the capacity for self regulation. Reich believed that drives become destructive only if frustrated, and that the original impulses are by nature spontaneous towards wanting contact. The destructive impulses (the death instinct) belong to the secondary level. The secondary level – the character armour – contains the distorted impulses (Freud's repressed unconscious) and it was this layer that Reich focussed on in his character analytical approach, with the aim of reaching the deeper primary level.

In his introduction to *Character Analysis*, first published in 1933, Reich elaborated on the concept of *resistance analysis*, inspired by Freud's plea to focus more on the defences of the patient. Reich invited the expression of the resistance, which manifested in the form of mistrust or unconscious negative attitudes, and he believed that these were part of the secondary level, restricting the deeper life force. His approach gradually became more confrontational and directive and he criticised his contempories for colluding with the positive transference of the patient, which he believed prevented resolution of the basic character issues.

> Character resistance is expressed not in terms of content but formally, in the way one typically behaves, in the manner in which one speaks, walks and gestures; and in one's characteristic habits – how one smiles or sneers, whether one speaks coherently or incoherently, how one is polite and how one is aggressive.
>
> Reich 1990: 51–52

Character structure

Reich observed different character patterns and developed a system of six basic character types. Figure 1 shows where the Reichian system fits with other developmental systems. Reich (1990: 160) formulated six factors which determine the kind of defence a child would adopt and eventually manifest as a character structure.

1   The developmental phase at which a trauma occurred, or an impulse was frustrated.
2   The intensity and frequency of the frustration.
3   The nature of the impulse against which the frustration is chiefly directed – for example against expression of anger or against tender feelings or expressions of need.

	0–2 months	5 months	10–15 months	2 years	3 years and on
Core issue	The right to exist	The right to need	The right to be independent	The right to be assertive	The right to love sexually
Reichian/Lowenian character structures	Schizoid	Oral	Psychopath	Masochist / Rigid →	Phallic / Narcissist / Hysteric / Rigid
Johnson's model	Schizoid	Oral —— Symbiotic ——	Narcissistic	Masochistic	Rigid
Ron Kurtz's character structures	Sensitive/analytic	Dependent/endearing / Compensated oral/self-reliant	Tough/generous / Charming/seductive	Burdened/ enduring	Industrious/over focussed / Expressive/clinging
Rosenberg	Attachment stage	Reflection ———	Differentiation / Healthy introversion →	Rapprochement →	Adulthood
Object relations	Autistic phase	Attachment phase	Differentiation / Practising	Rapprochement	On the way to object constancy
Developmental task	Unity with life/mother / Bonding	Establishment of sound symbiosis / Merged self-representation	Discrimination of mother as separate / Management of anxiety / Healthy narcissism; confidence in separate self	Resolving conflict between autonomy/ separation, good/bad	Internalisation of love object- realistic & unified
Ego defences	Fragmentation / Projection / Denial / Intellectualisation	Identification / Displacement / Rationalisation	Splitting / Projection / Idealisation-disillusion / Illusion of grandiosity / Denial	Denial / Undoing / Reaction formation / Passive-aggression	Identification- repression / Fixation

Figure 1 A comparison of developmental models.

4   The correlation between indulgence and frustration.
5   The sex of the person chiefly responsible for the frustration.
6   The contradictions in the frustration – for example, at times something is acceptable and at other times not but there is no logical explanation for this.

The basic character structures as further developed by Neo-Reichians – schizoid, oral, psychopathic or narcissistic, masochistic and rigid – are illustrated below. These structures can never define a person – each human being is so much more individual – but they can be explored as dynamics and signposts to the deeper truth of each person's core issue, and provide a framework for understanding. Some of us clearly embody predominantly one structure, as the damage occurred severely at that particular stage of development, whilst others show traits of several structures as layers of personality within the psyche; when working dynamically with it, each layer will reveal its own story.

The drawings show stereotypes that illustrate basic characteristics which may be used as guidelines, rather than the truth about an individual's body-mind expression. I refer to other authors such as Lowen, Conger, Kurtz and Cotter for a fuller description. An up-to-date and useful integration is presented by Stephen Johnson, who draws together the object relations theory and the character analytical theory (Johnson 1994).

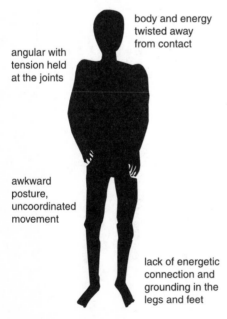

body and energy twisted away from contact

angular with tension held at the joints

awkward posture, uncoordinated movement

lack of energetic connection and grounding in the legs and feet

Figure 2 Schizoid structure.

The schizoid personality is injured by absence of adequate bonding during pregnancy and up to the first six months. The right to exist, to be welcomed and held physically and given a sense that the world is a good place to be in, has not been sufficiently met. The infant has been hated, rejected or abandoned and human warmth and connection denied, so that he learned to be self reliant, covering up a deep despair and terror. The initial trauma is severe and life threatening and profoundly overwhelming to the organism, because it occurred before any real organisation of the ego had taken place. For someone with a schiziod injury the core energy is withdrawn; the person has a tendency to live in their head, in ideas, having little contact with reality. The body shows fear in the form of fragmentation, it twists and turns away from contact showing various splits between different parts of the body. The body appears angular and there is a deep tension in all the joints. The body holds together against the fear of falling apart which manifests itself in movement as a lack of co-ordination or robotic movements. The energy does not flow harmoniously and there is an unreachable quality to the person.

The oral character forms in the first eighteen months, when the 'right to need' is negated, leaving the infant with the experience that the world does not respond enough to the need to be fed, talked to, played with, cuddled, etc. This results in a tendency to collapse into weakness, to be dependent, or the denial of any needs as a defence against the pain of abandonment. The person feels unfulfilled and powerless with weak aggressive impulses. The energy system is low and undercharged, and the body appears immature and underdeveloped in muscle tonus, often tall, thin and elongated, with a collapsed sunken chest and tensely held shoulders.

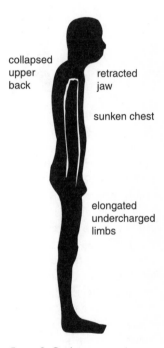

collapsed upper back

retracted jaw

sunken chest

elongated undercharged limbs

Figure 3 Oral structure.

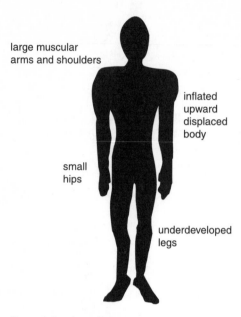

large muscular
arms and shoulders

inflated
upward
displaced
body

small
hips

underdeveloped
legs

Figure 4 Psychopathic structure.

The psychopathic character structure defined by Reich is more or less identical with the narcissistic structure according to recent research (Johnson 1985). The word 'psychopath' is also used in common parlance to describe a person without moral conscience and therefore needs to be distinguished from the extreme negative version of the sociopath.

It is probably today the most common structure in our society, driven by will to power and succeed. The psychopathic or narcissistic personality struggles with the right to be autonomous and separate and lacks the affirmation to be their own person. The injury occurs at the developmental stage of 18–24 months, when the child's natural omnipotence needs limits in order to learn about the need of others. Instead the toddler is used by the caretaker and pushed to be more than he can be, rather than being supported in his real needs. Alternatively the child has been humiliated when he shows his emerging vulnerability. As a result helplessness and the need for support are denied and a powerful false self is presented to the world. In the consulting room we may meet an aggressive, domineering type or a soft, seductive type. The first one typically presents an inflated, upward displaced body with massive shoulders and arms, piercing eyes, a narrow pelvis and less well-developed legs. The latter has a more harmoniously balanced and flexible body and the pelvis is overcharged. Both types are driven and have a lot of energy which is used to keep control over others as well as control over too much free-flowing energy from inside.

The masochistic character structure (The term 'masochist' as a character structure was first used by Reich, and it is not to be confused with the meaning of the word in the sexual context, where pain is inflicted in order to gain pleasure.) The developmental arrest is between 18–30 months, when the child is able to reason and agree to decisions and contracts. The injury is a crushing of the will, just as the child begins to assert herself. This results in an ambivalence between dependence on and resistance to the primary object. The free assertive expression has been impeded by the threat of loss of parental love, which is a strong part of the relationship. The child appears to capitulate and hold the expression inside by being good and well-behaved. She does not really give up herself or lose her sense of self altogether, but holds anger, spite and resentment, as the ego becomes more formed. In adult life masochistic types are responsible, reliable, warm, kind and relaxed with people and able to do a lot. They have a highly charged, robust body and an enormous energetic resource. The energy is

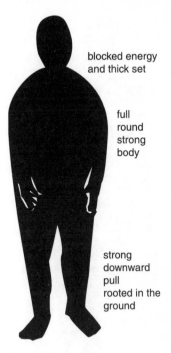

blocked energy and thick set

full round strong body

strong downward pull rooted in the ground

Figure 5 Masochistic structure.

physically blocked as it would move into expression, which is located in the body at the junctions between the torso, the limbs and the head. The typical masochistic body is full, compact and squarish, burdened around the shoulders and neck to keep a lid on the internal pressure. The voice may have a blaming quality. The bottom is squeezed and tucked in and the limbs are strong and full. Overall the body shows a defeated expression, heavy, rounded and rooted in the ground, as if held in a vice. There is a lack of dignity and pride with little upright assertive force.

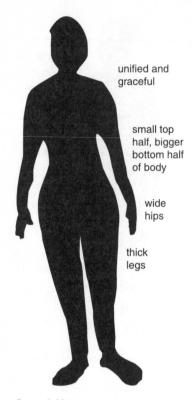

unified and
graceful

small top
half, bigger
bottom half
of body

wide
hips

thick
legs

Figure 6 Hysteric structure.

The rigid character structures are formed during the Oedipal stage of development, mainly between the ages of three and six, when the struggle with gender identity and gender issues dominates. At this stage the ego is strongly established in relation to the external world as well as internal needs. 'Object constancy' – the capacity to hold a constant internal representation of significant attachment figures – has now been established and enables the child to tolerate the frustration of the Oedipal conflicts, where a true relating in a triangle situation is tested.

The rigid personality can manifest in four different reaction formations: on the male side the phallic-narcissistic and the passive-feminine types, and on the female side the hysteric and masculine-aggressive types. The phallic-narcissistic man and the hysteric woman could be seen as being over-identified with their own gender and as living the stereotype. They have been affirmed in their sexuality by both parents, but may sometimes have been both over-stimulated and inevitably rejected as well. They learned to identify with the same-sex parent as a better way to be in the world. The passive-feminine man and the masculine-aggressive woman are more split in their identification. They have internalised a negative image of their own gender and identify more with attributes of the other sex, e.g. the boy tends to be soft and gentle and the girl rough and tough.

The term 'rigidity' itself refers to a general muscular stiffening which occurs when the body holds back an internal 'charge' of an impulse and remains tense. Their bodies are typically attractive, athletic and well proportioned, with an erect posture expressing confidence and pride and a sense of aliveness, possibly with a grace of movement and holding a lot of energy within an overall hypertonic, tense muscle structure. The tension is particularly held across the chest and in a retracted pelvis which may create strain in the lower back.

Reich conceived the '**genital character**' not as a character structure as such, but representing the healthy human being, who has overcome the restrictions of his character armouring. It is an 'ideal' to strive towards, having been freed from the chains of the past. This person enjoys his aliveness, the body is flexible and open to the energy flow. Life has a purpose and meaning. Transforming one's character could mean experiencing moments of such inner wellbeing. This has the potential to become a resource available at bad times. The 'genital character' is perhaps analogous to what the psychoanalysts D.W. Winnicott and R.D. Laing called the 'true self', and body psychotherapist Gerda Boyeson calls the 'primary personality'. There is an ongoing debate as to how much this concept includes the soul and the dimensions beyond the physical.

Figure 7 Phallic-narcissistic structure.

The development of vegetotherapy

Reich's formulations about character armour led him to a new concept which he called vegetotherapy (1933–1948). He came to the conclusion that body and psyche are functionally identical, and that mental structures and neurotic patterns have a physical manifestation in the form of muscular tension (either over or under-toned). Vegetotherapy became a way of working directly on the muscular holding in order to free blocked energy, expressed emotionally or physically through involuntary movements. It aimed to free physical mobility and breathing and lead to a capacity for more intense emotional experience of self and other. Vegetotherapy techniques became a powerful tool to access deeper unconscious processes. Reich explored how a certain breathing pattern could control underlying emotions.

This new approach included more direct hands-on work, using pressure and massage to reduce the muscular tension, and working directly with the breathing pattern (e.g. supporting via touch either ex- or inhalation). This could lead to an emotional discharge accompanied by involuntary body movements such as trembling or even convulsions, followed by a deeper sense of relaxation of the whole organism and a deeper sense of wellbeing. The client reported a sense of inner connectedness and a new-felt intensity, sometimes a sensation of streaming, as if being carried by waves of water, an oceanic feeling, which Reich also called 'vegetative streamings'. The term 'vegetative', first used in 1927 by the German medical doctor Friedrich Kraus (Boadella 1974: 102), relates to the vegetative or autonomic nervous system. Vegetative responses are involuntary responses beyond the conscious control.

Reich's focus became the *process* (the 'how') rather than the *content* (the 'what'). He also illustrated how unconscious material can be evoked by focussing on a particular body gesture, a special breathing pattern or sometimes through a suggested physical exercise. He elaborated his understanding of the muscular armour by dividing the body into seven segmental rings of tension (Figure 8), wrapping horizontally around the body and constricting the vertical flow from head to feet. His segmental theory resembles the Eastern system of chakras, although he did not make this link.

Muscle armouring also restricts the free flow of sexual energy; sexuality was central to Reich's theory. In 1924 Reich defined his concept of 'orgastic potency':

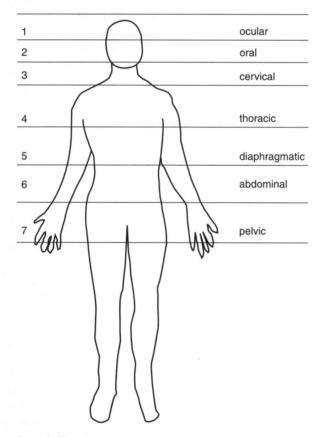

1	ocular
2	oral
3	cervical
4	thoracic
5	diaphragmatic
6	abdominal
7	pelvic

Figure 8 The segments.

Orgastic potency is the capacity to surrender to the flow of biological energy, free of any inhibition; the capacity to discharge completely the damned-up sexual excitation through involuntary, pleasurable convulsions of the body.

Reich 1983: 102

Reich expanded his therapeutic goal to include the attainment of the 'orgasm reflex', when dissolving the muscular armour. He moved beyond Freud's dilemma of the libidinous drives being seen to be in conflict with the demands of culture. He declared sexual expression as essential to health and supported the individual to find a self regulation out of an internalised moral position. Reich expanded his therapeutic goal to achieve more pleasurable physiological reactions when dissolving muscle armour which could lead to a fuller sexual expression. Reich had to battle with the issue of sexuality being somewhat publicly contentious at the time, and his ideas were later partly misused in the sexual liberation movement. It remains a question how much the distortions of this part of his work have set back the reputation of body psychotherapy.

Reich's thinking was dynamic and holistic, forecasting the new paradigms (Capra 1983: 384). He presented a holistic concept of human personality in his acknowledgement of the interdependence between the individual and the society. He also revolutionised psychotherapy by changing the therapeutic setting, believing that contact was key to the process: facing his clients, looking into their eyes and occasionally touching them. It remains a question how much he could really have entered the therapeutic relationship whilst maintaining the medical model and remaining 'the expert' who held the notion of how the patient should be. However, although the model of the therapeutic relationship has since changed and developed across the spectrum of approaches within the field of psychotherapy, Reich's ideal remains a challenge – to both client and therapist – to establish a 'core' contact beyond character armour.

Personal reflections on post-Reichian body therapy

Reich is now seen as the founder of body psychotherapy, yet the field of body psychotherapy today must be considered in the light of the developments within the Humanistic movement and the British and American School of Object Relation Theorists which subsequently took place. There were influences of other important voices such as Sandor Ferenczi, and the neo-Reichians such as Alexander Lowen, John Pierrakos, Stanley Keleman and Ron Kurtz as well as Gerda Boyeson and David Boadella. Reich was adopted by the Humanistic movement in the late 1960s and 1970s because of the philosophical implications of his work – in particular the demand for societal change, since he believed that existing societal structures produced character

structure. Probably he was popularised more in connection with the movement for sexual liberation.

I and many of my colleagues at that time came to the Reichian work
through the political movement. The application of Reich's ideas seemed a
step towards changing society. We were a political discussion group, and we
felt the need to make some of the changes Reich was pointing to, so we began
to use exercises with each other and share more experiences together. We
didn't learn from experts – it was a self-help group. This was in the early
1970s. No financial gain was involved, and there were no leaders; we simply
wanted to spread the ideas: we organised open evenings where people would
pay a small amount to cover the room fee, and one of us would prepare a
focus for the meeting and introduce exercises, sometimes out of a book such
as Rosenberg's *Total Orgasm* (1973). For most people it was just a gentle
opening, but at times someone would enter a deep involuntary body process.
This was rather frightening because none of us knew what to do, but it was
also self-regulating – knowing that there was no 'expert' to assist them, the
person would have to pull themselves together and not regress too deeply. I
don't think any real damage was done.

People at that stage were not interested in an analytic body psychotherapy,
but in the experience that body therapy gave them. The politics of that time
meant that they wanted autonomy within this; a medical model such as
Reich's would not be accepted nor would anyone taking authority, and therefore the work was restricted – the transference and the symbolic level was
ignored. The work could not be expanded until these elements were
reintroduced, and the work became a psychotherapy, but this happened much
later.

In a sense I would see Ferenczi more as the father of the humanistic
movement; he was an early psychoanalyst who, like Reich, did not agree with
the touch taboo; he also objected to the distant and neutral position of the
psychoanalyst and demonstrated practically and theoretically a need for a
more human relationship with the patient, especially the need for a loving and
authentic presence. He believed that the neutral attitude of the analyst could
be retraumatising for the patient, and he included physical interactions and
catharsis and also worked with relaxation to reach a deeper level of contact
with the client. He came to believe that through physical contact he was
addressing early developmental needs in his clients, and this focus on the pre-
Oedipal stages prepared the way for object relation theory – Melanie Klein
and Michael Balint were amongst his pupils.

Object relation theorist D.W. Winnicott also moved away from Freud's
drive theory; he regarded the 'holding environment' as essential for the emotional development of the child, and thus emphasised the relational aspect in
therapeutic work. The needs of the emotional body-self were eventually
taken more into account and considered. The classic setting of the client lying
on the couch and the analyst sitting behind was also changed to a more

relational setting with the possibility of having eye contact. Sensual and tact-ile needs were no longer characterised as sexual needs; rather it was seen as crucial for the individual to have joy in bodily activity and tactile experiences. These were seen as necessary to build an embodied sense of self – the body as a container of the self.

These developments, then, led to an understanding of nurturing touch, as distinct from sexual touch, as an expression of being supported, held and loved through the body, sexual gratification being secondary. In this view, physical contact does not necessarily gratify an instinct (drive); it can simply facilitate a bodily experience. Bowlby and his followers focussed on the for-mation of attachment as an important factor for the function of the self rather than simply the satisfaction of internal drives. Stern's research (1985) confirms even more radically the impact of relational and interactive aspects on the developing inner world of the infant. All these developments have questioned the drive theory as the basic paradigm for psychotherapy, and allow an opening of discussion about the use of the rules of abstinence and neutrality amongst psychoanalysts.

The co-founders of the Chiron Centre – myself, Jochen Lude and Rainer Pervoltz – came to London in 1978 to study with Gerda Boyesen and her team; by that time our self-help group in Berlin had developed into a training group in bodywork and this proliferated in the years that followed. Lowen and Pierrakos had worked together for a long time, developing the bio-energetic analysis model that took hold in the United States and also a little in Britain, but for various reasons it never really got established here. Differ-ent schools within the developing field of body psychotherapy chose to focus on different aspects of the work.

Basing his work on Reich's character structure model – a theoretical sys-tem and a practical approach concerned with raising consciousness about how we use our 'life energy' – Lowen's system of bioenergetics works actively with the breathing and a range of body exercises to facilitate emotional expression. Following Reich's emphasis to focus on the latent negative trans-ference as the major resistor, the bioenergetic therapist tends to concentrate on the expression of negative feelings such as anger, resentment or pain espe-cially in the early stages of the process. The therapist actively confronts the defence system to break down the armouring. Lowen was particularly good at diagnosis and bodyreading, out of which he would adapt bioenergetic exercises to suit a person's structure. Lowen expanded Reich's character analysis and he worked with it in a much more detailed and systematic way, though it is also true to say that, in my experience, there was a lot of energetic work and not much analytic integration. However, my main experience of his work was in workshops, and this integration may have taken place more in a long-term one-to-one therapy.

Pierrakos split from Lowen to develop his own work which he called core energetics. Included in his work was the understanding of the subtle energy level, how energy is distributed in the body through chakras and an understanding about our spiritual essence. He continued to base it on the character structure theory, in the sense that he worked first to mobilise the negative layer of the structure, the resistance, but he would then direct the focus to the heart, to energetic expansion and 'melting'. He also worked with subtle levels and the aura within each structure. I experienced his work as gentle, deeply moving and touching.

Keleman developed his own system of body structures which was more anatomical, describing the pressure and 'ballooning' of energy which is constricted or supressed. His way of working was very subtle and detailed. He would guide the client into small motions, breaking down an expression into five or six steps to really feel 'how' this gesture or movement is made, and to understand it through the felt experience: 'How does your body do it? . . . Listen to what your body tells you . . .'. I like this aspect of his work and I find it very useful. It is more of an energetic than an analytic character structure system, and this distinguishes it from Reich and Lowen, and represents a different focus and direction for the work.

In biodynamic psychology, developed by Gerda Boyesen, the central focus became the vegetative processes and the movement of energy from within, emphasing the essential bodily pleasure of existence. The biodynamic psychotherapist is not so much intent upon unmasking the client's ego defences as working with the body and inner movements, allowing the dynamic of the life force at other levels than the ego to be felt and experienced. In a biodynamic vegetotherapy session the psychotherapist allows 'it' to happen, aiming to allow the deeper life within the body full rein, so that the 'id' can emerge and evolve. The therapist is interested in whatever is happening in the client's body, starting at the edge of awareness, often with the smallest sensation or emotion, however tentative the movement. Gradually these sensations, images, impulses and emotions grow stronger, as they are encouraged and they begin to take gestalt (perhaps a form which is without words): a gesture or eruption of emotion. This biodynamic work continues to be practised at the Chiron Centre.

David Boadella was another teacher in this neo-Rechian movement whose clarity had an influence on the developing work which we brought to the Chiron Centre. After years of research he initiated the school of biosynthesis which integrates three essential aspects of human existence: the body existence, the psychological experience and the spiritual essence. When working with the body, the therapist focusses on the balance of breathing patterns, muscle tone and the expression of emotions with the aim to experience more fully the qualities of the essential core.

Body psychotherapy as a discipline

Body psychotherapy is established as its own discipline and is now represented in the United Kingdom Council for Psychotherapy (UKCP) as a branch within the main field of psychotherapy. Three schools represented within the UKCP now adopt a body-oriented approach: the London School of Biodynamic Psychotherapy (previously Gerda Boyesen Institute), the Chiron Centre and Karuna Institute, as well as several independent trainings in body psychotherapy (see Appendix for details).

At the Chiron Centre we include the study of the post-Reichian schools mentioned above as a foundation for an approach which is eclectic and integrative, a combination of three main forms of body psychotherapy: biodynamic psychology, Reichian character analysis, and Gestalt body psychotherapy.

The term 'body psychotherapy' was coined by the European Association for Body Psychotherapy (EABP) in 1991 as the accepted label for psychotherapists whose theoretical and metapsychological position together with a range of techniques and interventions include the body. Other modalities such as Gestalt and psychosynthesis use some principles of body psychotherapy, and there is an increasing awareness of the body as a vital ingredient within the complexity of the therapeutic process.

Body psychotherapy differs from body treatments such as the Alexander Technique, Rolfing, Feldenkreis, etc. Body psychotherapy is an in-depth approach, addressing unconscious material and working through a therapeutic relationship towards integration into consciousness. Some body psychotherapy approaches focus much more on subtle energy processes, working with the aura of the body (see Chapters 8 and 9). Techniques of body work are not used as a treatment and 'done to the client by the expert', but used appropriately within the therapeutic relationship. Change only occurs through the relationship with another human being, as it is in a relationship in the primary scenario where the damage originally occurred. This implies an understanding of the dynamics of transference and countertransference and how to use these in the therapeutic relationship. In addition, body psychotherapy addresses the psychological implications and meaning of bodily expressions and in doing so works against the fundamental split between the body and the mind (Eiden 1999).

Body psychotherapy today

It is agreed as a basic principle in body psychotherapy that neurotic symptoms have a psycho-physical correlation. Vegetative discharge is therefore considered vital for the completion and healing of a suppressed psychic complex. Emotional discharge needs to be accompanied by vegetative discharge, because any emotional repression has its physical equivalent and the neurotic symptom is bound in the physical structure. Different body schools locate the root of this equivalent correlation partly in the 'endoderm' – the deep organic level in the intestines, the 'mesoderm' – connective tissue, the skeletal and muscular system, the blood and lymphatic system, and the 'ectoderm' which forms the skin and nervous system. Freud's 'id', the reservoir of the primitive drives – the sexual and aggressive forces – is related to the endoderm, while the ego and superego are related to the ecto- and mesoderm respectively.

The vegetative discharge reaches the deeper layer of the neurosis, the layer in the biological system. If a tense muscle holds inhibited aggression or binds anxiety, it is easy to understand that relaxation might at first produce restlessness or fidgeting movements before deeper bodily sensations, such as trembling, twitching of muscles or itching, surface as somatic manifestations of anxiety, anger and pleasure. These reactions in the vegetative or autonomic nervous system are necessary for the undoing of the repressed energy in the somatic realm.

A key concept is the therapist's attunement to the 'id' and the 'ego' functions of the client. Both the id and the ego are functions of the life force. The id relates to the unconscious, to primal instincts, involuntary impulses and raw emotions and is governed by the 'pleasure principle', while the ego is the home of conscious awareness, of the capacity to think and make voluntary responses. The ego follows the reality principle and mediates between the raw id energy and the external world in action and regulation. Biodynamic vegetotherapy encourages the unconscious or the repressed id to come to the surface by allowing this energy to impinge and be stirred from within. The therapist aims to speak directly to the id, using language specifically to encourage this 'dynamic updrift': 'Let it happen . . . feel the energy in the hand . . . see how it feels . . . go with the movement.' The essence of this work is the energetic process: to liberate the repressed energy and help it to become integrated in the client's circulation and consciousness (Southwell 1988).

Vegetotherapy

The application of vegetotherapy, as originated by Reich, has become a fundamental principle in body psychotherapy, refined and adjusted by the different approaches according to their own methodology. Vegetotherapy aims to release physical tension to free the mind, the mental belief structure. It can be likened to the technique of 'free association' in the analytical approach, but is instead a 'free association through the body'. It is a system of therapeutic techniques with the aim of accessing the body's inherent life energy and dissolving the defence system, the armouring of the body. It takes place in various ways: the client might stand, move or lie down and be asked to pay attention to the body and encouraged to be in touch with internal movements, sensations and emotions. The therapist may encourage the breathing, use a supportive hand or facilitate the process by means of a more confrontational physical exercise.

Working with the resistance in its physical manifestation has became an established way of working in body psychotherapy: to mirror the resistance back to the client and help them to identify with it and explore its meaning and intent, before engaging further with the underlying content. The 'resistance' often encapsulates a 'charge' – 'charge' can be described as the flow of energy carrying the emotions and releasing tension. The therapist encourages the client to express this hidden charge which is held in the body in the form of rigidity or frozenness, or in collapse and loss of feeling. Loosening the body armour results in the release of anxiety, aggression or libidinal impulses.

The work with the breathing is a crucial technique. By conscious and voluntary manipulation or control of the breath a person affects his involuntary responses. The aim of this method of vegetotherapy is to actively mobilise and facilitate the involuntary expression beyond conscious control, often leading to emotional release. This moment of spontaneous uncontrolled movement is in itself therapeutic, because it reaches the deeper self beneath the defence structure. It not only provokes/elicits repressed images together with an emotional release, but also confronts the somatic structure which contains the suppressed experience.

Gerda Boyesen's concept of the 'emotional vasomotoric cycle' illustrates how neurosis cannot be fully eliminated without the accompanying vegetative discharge, because residual tension remains stuck in the armour of the tissue, muscle and viscera. Residual tension remains when an upsurging emotion has not been expressed adequately and has been interrupted. The startle reflex pattern is the most common factor for such interrupted cycles and causes physical armouring: tension in the diaphragm, a slight overemphasis on the inhalation and hypertonus in the secondary respiratory muscles (Collected Papers of Biodynamic Psychology 1980).

Reich developed a formula for the healthy energetic cycle: tension-charge-discharge-relaxation. The understanding of the energetic cycle, and how energy is circulated and expressed through the body, has been further developed since (Figure 9).The functioning of the autonomic (vegetative) nervous system with its sympathetic and parasympathetic parts follows this cycle of tension and relaxation.

The following experience, described by a client from a session with a body psychotherapist, demonstrates the effective release of a 'block' within the cycle of expression.

My limited experience of bodywork has come to me without the intellectual baggage associated with either a formal training or even informal learning about this particular approach. However, I did already hold the view that repressed emotional responses can be held within the body in a form that may potentially find direct expression at some later date. This is an attempt

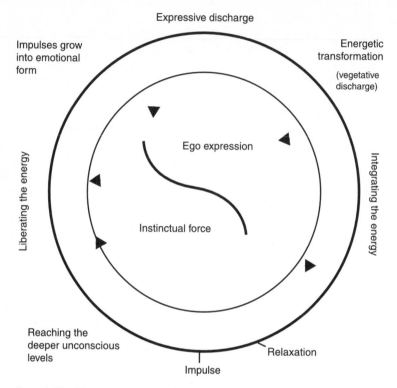

Figure 9 The Vasomotoric cycle. Based on Reich's 'orgasm cycle' (1973) the Vasomotoric cycle traces the client's 'cycle of expression' which could be described
as their circling around within the restrictions of their character structure.
It is their mental/emotional/physiological process which is habitual and
repetitive, whatever the content of what they are saying.

*to describe my most recent experience of bodywork that comes after two or
three previous experiences of working in this way.*

*I arrived at the session aware of a physical sensation in my stomach that
I had associated with an image from the previous session. I had linked this
image with a sense of being alone. It was dark, organic, in a state of flux,
about the size of a human liver and located in the pit of my stomach. This
theme of finding it difficult to be alone and without distraction was one that
has been an issue for me for as long as I can remember. I had determined in
advance of the session that I wanted to explore it and see where it might
take me.*

*To begin with, this physical sensation was faint and I had doubts about
my ability to access it. However, I knew from past experience that regular,
long, deep breathing might help intensify it. The physical sensation started*

to intensify intermittently, and then I found myself almost gagging on surges of energy that seemed to emerge silently from my mouth. It was as if I wanted to cry out, but the sound did not come. At this point, I felt the need to clarify with my therapist that it was indeed all right for me to cry out; that I would be accepted and not ridiculed or diminished in some way. I then took a deep breath and gave myself permission to continue regardless of these concerns which were being raised, in part, by the transference to my therapist of feelings I have about my parents. I needed my therapist to be there to witness my self-exploration and expression, as well as offering me containment and intervention, if necessary, to help facilitate this process.

I continued with long, deep regular breathing and began to experience numbness in my wrists and ankles, and a little light-headedness. I began to vocalise with timid, low-level moans on the out breath. My therapist then asked me how my body might want to move, if I allowed it to do so.

The effect of this intervention was immediate and powerful, as if something had been unblocked. My upper body fell forward across my legs and the vocalisation of my out breath intensified. I was now crying out like the young baby I had once been, left alone by his parents on a bed in a darkened bedroom. I desperately wanted their physical presence and comfort, to be held, but instead I was expected to remain quietly in my bed. This became an outpouring of emotional distress at the fear and pain of feeling abandoned.

Throughout this experience there was a disidentified part of me, conscious that I was allowing myself to undergo this experience for therapeutically beneficial reasons. There was also a fully identified part of me that was being taken on a journey over which I had little conscious control. There were surges or waves of emotion that seemed to be released spontaneously from my body, simply by allowing myself to notice and consciously intensify the experience of the physical sensations within my body. I would then ride the wave of emotion that was released and connections between these emotions and my early childhood experience made themselves apparent almost as spontaneously.

Just when I thought this session had come to an end, my therapist asked whether I was feeling anything in my jaw, as I was holding it at the time. There was a little tension that I thought might be associated with anger, as that is what I had read though not directly experienced.

My therapist then held my jaw and asked me to push against her hand. The impact was immediate, a rush of anger and fury. I felt like a wild dog, snarling and ferocious. I wanted to tear limb from limb those parents who had left me alone in that darkened room as a baby. This was anger that I have felt sure was within me because it would occasionally be expressed explosively, triggered by the most apparently minor frustration. At last, I felt I was connecting directly with this repressed emotion and one of its sources, and it felt liberating.

Finally, as the session drew to an end I began to recover my composure

*and feel a sense of exhaustion, elation, empowerment, connection with my
early self, release, joy, lightness and wellbeing.*

In an ongoing process vegetotherapy sessions are used intermittently, either
to stimulate new layers and bring more material to consciousness, or to process and release material which has been stimulated. It may therefore be used
less frequently in the later stages of the work. The client may have opened up
enough to the therapeutic process so that talking is connected to the deeper
feelings. Working with the energetic charge in the therapeutic relationship can
then be enough to hold the process, and have an impact on the vegetative level.
The therapist uses his own emotional responses as a barometer. Somatic
resonance is an important tool for the body psychotherapist. Having been
trained to be in tune with their own body sensations, they use this resonance as
countertransference to address the client's internal process.

Working with the therapeutic relationship and recognising its importance
as part of the body work – an aspect of Reich's work which was dropped
during the early days of the Humanistic growth movement – has become re-
integrated into body psychotherapy. This progress implies an inherent criticism of the earlier ways of working: because the focus in body psychotherapy
can be directed inward on the internal circulation and flow of energy, it can
sometimes neglect the relational aspects; furthermore it is now appreciated
that even the gentle ways of working with the body are too overwhelming for
certain clients. It may also be that body psychotherapists are more willing to
integrate different approaches and experiment more freely with the polarity
between the psychodynamic and body psychotherapy position.

Working with character structure

Character structure and its transformation remains a cornerstone of body
psychotherapy today. The theory of character structure enables the therapist
to form a diagnosis and develop a working strategy. As developed by Reich
and described previously, the character armouring is the manifestation of the
frozen life history of a person. A hardening of the ego occurs during the
process of adapting to an adult life with all its responsibilities, compromising
primary needs and wants in order to adjust to the social reality. This results in
blocking the flow of the life force, manifesting in neurotic and somatic symptoms. The formation of ego defences goes in tandem with the somatic
armouring (see Figure 1).

Insofar as the ego is involved in those functions of the individual that relate
to their interaction with the world, it is a key to the working of a therapeutic
alliance. Ego-strong structures are those formed in the later stages of development when the reality function of the infant and the 'object constancy' has
been well established, as it is for the rigid structures and partially for the
masochist. Ego-weak structures are those formed in the earlier stages of

development – borderline, schizoid and oral as well as the narcissistic/psychopathic structure.

From today's perspective I would strongly underline that the characterological approach in body psychotherapy overemphasised the 'de-armouring' or 'de-structuring' of the personality and did not give enough recognition to the fact that clients who have a weak and fragile ego need containment and support to keep their defences as a resource. It follows that the character analytical approach can be applied for neurotic, but not for psychotic, structures. Psychosis can be understood as the failure of the ego to contain the id energy. A fair criticism of body psychotherapy is that it has in the past sometimes contributed to a breaking down of the personality structure, and out of this understanding a different way of working has developed where the therapeutic relationship is paramount, taking priority over the application of techniques. It is the relationship that provides the containment and holding for the client in order that the deeper process can emerge. In my experience this does not mean that in maintaining the ego defences, the ego weak-structures will remain untouched; rather that the expression of emotion is less necessary than an understanding and mental framework as a container for the updrifting memories and experiences that arise. The unconscious dynamics will emerge and can be looked at when the client is held in the contact of the therapeutic relationship.

Assessment and diagnosis in body psychotherapy

'Body reading' when used in a systematic way to identify the character structure, gives the body psychotherapist essential information with which to approach the therapeutic work, and it can help the client to identify with a part of themselves which they do not connect with or which is not the most obvious. Since core issues may be identified through body reading, the therapist is sensitive to the possible intrusion this may represent to the client and sharing this information may or may not be appropriate. Some of the questions considered when body reading include (Dychtwald 1997):

- What is the overall non-verbal message the body gives? For example, 'Don't come close!' 'Please come and help me!'
- Is the body as a whole harmonious and balanced, split or displaced? Check the proportion between lower and upper body, front and back, right and left, extremities and torso, head and torso.
- Is the body charged or undercharged, hyper- or hypotonic in muscles and tissues?
- Do different parts of the body give conflicting messages?
- Is the energy flowing?
- Where is it held?
- Are any parts specifically drawn to your attention?

- What is the shoulder position (forward, downward or upward)?
- What is the facial expression like?
- What do the eyes look like and tell you?
- Is the person connected to the ground and is the energy going down into the legs?
- What does the position of the pelvis tell you?
- The position of the head?
- How is the breathing pattern?

The psychotherapist not only listens to the story, but also observes the posture, gestures, facial expression, breathing and unconscious movements – often the body language speaks a different truth. If the client smiles when talking about anger or talks about feeling good with eyes wide open and frightened, this information suggests to the therapist that the person is not integrated and not in touch with their inner life.

Clinical reflections on working with the character structures

Working with the schizoid structure

The therapeutic process with a schizoid client is a journey which starts from an isolated, terrified, mistrusting and hopeless position, and leads eventually to the discovery of an inner self that can be life affirming. A non-invasive, accepting presence from the therapist is essential in order to establish safety and trust. Gradually the therapist attempts to develop in the client the capacity to tolerate body sensations which eventually connect to feelings. This can include physical contact, body awareness and work with breathing. Massage can be very beneficial as well as gentle body work to provide a kinaesthetic experience and to help to connect to inner movements and sensations. Physical exercises, to get out of the head and to ground experience in concrete reality, can be helpful, with the emphasis on controlled release until the client can overcome the terror of being out of control. For someone with this injury the emergence of strong feelings can be experienced as annihilating – as if they are falling apart.

The schizoid structure is based on primitive ego abilities and defences prior to reality testing, e.g. splitting and projection/denial. The fear of becoming overwhelmed needs to be balanced by verbal contact. There is no need for use of powerful techniques; this could lead to uncontrolled release, reinforcing the fear of falling apart. As the tolerance for aliveness develops in the body, and as trust is established, the deeper feelings can emerge in a controlled way: the deeper fear and terror and eventually the hostility. The integration of the explosive anger and the grief for the love that was never given are the pivotal points for change. Gradually the client can learn to trust her impulses, needs and feelings as she experiences them being contained and met in the thera-peutic relationship. Contact is no longer so threatening and the internalised belief, 'something is wrong with me' or 'I am not lovable', can be modified. As the therapist withstands the deeply feared moments of mistrust, hatred and coldness, the schizoid client can sustain more and more of her own aliveness.

Although these clients can be helped through bodywork, they are very vulner-able to becoming overwhelmed if techniques stimulate strong impulse discharge from within. Slow and deep reparative work is needed, building the resources. A gentle somatic approach – small inner movements and sensations which can then be connected to feelings in a contained way with the aim of helping the client to be in touch with the body and the inner life whilst also in contact in the relationship – offers the possibility to repair the 'splitting' dynamic (self *or* relationship, inner *or* outer etc.) which is a feature of this structure.

A clinical example from my own practice demonstrates the process of gradual re-integration of the somatic reality. I worked over a five-year period with a man of predominantly schizoid structure. He came originally because he was particularly interested in the ideas of Reich and he wanted massage. During the massage process, as his breathing deepened and as he expanded more physically, the startle reflex would suddenly be activated, and his body would contract and sometimes convulse. Old memories resurfaced: experi-ences of an abusive father for example. Over the years he was gradually able to tolerate more and more expansion, and the convulsions became less and less. On the physical level this was the undoing of the startle reflex: as he talked it through he gradually became less afraid of his body's response; he associated it with memories and events, and began to understand it more. The body became a less frightening place to be.

Working with the oral structure

The underlying depressive pattern in this structure can be covered up with an eagerness to talk and gain attention. The person may appear open and relaxed, or the repressed need may be compensated with an overlying rigidity and the message 'I can do it on my own'. The most common defences are projection, identification and displacement. Other people are often objecti-fied, seen as potential need gratification; the person will therefore often attach themselves to others to gain a sense of self.

Physical work, including massage, can be very beneficial, especially in the initial stage in the process. The aim is to vitalise and energise the undercharged system, help to develop the muscles and access the libidinal energy in the body. Once the energy is awakened and activated, this can be a step towards self nourishment. The therapist aims to help the client to sustain the charge and contain the energy rather than lose it and become depleted.

The deeper tension held in the shoulders and arms needs to be worked with and will connect to the deeper pain and despair about the original loss or absence. The client will regress and need to have a witness for the justified pain and anger. They need the security of being understood, seen and met this time in the therapeutic relationship, and to see that it is worthwhile reaching out. An important turning point in the further process of differentiation is the realisation for the client that the therapist can never make up for the original loss. This can liberate a deep rage which can turn into a constructive assertive force: 'I can take care of myself and I can express my needs'.

Working with the psychopathic/narcissistic structure

The challenge in the therapeutic relationship is to build trust and support, to reach and nurture the real and vulnerable person, and to respect and acknowledge their deep fear of being controlled. Working directly with the body helps to connect the client to their inner aliveness which is poorly felt and not easily available. Gentle breathing work and body awareness help to establish the downward flow of the energy and to open the involuntary process. In doing so the therapist may encounter a strong resistance in the client, who prefers to be active and possibly angry and outwardly aggressive. These are defences against the underlying panic, fear of being alone, and feeling lost and vulnerable. The fear is that other people may recognise that he is not so powerful and self-sufficient, revealing the lack of knowledge about the range of human feelings.

A turning point in the process with this structure comes when the client opens up to the vulnerability and the acknowledgement of the helplessness which is experienced as humiliation. There is a deep loneliness and pain for having abandoned the real feeling self. The superiority and contempt for others, which covers the need to be loved, to belong and be emotionally connected, needs to be addressed. For this structure the denial of feelings is the denial of need, which represents vulnerability. It can be easy for this person to put on a display in a bodywork session and to produce an impressive act of anger, especially in a group setting. He might need to do this again and again, in order to touch the vulnerability after the catharsis, which opens for him the contact to the real injured self.

Working with the masochistic structure

The release of this blocked assertive energy is a key for therapeutic progress. A more physical approach can be most effective here, because a lot of charge is held underneath the surface. It is important to combine the physical work with character analytical interventions. It is crucial for the therapist not to push the masochistic client. Any direct impingement on the personality could be experienced as re-enactment of the original injury. It is best when the therapist explains the therapeutic interventions and leaves the choice to the client, remaining an assistant to the process. Any energetic work using voice and physical movement helps to liberate the held-in energy and creates an energetic expansion which will be followed by fear and a tendency to give up/collapse. Resistance has been a life-saving strategy for the masochist to keep the inner self intact against external demands, and any expression is frightening. The therapist needs to educate and encourage the client, until she is ready to let go of her compliant or self-sacrificing or passive-aggressive behaviour.

Working with the rigid structures

The rigid personality is dynamic and highly energetic, achieving in life but living in a way which is out of touch with their deeper self. They are socially adept, confident and competitive personalities. Feelings might be easily expressed, but only superficially to defend against the deeper self, and the heart remains locked away. Feelings are controlled by the thinking function in order to avoid failure. The different rigid character types have in common that emerging sexual feelings were compensating a betrayal with an attitude of 'you will not get me'. Although later in life sexually expressive, these structures are not able to surrender deeply and tend to split between romantic and sexual love.

The therapeutic work will aim to support the possibility of surrender instead of holding back. Intuition and deeper feelings are likely to be disregarded as not important and therefore they need to become experienced and valued in order to be connected to and more fully embodied.

The tasks to be learned from the conflicts in this phase are complex, but could be summarised as follows:

- to establish a gender identity and identify with male or female qualities;
- to establish a sexual identity and affirmation in being sexual;
- to learn to accept defeat and rejection; to handle disappointment; to hold on to the loving object inside;
- to accept boundaries and reality through the experience that erotic drives cannot always be fulfilled; to be able to sublimate sexual impulses;
- to learn a 'capacity for concern' and the development of empathy as a foundation for a moral position;
- to be able to sustain strong conflicts;
- to develop healthy competitiveness; to be assertive and goal orientated.

Physical work, such as vegetotherapy or therapeutic massage, can be beneficial to open up the client's feeling response, to access their sensitivity and the inner world of sensations, images and feelings. Often the deeper feelings are not buried far beneath the surface. This process of helping the client to fall into themselves will bring up unfinished resentments and hurts, but may eventually lead to a deeper level of contentment, fulfilment and inner peace.

The borderline personality has only been distinguished and thoroughly researched in more recent years and has been included since 1980 as a definition in the *Diagnostic and Statistical Manual of Mental Disorders* (DSM-III). In every psychotherapy practice there are some people who display at least some traits of the borderline personality. It is different from the neurotic character structure described above, being a personality disorder on the border between neuroses and psychosis with a more severely defective ego development. This personality does not have the same inner resources available as a neurotic structure and can fragment under stress into depersonalisation, extreme confusion, psychotic behaviour, paranoia or acting out with self-destructive behaviour, such as suicide attempts, addictions, self-harming or eating disorders. Such people are not able to differentiate between the internal and external reality or the real and the symbolic.

The physical appearance of the borderline does not show any typical shape. It could be associated with some schizoid characteristics in which case the body might appear underdeveloped with a low charge. However it could also show the characteristics of a well-functioning, competent 'false ego' personality with a strongly developed body.

The borderline personality is formed during the separation stage or rapprochement phase (15–24 months), occasioned by the caretaker's withdrawal of support and encouragement in response to the child's attempts to separate. This abandonment is experienced as highly traumatic, leading to a loss of self. This structure typically displays idealising and splitting as strong defence mechanisms, as well as denial, projection and projective identification. The core issues revolve around identity and relationship problems. Identity is sacrificed, and a symbiotic attachment is formed in the hope of gaining love. This idealised love and closeness inevitably results in a loss of self through engulfment or abandonment, and this provokes panic. When fears of engulfment are dominant, the client will keep distant, and when fears of abandonment dominate, the client will be clinging and very demanding. Both scenarios will be acted out in the dynamic with the therapist. The therapeutic relationship becomes the main vehicle for the work, since there are intense relational dynamics in the foreground.

The therapeutic process is aimed at helping the client to move to independence and to be able to tolerate the anxiety of separation – what Masterson calls 'abandonment depression' (Masterson 1976). Physical work needs to be applied carefully, if at all. Body psychotherapy has been designed for neurotic structures rather than for borderline. Due to the poor sense of self, a weak ability to differentiate and a strong projective tendency, a physical intervention is likely to be received in a distorted way, experienced as either magical or abusive. Physical interventions can be helpful if used selectively in moments when the working alliance is intact, e.g. to help alleviate feelings of panic and unreality and to provide grounding or help to express anger and rage which is turned against the self in self-destructive behaviour.

Sometimes I find it more effective therapeutically to be more directive with such clients in order to avoid regressive episodes in sessions. A recent experience with a client in a couple session reinforces my belief. The woman, whom I would describe as a borderline personality (symptoms of eating disorder and self-harming behaviour) had come with her partner to discuss how these problems affected their relationship. During the session she felt deeply threatened by what her partner said, and she regressed: her body began to shake and tremble. I did not manage to intervene early enough to direct her away from the regression, and I followed the process through as she entered a full body catharsis; eventually I got her to stay in contact with the partner and complete the cycle. But the result was that she suffered a great deal in the weeks that followed; she had involuntary movements in her body which she could not control and she felt very frightened and overwhelmed and was unable to spend time alone. I believe that in the end it is good for a client to enter this process – there is a terrified abandoned child who cannot believe she could be acceptable being like this – but I prefer to do this in little steps, and I don't think it is necessary to go through such a painful process which interferes with daily life.

Working with trauma and the use of touch

As therapists we are alert to the fact that hands-on work with trauma victims may activate overwhelming memories, or be experienced by the client as an intrusion of boundaries which consequently might lead to further dissociation. Touch is therefore either contraindicated or needs to be applied very carefully. However, in my experience touch can be a useful intervention, after boundaries have been explicitly set and agreed in the therapeutic relationship, when the relationship is safely established and when the client is able and willing to explore the bodily interventions in an ongoing verbal dialogue.

There seems to be a growing popularity for body psychotherapy in the field of trauma work. Babette Rothschild's somatic approach is based on body psychotherapy with no touch (Rothschild 2000). I would like to reflect on the potential value of touch, when applied mostly in the later stages of the trauma work. Dissociation and disembodiment are common symptoms for trauma clients, and therefore physical sensations and needs are numbed or not experienced. Automatic hyperarousal is a residual symptom from a trauma and leads to an inability to relax. The gradual experience of a 'safe touch' can eventually heal the effects of the original trauma and help the body to awaken to sensory experiences. Touch is likely to evoke further repressed emotional memories, hence more hyperarousal. It is the body psychotherapist's assessment skill which guides the process: to help the client to say 'no'; to validate the client's physical experiences and help to make meaning of the sensory experiences instead of dissociating from the body. This eventually helps the client to experience the body as a container for intense feelings; to help the client to relax more and reduce tension and to experience a change in the muscles or tissue. This experience affects the mental state: in general to facilitate a process leading to the integration of an embodied sense of self, experiencing the self in and through the body.

However, the use of touch with trauma clients remains a very controversial debate. My experience shows that a body psychotherapy approach can sometimes work more time-effectively, while a purely verbal approach demands a much longer process. This is also generally true for very early disturbances which are more difficult to reach by means of language; it also applies to clients with psychosomatic symptoms. Psychosomatic symptoms can be understood as *a somatised response to undesired affects or emotions*, and may stem from a repressed memory of an event experienced early in infancy, prior to the capacity to symbolise. The body symptoms signal the need to express something which is not accessible as a feeling nor able to be verbalised. A holding, supportive touch is a means to enter a somatic dialogue.

Conclusion

This chapter details how body psychotherapy has developed in the post-Reich era. It also conveys the two-way interaction between psychic and physical expression as fundamental to body psychotherapy, illustrating how the bodily approach and method can deepen and enrich the practice of psychotherapy. Above all, the quality of meeting and the contact with the client is what remains most central, whether this is achieved through a verbal or a physical method or both.

References

Biodynamic Psychology, Collected Papers, Vol 1–3. Biodynamic Psychology Publications 1980. Printed originally in *Energy and Character – Journal of Bioenergetic Research* edited by David Boadella (1972–1982)

Boadella, D. *Wilhelm Reich: The Evolution of his Work*. Chicago: Henry Regnery Comp. 1974

Boadella, D. *Lifestreams – An Introduction to Biosynthesis*. London: Routledge & Kegan Paul 1987

Capra, F. *Wendezeit*. Bern: Scherz 1983. English edition: *The Turning Point*. New York: Simon and Schuster 1982

Conger, P. *The Body in Recovery. Somatic Psychotherapy and the Self*. Berkeley, CA: North Atlantic Books 1994

Cotter, S. 'Bioenergetics at Cranfield'. *Journal of Management Development* 1996; 15 (3): 3–76

Dychtwald, K. *Bodymind*. US: Tarcher, Second edition 1986 [1977]

Eiden, B. 'Reich's Legacy'. *Counselling News*, January 1999; 12–14

Ferenczi, S. *Further Contributions to the Theory and Technique of Psychoanalysis.* London: Karnac 1994a

Ferenczi, S. *Final Contributions to the Problems and Methods of Psychoanalysis.* London: Karnac 1994b

Freud, S. *The Ego and the Id*, S.E. 19. London: Hogarth 1923

Gomez, L. *An Introduction to Object Relations.* London: Free Association Books 1997

Johnson, S. *Characterological Transformation: The Hardwork Miracle.* New York: W. W. Norton 1985

Johnson, S. M. *Character Styles.* New York/London: W. W. Norton & Company 1994

Johnson, S. *Humanising the Narcissistic Style.* New York: W. W. Norton 1985

Journal of Biodynamic Psychology, Vol 1 (Spring 1998); *Vol 2* (Summer 1981); and *Vol 3* (Winter 1982). Calvert's North Star Press Ltd

Kurtz, R. *The Hakomi Handbook.* Boulder, CO: Hakomi Institute 1970

Kurtz, R. *Body-Centered Psychotherapy: The Hakomi Method.* Mendocino, CA: Life Rhythm 1990

Lowen, A. *The Language of the Body.* New York: Collier Macmillan 1958

Lowen, A. *Bioenergetics.* London: Arkana 1975

Masterson, J. *Psychotherapy of the Borderline Adult: A Developmental Approach.* New York: Brunner Mazel 1976

McNeely, D. A. *Touching – Body Therapy and Depth Psychology.* Toronto: Inner City Books 1987

Pierrakos, J. *Core Energetics.* Mendocino, CA: Life Rhythm 1987

Raab, I. *Touch in Psychotherapy – Controversies and Applications.* Dissertation: Massachusetts School of Professional Psychology 1996

Reich, W. *Character Analysis.* NY: Noonday Press 1990 (Copyright date 1945)

Reich, W. *The Function of the Orgasm.* London: Souvenir Press 1983 First British Edition

Rosenberg, J. *Total Orgasm.* Berlin: Orgasmus 1975

Rosenberg, J. *Body, Self and Soul – Sustaining Integration.* Humanics 1985

Rothschild, B. *The Body Remembers – The Psychophysiology of Trauma and Trauma Treatment.* New York/London: Norton 2000

Southwell, C. 'The Gerda Boyesen Method: Biodynamic Therapy'. In: Rowan, J. and Dryden, W. (Eds) *Innovative Therapy in Britain.* London: Open University Press 1988: 178

Stern, D. *The Interpersonal World of the Infant: A View from Psychoanalytic and Developmental Psychology.* New York: Basic Books, 1985

Totton, N. and Edmondson, E. *Reichian Growth Work – Melting the Blocks to Life and Love.* Prism Press 1988

Totton, N. *The Water in the Glass – Body and Mind in Psychoanalysis.* London: Rebus Press 1998

Winnicott, D. *The Maturational Process and the Facilitating Environment.* London: Hogarth 1965

Chapter 3

Sexuality and body psychotherapy

Tree Staunton

> If we were men, if we were women, our individualities would be lone and a bit mysterious, like tarns . . . and fed with power – male power, female power – from underneath, invisibly. And from us the streams of desire would flow out in the eternal glimmering adventure, to meet in some unknown desert.
>
> D.H. Lawrence: 'Love Was Once a Little Boy' from
> *Reflections on the Death of a Porcupine and Other Essays*

This chapter offers a brief overview of psychotherapeutic understanding of sexuality, and describes the underpinnings of a body psychotherapy approach. It takes a look at the sexual issues connected to the different 'character structures' and how to work with sexuality; it discusses the psychodynamics of sexual relating and the issues of touch and sexual transference. Finally it touches on the ethics in working with sexuality and the body.

Body psychotherapy and sexuality: placing it in the field

Freud, Reich and Jung have clearly been enormously influential in the development of the theory and practise of body psychotherapy today. Although all three agreed that the integration of the instinctual-emotional life was a fundamental aim of therapy, the centrality of sexuality as a root cause and key focus for the work was a major cause of difference. The most significant of Jung's doubts about Freud's theory concerned sexuality which he 'did not wish to place so firmly in the foreground or to endow with a psychological universality' (Jung 1997: 93).

> I wished no longer to speak of the instincts of hunger, aggression and sex but to regard all these phenomena as expressions of psychic energy.
>
> Jung 1995: 234

Whilst Freud understood sex as a basic instinct, ruled by the Pleasure principle, Jung's addition of the spiritual instinct – 'an instinct towards individuation' (Stein 1984: 134) – which he also called the *creative instinct*, opened the door to an understanding of sex as a *drive towards wholeness*, a quest for creative union within the psyche. More recently, Archetypal psychology has suggested that the creative instinct is 'similar if not identical to the nature of eros' (Stein 1984: 135) and this leads to an understanding of the sex drive as *part* a desire for sensual gratification and discharge and *part* a spiritual quest for psychic wholeness.

> . . . the understanding and ultimate resolution of the body/mind split in modern people necessitates a thorough exploration of the relationship between the sensual and spiritual aspects of the soul.
>
> Stein 1984: 134

Reich's focus remained on the theory of sexuality, using Freud as the groundwork and expanding into orgonomics (see Chapter 1). Reich believed that all neurosis was caused by an unholy alliance between a psychic conflict and dammed-up sexual energy, that the blocking of the life force in the very tissue of the body was the cause of the misery in the psyche of man [sic] and his world.

Although most body psychotherapists base their work on Reich's ideas of character armour and orgonomics, Jung's conception of sexuality comes closer to the working understanding arrived at by many practitioners today: a conception of libido as a 'psychic analogue of physical energy' seeing our drives as 'various manifestations of energetic processes'.

> Just as it would not occur to a modern physicist to derive all forces from, shall we say, heat alone, so the psychologist should beware of lumping all instincts under the concept of sexuality.
>
> Jung 1995: 235

This view of 'energetics' is very akin to the Body Psychotherapist's working assumptions about sexuality and its function in the psyche.

There is no doubt that both Freud and Reich's theories were based to a large extent on the medical model in relation to treatment of illness, cure being achieved by the successful application of techniques. The focus on a single root cause – sexuality – meant that a cure could be efficated if one applied treatment to this cause.

Jung had no such illusions, and perhaps because of the depth of his own journey accepted that surrender to the mystery of transformation was the only view possible. A natural consequence of this view was the development and strengthening of a Witness or Observing Ego position, which is in any case a developmental goal in all psychoanalysis and psychotherapy.

It is to Jung, therefore, that Humanistic psychotherapies owe our present-day relational model which attempts to collaborate rather than treat, in which the practice is based on a very real principle: that the wounds suffered in relationship must be healed in relationship. All the training and preparation which the practitioner undergoes in order to gain knowledge and understanding, and refine skills and techniques are geared towards this aim – to be as available as they can be for the unique relationship which will unfold with each individual who seeks help. This is never more true than in working with sexuality.

Sexuality and body psychotherapy today

Freud spoke of instinct and duty, of repression and sublimation; Reich spoke of instinct and liberation, discharge and release; whilst Jung elevated the instinctual to a mystical symbolic union. But nowhere are these approaches at understanding human sexuality linked to *love*.

How can we base our work with clients on issues surrounding sexuality if even the theories do not link sex and love? Reich's idea was to unite heart and genitals by working to release the energetic/emotional blocks preventing energy flow between them – but is this a language of love? How can we speak of these intimate matters with clients when we have a clinical understanding that is alien to our experience or does not speak to our nature? It seems that at least part of the solution is developing a language – one that will be allowed to emerge from the working relationship – which can truly describe the nature of the experience. And for this purpose we must borrow from different sources as well as invent our own.

Every new generation moves on in consciousness, and in practice the work of change is much more complex than Reich conceived. Though revolutionary in his thinking at that time – he was passionately addressing liberation from an implicitly socio-political stance – as body psychotherapists in the post-Reich era, we can experience the shadow of his work. Reich's idea of sexual liberation for individuals and for society, though sound in principle, was an ego-ideal, and as such must be resisted by the organism. Reich's approach was to achieve a *destructuring* of the 'civilised' ego in order to liberate the instinct, and he believed that, if given a free rein in childhood, self-regulation would lead to a more healthy expression of love and sex. He did not concern himself with *restructuring*, or the ego-building necessary for primitive levels to be integrated, nor with an inter-relational field between individual and society. Post-sexual revolution, half a century later we have more a sense of the need for 'creative regulation of the instinctual-emotional life' which Stein speaks of (1984: 152) and a respect for an individual journey towards wholeness which may be less 'liberated' than Reich deemed desirable. Liberation comes through acceptance of what is rather than through a programme of change aimed at liberation. Humanistic therapies today – and increasingly more analytic approaches too – favour a less prescriptive approach over the previous rather reductive and clinical way of assessing life function. They move towards acceptance of individuals' choices of self-expression and are supportive of a variety of expressions of sexuality as healthy, provided that individuals are not imposing on the happiness of others. Whilst sexuality has remained at the centre of psychotherapeutic theories, the emphasis has changed considerably.

Neo-Reichians such as Lowen (1977), Pierrakos (1987) and Boyeson (1980, 1981, 1982 and 1998) all worked with sexuality as if it were an independent force in the body. Lowen developed his system of bioenergetic exercises to break down the muscle armour, whilst Boyesen applied her massage techniques with little explicit reference to the therapeutic relationship. 'Sexuality' was termed synonymous with 'life force'. There was a notion of removing blocks in the energy expression without reference to the internal objects and relational dynamics that created and maintained them; they had taken on and developed the orgonomic aspect of Reich's theory but dropped the psychoanalytic aspect. The drive theory was no longer underwriting the understanding of the work.

Many body psychotherapists today include the understanding that whilst sexual energy is cathected in particular ways in the body it *is* psychic energy and the cathexis is linked to internalised objects in the psyche. We return to the understanding that all love is object related.

The Oedipus Complex

Can any psychotherapist talk about understanding and working with sexuality without talking about the Oedipal myth? The instinctual life – that which obviously includes one's relationship to one's bodily experience and one's drives and impulses – is a thing unto itself, moving and operating in each of us. But the Oedipal myth refers to an object towards whom one directs these impulses and desires. And it suggests a universality about that, that indeed we *all* have wishes and fantasies and desires related in a specific way to each of our parents. It will be clear from Chapter 2 that Reich's character structures are constructed around this constellation.

In theory I do glean some important information from the story, though I do not necessarily see its application as a story representing the internal mythology of each individual's psychic makeup. Oedipus is afraid of his incestuous desire; by doing everything in his conscious power to avoid transgressing, he does exactly that. His parents, too, fear the incest that is predicted and they cannot face themselves with such a possibility; perhaps this speaks more of avoidance of the intimacy which borders on incest than the pre-determined nature of family relations.

Traditionally psychoanalysis used it as a parable, a prediction of inevitable dynamics that should be faced in order to be overcome. As women we should face and then overcome our desire for our father, lest we spend our whole lives trying to recapture this lost desire and never find fulfilment elsewhere. Likewise with sons and mothers. There is a fatality, an inevitability of enactment within the myth that tells us more broadly something important about the nature of the unconscious: *that which we avoid or deny will manifest itself again and again until we have faced it* . . . it cannot be consciously avoided. If we cannot contemplate something it is necessary to live our life around it in attempts to avoid it – and it will catch up with us in the end. Much of our work is centred on assisting clients to face up to their greatest fears so as to interrupt their self-fulfilling fantasies.

So is the myth itself valuable and important and, if so, how can it be applied? In practice, can one suggest a particular interpretation to a client and then call it resistance if they deny it? It is questionable ethically in a Humanistic approach to the work. This does not mean ignoring the defence mechanisms or colluding with a false reality, but rather embracing a third reality which is waiting to emerge from the relationship dynamic. As a psychotherapist I must recognise the enormous symbolic significance of a father to each woman's psyche, just as there is a great influence from the family dynamic and the person's position in the family. But myths are live forms that are recreated and reconstellated over time. Archetypes, too, alter over time in a collective unconscious as well as in different cultures and societies. As we become an increasingly mixed-race society in the West, our sexual mythology adopts new dimensions. There are many different ways in which we now live out our sexuality – women and women, men and men – and gender roles, too, shift and change; many mothers adopt a father role, setting the rules and boundaries, expanding horizons in the world of ideas and introducing a bridge to the outside world, whilst fathers may adopt a more traditionally female position.

The psychic need of the individual remains to find a creative expression of their sexuality through the internalisation of a workable relationship between parents which nurtures the desire of the child whilst refusing to fulfill it.

Sexuality and differentiation: developing our own approach

We have taken a brief look at the roots of our work in Freud, Jung, Reich and the neo-Reichians. Each practitioner is led by a desire beyond and besides the content of their particular thesis: Freud's deep search for truth was in the realm of ideas, the mind; Reich saw salvation or redemption in the body; whilst for Jung it was clearly the spirit itself. Many psychotherapists today use the term 'integrative' to describe their work, because they see themselves trying to integrate these different aspects to form the whole (mind, body, spirit – a holistic approach).

But whilst we may follow a 'school of thought' we must all work from our own source. We each have a desire beyond the content of our chosen approach to the work – the spirit that motivates us toward our work as therapists, our central guiding imago. It is essential that as therapists we come to understand this imago, so that we may draw our inspiration from it but so too that we learn to stand outside or beside it: to know which lens we are looking through, and to recognise our blind spots.

The *idea* of sex and the subject of sexuality occupied Freud for his entire life. Jung said of him

> There was no mistaking that Freud was emotionally involved in his sexual theory to an extraordinary degree . . . I had a strong intuition that for him sexuality was a sort of *numinosum* . . .
>
> Jung 1995: 173

This kind of inspiration or 'guiding light' exists for all of us. It may be constellated around the Archetypal Mother–child relationship (depicted in the religious icon of the Mother of Christ holding the babe in her arms) or it may be an image of Wholeness in which a Unity of self is represented (the Mandalla); or perhaps it is the image of the Lovers, of union as represented by 'sex'. Perhaps less commonly in psychotherapy, it can be a Father imago, or a Logos principle that holds the chaos of inner life with a structured yet open mind.

We sometimes find in exploring images through bodily experience (see Chapter 6) that this meaning is held in or represented by a particular part of the body. For example, the heart may be key to this deep connection to the Life Force; the hand which gently caresses, or the eyes which hold a deep and powerful resonance, an experience of being met, of belonging. It is our life's work to connect to and work from this place of meaning and purpose.

Love and sex

It is astonishing that Freud used the words 'sex' and 'love' interchangeably, given the degree of thought he gave the subject of sexuality.

C.S. Lewis in *The Four Loves* (Lewis 1960) describes four types of human love: Affection, Friendship, Eros and Charity. Rollo May (May 1974: 37) also defines four types of love in Western tradition as Sex, Eros, Philia (friendship or brotherly love) and Agape (love devoted to the welfare of others). Debatably, we should add a fifth type of love – Transference love – though Mann (Mann 1997: Chapter 2) tells us that no analyst from Freud onwards has managed to successfully distinguish transference love from 'normal' love. Lewis is considerably more differentiated than Freud – and indeed Mann – in his distinction between *eros* and *sex*: 'Sexual desire, without Eros, wants IT, the thing itself, Eros wants the Beloved.'

Sex, lust, libido may or may not be contained within love but, like all other instinctual needs, it is a statement about ourselves, rather than a relationship to another. Sexuality in this sense is animal desire, instinct, sensory pleasure, the impulse for sex for the sake of sex.

> We use a most unfortunate idiom when we say of a lustful man prowling the streets, that he wants a woman. Strictly speaking, a woman is just what he does not want. He wants a pleasure for which a woman happens to be the necessary piece of apparatus. How much he cares about the woman as such may be gauged by his attitude to her five minutes after fruition (one does not keep the carton after one has smoked the cigarettes).
>
> Lewis 1960: 109

On the other hand, Lewis tells us that eros

> . . . makes a man really want not a woman, but one particular woman. In some mysterious fashion the lover desires the Beloved herself, not the pleasure she can give.

Eros can be defined further as the drive of love to procreate or create; the urge, as the Greeks put it, towards higher forms of being and relationship. It is the force that changes and invents new structures and forms new ways of being; it is the energy at the growing edge of change and renewal because it is the desire for union or communion; a dynamic ebb and flow, meeting and parting. It is in this understanding that Jung equated eros with the creative urge towards individuation (Jung 1960: 45).

Transference love

David Mann (Mann 1997: 31) tells us that when the British psychoanalyst J.C. Flugel asked Freud why analysis cures, the answer he gave was: 'At one moment the analyst loves the patient and the patient knows it and the patient is cured' (quoted from LeShan 1989).

Much more famously, of course, he is quoted as saying that the love the analysand feels is always a resistance to analysis and the analyst should remain detached and uninvolved at all times. After some searching discussion on the subject, Mann concludes

> . . . our understanding of transference love has not developed very far since Freud's 1915 paper (*Observations on Transference Love*). Transference love is still a muddle for psychoanalysis.
>
> Mann 1997: 52

On the whole both psychoanalysis and psychotherapy now view the counter-transference as an essential therapeutic tool rather than an obstruction;

reference is often made to the fact that both therapist and client are transformed in a successful therapy, and that transference and countertransference operate both ways and are a 'joint creation'. Both client and therapist are 'moved'; love is implicit in the healing dynamic.

However, I agree with Mann that when it comes to the sexual dynamic, the 'transference love' is, for a number of reasons, frequently attributed to the client rather than being acknowledged as also belonging to the therapist. Frequently, the therapist prefers to adopt the more powerful and passive-receptive 'mother' position in the relationship, which can be a major defence against relating; furthermore, the therapist is more in a position to defend themselves from unwanted feelings than the client, with the justification that it is the client's feelings which require attention and not theirs.

> By and large, what tends to be described as projective identification are those qualities that conflict with the ego-ideals of most therapists.
>
> Mann 1997: 77

In other words, if I did feel it, you made me feel it. As therapists we are comfortable with the presence of *agape* – the love evoked by the pain of another, the desire to care for another, putting aside our own needs. But what of other forms of love? It is possible that Humanistic therapies are conceived of – perhaps by therapists who choose this orientation as well as clients – as a more 'philial' relationship; whilst the analytically-oriented therapist is seen as more potent and perhaps threatening, a more menacing subject for the containment of the client's unconscious forbidden desire. What is clear is that potency and desire, attraction and aversion are elements that do not sit comfortably in the therapist's chair, more especially in same-sex dyads.

Psychodynamics of sexual relating

Sexuality is complex relationally. It requires considerable maturity and a certain level of integration of primal realities to maintain an adult sexual relationship. The loss of ego and the intensity of instinctual force ('updrift') severely compromises the person just on an 'organismic' level, never mind the complexities of interrelating and negotiation of different needs and desires. Sex evokes and reawakens early issues of identity and selfhood. May ([1969], 1974: 65) talks of sex as 'the struggle to prove one's identity and personal self-worth'. Horrocks (1997: 74) tells us that sex takes us to the root of selfhood, it 'plays around with identity and loss of identity'.

> The orgasm for both sexes seems to encapsulate this explosion of boundaries: at the point of orgasm, one may not be very sure who is who, or who is doing what. Isn't that part of the delight?
>
> Horrocks 1997: 73

Yet for some this 'playing with selfhood' provokes extreme terror. Whether the loss of self-boundary is experienced as a joyous expansion or as a threatening annihilation depends largely on the *embodied* ego capacity of the individual.

In terms of development a person needs to be at least capable of Object Constancy (see Chapter 2, Figure 1) to sustain a long-term sexual relationship. There is no doubt that many clients seen in psychotherapy have problems with their sexuality due to an unformed or inadequate Self-Boundary and crippling pre-sexual internal dynamics.

In order to relate sexually as adults we need to feel that we can face *another* – man or woman – with our fears and our needs and be prepared to be rejected, dismissed or abandoned without losing our sense of ourselves and our secure identity. Being in a relationship where there is 'too much to lose' to be able to say who we really are is a recipe for avoidant or absent sex. Emotional honesty and transparency are the keynotes to our ability to openly express ourselves sexually.

We need to be able to feel entitled to be met without necessarily being gratified, daring to be with our desire whilst capable of sustaining a belief in ourselves when it is not welcomed by the other. It is a negotiation – inner and outer – so full of pitfalls and potential disappointments that many people find it easier to avoid or compromise, accepting much less than they really want. This resignation represents the 'character armour' which has been discussed in Chapter 2.

If a client wants to 'have' their sexuality they need to be emotionally 'behind' their own impulses, able to withstand challenge and disagreement, not dependent on acceptance. Sexual relating brings with it much insecurity, because it is a 'putting oneself on the line', an identification with one's desire; it cannot be – and is not usually experienced internally as – a half-hearted affair. It is or it isn't.

In order for there to be intercourse there must be two discrete entities which, coming together, may then surrender their separateness and merge to form a union. The relationship which is thus formed is a third 'other' entity; and rather than a bond between two – a 'merging' that psychically resembles the mother-child relationship with all its concurrent limitations, restrictions and inhibitions, as well as positive bonds and dependencies – the adult sexual relationship demands a commitment to this 'other', which one is participant in, and responsible for co-creating (see Figure 10).

Character structure and sexuality

We have to remember that character structure is a defence – a defence against contact and relationship now as much as a defence against experiencing a past injury; a defence against one's own desire for erotic and heart connection. Whilst we are supportive and empathetic with the various mani-

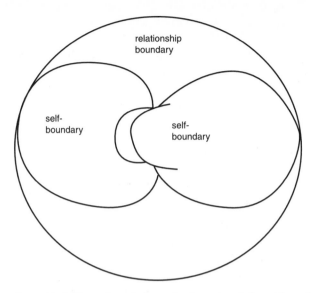

Figure 10 Self-boundaries/relationship boundary (adapted from Rosenberg 1985: 234).

festations of our client's habitual stance, if we are to be of therapeutic use to them, these defence structures need to be disrupted and challenged. Reich's method of disruption – to interrupt the breathing pattern in order to disturb the neurotic equilibrium – is still used by some body psychotherapists in some situations. But, as Bernd Eiden points out in Chapter 2, this is not always appropriate, and more often we are engaged in a delicate balance of supporting the ego structure and working *with* the defence in such a way that there can be a position outside of it. The therapist needs to ally themselves to a part of the client which can reflect on and experience the feelings of their conflict so that they can separate themselves from the defence. If the client identifies with their defences, then they will experience a sense of annihilation if those defences are disrupted or dismantled.

Whilst all character structure presents a difficulty in intimacy and sexual relating, there is not the linear or hierarchical relationship implied in the developmental model, such that if there is earlier damage then a person is 'further away' from reaching the genital phase, and therefore has less possibility of satisfaction in terms of sexual relationship. In fact, in my experience there is a more palpable sense of eros with the so-called ego weak structures, where an absence is felt: there is a strong sense of something missing, a greater longing for union to take place. With an ego-strong structure there is more of a defence against this longing, and the desire for power replaces the desire for contact. Problems arise in the extremes of both – a fragile, uncontained ego-weak structure or an over-bound and defended ego-strong one.

Quality of contact may be more important than 'quantity' in terms of the expression of one's sexual life; contact with it may be more important than expression, and very few people nowadays adopt Reich's literal way of looking at the organism and the instincts – the suggestion that a 'healthy' person discharges fully and often. If we accept the view that there is a 'spiritual' dimension to the erotic, then the quest for an inner union is also central to fulfillment. There must be a balance between inner and outer, being *with* an experience and acting or expressing, and this will be different for different individuals depending on their desire in life and, on a more transpersonal level, the meaning of their soul's journey.

It follows from the description of the orgasm cycle (Chapter 2, Figure 9) that the ability to engage sexually in an enjoyable and fulfilling way depends on the ability to contain 'charge' or excitement, to allow it to spread throughout the body and to surrender to its pleasurable release. Rosenberg (1985: 232) talks about the use of breathing in developing arousal, and the importance of containment and boundaries in the body ego. Some of the breath work in which he engages his clients is, he says, 'Like the Hindu practice of Tantra, which also involves intense eye contact while the energy is circulating from the genitals through the whole body up to the eyes'.

The armouring of muscles and tissues of the body in character structure is developed to prevent the charge from building or releasing, and the emotional issues 'held' in this armouring are at the root of each person's sexual identity. Without basic security and primary self love, sexuality in all the structures may be usurped by basic needs for love and acceptance: the person looks for love by offering themselves sexually. When they are relating sexually from this condition they will never feel loved and will always feel used – regardless of the feelings and intentions of their lover – because they are allowing access to one part of themselves in the hope of gaining fulfillment in another part; they are using themselves, and betrayal is inevitable.

If we now take a closer look at sexual issues within the different character structures we can begin to understand some of the influences on sexuality that arise out of pre-sexual dynamics. It has been suggested (Berliner 1993) that melting or fusing with the mother (actual or archetypal) is always part of the unconscious wish or fantasy in sex, dominating or conflicting to varying degrees in different character structures. I would add that the desire to melt and become one with an 'internal object' in the psyche can be expanded to the 'spiritual instinct' mentioned earlier, a desire for a cosmic oneness experienced through union physically with another, who comes to represent the divine during sex.

The schizoid structure presents a problem in 'letting go' into this melting, due to an energetically brittle and fragile boundary, and also problems with 'building charge' – the bodymind structure cannot contain charge easily. Berliner (1993) has stated that the schizoid may not experience pleasure in sex if they are unable to merge with the (m)other in fantasy.

For the oral structure, on the other hand, the desire to merge with the mother becomes confused with the sexual desire for an *other*, and whilst the desire for closeness brings the oral person into intimate contact with another, often their primary need is to be held and nurtured. Oral sex may be more pleasurable than penetrative. Again the energetic system presents difficulties in building and containing 'charge'.

Borderline and pure Narcissistic structures bring into their sexual life a chaotic and sometimes perverse quality, with many different partners and many ways of getting pleasure. At the forefront are psychodynamic elements of power and use of sex, seduction and conquering, so that although the energetics *per se* do not present such a problem as in the earlier structures, the intrapsychic confusion interferes with maintaining 'charge' and flexibility of boundaries.

Structures which arise at later stages of development are likely to involve issues of power and control in the expression of sexuality; the energetic issues concern *over-containment* of 'charge' and a loss of self is experienced in the letting go. Whilst the release of somatic 'holding' may be easier and feel less life-threatening than with the earlier structures, the psychodynamic 'holding' is more complex, and must be accessed through the transference dynamics.

Some clinicians in the field (notably Berliner) have delineated more detailed issues accompanying the different structures but it is more in fitting with the approach to avoid the prescriptive and to work with what arises, reflecting in the usual ways on somatic, energetic and relational dynamics.

Sexuality and the therapeutic relationship

> The soul connection between analyst and analysand is central to the healing process (. . . particularly where the wounds to the soul are in the area of love and sex, and mind/body splitting . . .) – and this is not possible unless the analyst is willing and able to reveal his or her own soul.
>
> Stein 1984: 6

Why should the client bring to the therapeutic relationship – or to their own conscious awareness – feelings of an erotic or sexual nature if the therapist is not also willing to engage at this level? The therapist working with the sexual is able to be in touch with their own desire for erotic connection, and to resonate with this in the client.

The wish for an erotic connection is always there. It may be buried under a dense and impenetrable cover of self-pity and resignation or anxiously present in an avoidant and unwilling participation. At times clients seek the connection through pathological behaviours – 'going for the sympathy vote' as one client called it. With others, the wish is palpable, a strong and magnetic current which pulls at the heart, the belly or the genitals. How is the contact blocked? How am I experienced by the client in wanting contact with them, and how do they treat me? How is the subject matter dislocated from the feeling in them and the contact with me? If we talk about sex, how present is the libido, how alive the desire? What is the nature of their sexuality? Is it a phallic thrusting energy or a seducing, magnetising one? Or is there a passivity which brings stalemate? All these qualities are experienced by the body psychotherapist 'energetically' as well as psychodynamically.

The therapist 'being available' has a meaning beyond attentiveness, active listening and therapeutic presence. It means that, as therapist, I can be reached: I can feel attracted, bathed, soothed, stimulated or aroused by the client. I can also feel repelled and disgusted, or feel a total lack of erotic interest. These things can be registered and acknowledged, contained within the therapist's 'self-boundary' and allowed to permeate through to the client as a healing and reparative experience. There is a boundless and overflowing sense of joy and wellbeing tapped in the client who feels 'received' and a tremendous sense of empowerment arises from the knowledge that they can make an impact on the other person. By the same token, the most difficult and unwanted reflections can be received by the client if they are held within the framework of this bond.

> The patient and the therapist come together in a psychic intercourse that will either lead to a new conception (gestation and birth) in the psychic development of both, or there will be psychic impotence and sterility.
>
> Mann 1997: 124

The exchange between client and therapist must bear fruit. A therapy, which painfully re-lives past experiences but does not stimulate a different experience in the here and now, is not resolving or healing. There needs to be something enlivening, with hope and possibility.

The work: towards embodied sexuality

> *While we have sex in the mind we truly have none in the body.*
>
> D.H. Lawrence 1929

Lacan would have us believe that human sexuality is inevitably disembodied, since 'sexual desire is saturated in fantasy' (Horrocks 1997: 74). Whether it is wholly or partially true, in the analytic sense, that we desire fantasised internal objects in our sexual quest, it remains true that for much of our lives most of us are engaged in the business of having sexual relations, and this is a very bodily-based activity. As Horrocks points out:

> Generally sex goes on in or around certain bodily orifices: the mouth, the vagina, the penis, the nipple, the anus . . . sexual energy seems to play

along the edges of the body ... seems to derive its charge from the oscillation between the I and the not-I ... Our orificial boundaries collide and mingle ...

Horrocks 1997: 71–72

In working with identity and boundaries, body psychotherapy involves the physical and energetic work of developing a more flexible body-ego, so that the transition of the movement from I to not-I can be more pleasurably experienced.

For the purposes of study, the work with sexuality can be divided into two stages, applied in an earlier and a later phase of therapy although in practise they will also operate concurrently.

1   Contact with the instinctual level, where the person begins to feel themselves as embodied and alive, 'stirring up' the unconscious material 'bound' or held in the bodily structure. In the sense that it is only 'about themselves' we are interested here in the intra-psychic level of their sexuality: their connection to it, their awareness of it, their physical and emotional 'response'. This includes breathwork, cathartic expression, movement, vegetotherapy or 'going inside'. It necessarily includes uncovering the meaning or symbolic aspects, fears and fantasies.

2   Bringing it into relationship: the psychic analogue to sexuality and what happens in relationship to another can be explored through the body *in relationship to the therapist*. The client who has come to feel somewhat at home with exploring their feelings through their body can access relationship responses, inhibitions, contractions and desires; movements towards and away from the 'other'; areas of feeling sensation in the body and areas of numbness. Consciously experiencing one's sexuality in the presence of another, whatever the nature of the sexual transference, initiates the projection of internalised dynamics in the client's psyche, offering the possibility of resolution.

When working with sexuality, then, we are focussing on power and empowerment, potency and impact, and on dynamic interchange and dialogue. In looking to create a possibility with the client of a 'two person' dynamic, the therapist is aware of shifting in quite a profound way from holding a 'maternal' position – supportive, allowing, encouraging, being able to give the client total priority – to a position not simply of challenging or confronting resistances from a therapeutic perspective, but a kind of inter-relatedness. Rather than one person taking care of the other, there is an expectation of mutual respect and consideration where what is given priority is the process of active engagement in the psychology of 'two' psyches, two perspectives and two positions being present in the relationship at the same time. This process can be subtle and implicit, and it in no way detracts from the client's agenda, or from following their interests. For example, a 'maternal' response to a client's sharing might be: 'I understand how you feel'. Translating this into the dynamic somatically, the therapist 'softens' their boundary, allowing the client to 'come forward' and take more space in the meeting. An 'other' response might be: 'That's an interesting way to look at it', whilst somatically there is more energy placed at the contact boundary, offering a stronger interchange, challenge or opposition.

What I want to know in the latter scenario is what is individual or unique about this person? I want them to experience how they are different from me; I am not pathologising their position or suggesting that mine is superior. I want them to share their world view: if it causes problems for them then I may be able to offer some insight as to why that is, and we can explore together the alternatives. I may self-disclose in the interests of 'being myself' with them, modelling an ease – or even an excitement – with being different.

In the 'maternal' response there is much more a tone of putting the person at their ease, reassuring them that they are 'normal' or that we have heard this kind of problem before. The priority is *safety*, whereas in the latter the priority is the *edge*, the *unknown*.

These different dynamics are translated into touch in body psychotherapy – a reassuring touch addresses pre-Oedipal material – and the therapist's countertransference response is palpable in the touch. At times we process our response *before* touching a client, whilst at other times it is a 'live' moment-to-moment interaction, trusting our intuitive reactions.

It is my experience over years of training and supervising that this shift from 'maternal' to 'sexual' is an enormously difficult one for therapists to make. The anxiety of 'what do I do if they are attracted to me?' reveals the underlying belief that the feelings of the client are the therapist's responsibility, to look after and 'deal with' in some way.

> So long as one party is responsible for the welfare or development of the other, a psychologically creative relationship is not possible.
>
> Stein 1984: 164

It is more demanding in a particular way for the therapist to 'show themselves' to the client. To be fully with themselves can be exposing of weaknesses, laying themselves open to attack or admitting to failure, fear or inadequacy. Hiding behind the role of carer may give the therapist a security which they lack. It may resemble the medical model of 'doctor' and 'patient', but is in fact more often disguising an idealisation which may be erotically laden, appealing to the narcissistic position in the therapist and in the client. To abandon this is blowing the whistle on implicit power dynamics that exist in the client-therapist set up, questioning the known 'frame'.

Some years ago a man came to see me saying that he wanted to work out something regarding his sexuality in the therapy. Early on in a beginning session he asked, 'What do I do if I have sexual feelings towards you?' I said, rather smartly: 'You can have your feelings.' After that he only ever talked about outside affairs. With my rather glib response I had dismissed his anxiety as unnecessary, as if to say 'that's not a problem here' and I had also missed his announcement to me that there was *already* a sexual attraction. My own anxiety had caused me to attempt to reassure us both that it would be fine, and in doing so, I deflected an exploration.

Working interrelationally requires a more differentiated psychic position in the therapist; he or she needs to have a strong enough ego-position to maintain contact with their own feelings within power dynamics rather than resorting to the use of power in the role. The role of supervisor is crucial in working with sexual dynamics: as the 'third' person in the triangle, they may pick up on collusions, cover-ups and unspoken suggestions of the erotic in the countertransference, experienced in the parallel process within the supervision sessions. In this sense the supervision relationship is an essential modelling for how the sexual dynamic can be embodied and contained.

The issue of touch and the expectations and dynamics which this creates presents an additional complexity for body psychotherapists.

To touch or not to touch: a question of transference

Body psychotherapists today are still regarded with suspicion when the subject of working with touch and sexuality is discussed, and they tend to see themselves out on a limb (pun intended). It is assumed that touching a client opens the door to sexual acting out. Some psychoanalysts talk of 'stimulating' the client sexually by touching them when working with sexual material (and some would argue that if you are not working with sexual material, you are not doing psychotherapy).

I believe this view is erroneous when applied as a 'principle' and that the use of touch applied with discrimination and awareness of the relational field can greatly assist the process of re-awakening the instinctual forces – libidinous streamings and pleasurable sensations of the body – as an important and necessary path to the individual's re-connection to their sexual self. Use of touch facilitates body-consciousness. Touch may be used to bring attention to an area of muscular contraction or holding or to invite the client to feel, or image a particular part of the body. It may be used specifically to relax or support an area of holding, or to assist expansion of breathing. Alternatively it may be offered as resistance to counter an inner pressure or to engage with a pushing movement. Perhaps more importantly it establishes a 'contact boundary' between client and therapist which amplifies feelings and experiences in the relationship.

But touch without discrimination is of no value in a psychotherapeutic context. If the use of touch is 'prescriptive' rather than relational – i.e. if therapists adopt the principle of 'I never touch my client' or equally if a body psychotherapist 'applies' touch as a matter of course – a valuable therapeutic tool is missing.

Analysts who see the 'touching taboo' in the work as equivalent to the 'incest taboo' are, it seems, literalising what is in all other areas treated as metaphoric or symbolic. What does the body represent when to touch it means to engage sexually or to cross some frontier psychically? Does it mean that 'I' am my literal body, and my skin is my psychic boundary? It is surely an individual matter where 'I' locate my Self-boundary – for some an intrusion into the 'mind' represents a far greater trespass than being touched physically. How can we come to understand what touch symbolises for someone if there is an absolute ban on touching them? In supporting the no-touch principle, Mann suggests that 'there is no point banning something which people do not want to do' and 'the intensity of a prohibition is proportional to the intensity of a desire' (Mann 1997: 57). Are we are all desperate to touch our clients and they us? This is surely a fantasy arising out of the prohibition. Yet in discussing the erotic as resistance Mann says that 'often the very act of treating the erotic as a resistance causes it to become a resistance' which 'becomes a self-fulfilling and perpetuating prophesy'.

So what of isolating physical contact and imbuing it with all the power and allure of the prohibited erotic? *The question of when to touch and when not to touch is not a theoretical one, but a relational one.* What is my sense of the contact and connection through the touch? Is it a tender touch I am inspired with, or a firm and solid one? Is there a tentative feeling in me as I touch? Perhaps there is a cold feeling, perhaps I do not want to touch or be touched by the client. I am required to experience the energy field of the client, their smell, *their* feeling of being 'them' in their body. What about feelings of disgust and alienation?

Physical closeness speeds up the processes that will happen in the therapy – internally in the client, internally in the therapist and interpersonally between the client and therapist. Simply the *possibility* of physical contact already stimulates all these things; clients may fantasise or interpret the possibility of physical closeness as sexual because they have an undifferentiated sense of self and bodily based identity, or because they sexualise as a defence, in order to avoid more primitive issues of contact and dependency. A sexual transference early on in the therapy is likely to be disembodied – a projection of an idealised image rather than a felt sense or an erotic dynamic, and the therapeutic work is towards grounding in the body and in the relationship.

When we touch, we cannot avoid the awareness of both the sexual *and* the primitive – in ourselves as well as the client – and the therapist's use of their somatic countertransference is a vital tool in differentiating.

Use of touch and bodywork has been characterised as inviting regression, and this is certainly a strong aspect of its therapeutic use; it can be used to encourage inner experience where a client seems too externally focussed and lacking in a core sense of themselves; it is also popularly employed in cathartic experiences where the 'organismic' process leads the client into unknown and regressive areas of the unconscious 'held' in the body. But what is not so commonly realised is that a body psychotherapist, unlike therapists from other approaches, makes an intervention by *not* touching or offering to enter into a body-based exploration.

If the use of touch encourages regression, then the witholding of touch encourages the here-and-now relational dynamic; the client who is 'in touch' with themselves may respond to the absence of touch with sadness or longing, anger or frustration; regression 'away from' the adult here-and-now contact can be monitored by the therapist who remains alive to their own relational needs, or senses the avoidance of the erotic encounter. It follows from all that has been said that the issue of touching is directly connected to the therapist's awareness of the transference and experience of countertransference.

Many love stories develop out of a woman in need of help coming to a man. The hero-rescuer motif is an erotically-laden one at the outset, and the male psychotherapist does well to inform himself of this and to distance himself sufficiently to recognise when he is in its grip.

For female psychotherapists the initial motif is much more likely to be maternally imprinted, which is no less erotically charged, particularly when the psychotherapy includes the use of touch. Whether the client is male or female, the touch of 'the mother' is a powerful and evocative one, re-awakening the sensations and memories of that first love, the basis for all other loves, and an opening to the instinctual realm.

Love in the time of Narcissism

Since sexuality is no longer culturally and collectively repressed to the degree that it was in Freud's time, we suffer from a blurring of distinctions between different types of love. May tells us that 'every human experience of authentic love is a blending in varying proportions of these four '(love, eros, philia and agape) and that in our modern day we require sex to carry all forms (May 1974: 38). Sex can be used indiscriminately. We have lost the erotic container; we can no longer allow these various forms of love to co-exist, we have an inablity even to experience some forms with people of the opposite sex because we fear being labelled and misunderstood – we fear being seen as offering the sexual whilst we may be experiencing philia or affection. Philia becomes impossible between men and women. We become engaged quickly in sexual activity, without allowing time for a love to grow, to speak to us in our hearts and our bodies and to differentiate itself fully. In our permissive society we have the freedom to act on our instincts, and because 'society' and/or religion no longer hold a boundary for us, we are not protected from the acting out of the multitude of needs and desires that comes flooding forth when someone shows a kindness or interest in us. We confuse our needs with our desire.

This lack of boundary and possibility for sex with a stranger creates anxieties of a kind that were never prevalent when repression operated in a more widespread fashion culturally. Much more is required of individuals in terms of self-development and differentiation if they are to evolve a psychic structure that is able both to protect against primitive processes in themselves whilst allowing for self-expression. It is in this context that we see far more 'borderline' psychotic character issues in psychotherapy today. Permission-giving can be a denial of the fullness and overpowering nature of the instinctive responses and archaic memories which begin to stir as we enter fully the sexual realm. The 'permissive' culture removes the structure or guidance, representing psychically an absence of Father; the 'child' rules, and can either collapse in fear or be as tyrannical as any paternalistic force. As a result, Narcissistic traits dominate our collective psyche today – grandiosity and self-interest, a wish to overpower and dominate, and an enormous difficulty in taking responsibility and being consequential.

In the arena of love and sex, this manifests as 'usage' of another; the sexual as non-relational; the Narcissistic incapacity to *inter*-act, the person whose need for the other is as a means of gaining access to themselves, in order to 'discharge' or empty themselves into another, or to be experienced in order that they may experience themselves. Using another person to meet our needs and appetites or avoid our fears, to discharge our tensions and fulfill our fantasies is the antithesis of sexual love. Whilst in Freud's time sexual repression was the 'big issue', the emptiness of the Narcissistic structure is possibly the biggest issue in love and sex today. In our work with the Narcissistic structure we are more often attempting to repair a Self-boundary than to lift repressions to release unconscious sexual desires. Gaining access to an inner sense of self may be blocked by the fear of humiliation and the attachment to the power imbued in the false self.

The feeling of being used, being done to in many different ways, is the everyday experience of the therapist; the sitting with and processing of the impact of this, and the gradual return of this information to the client is the dynamic interchange which forms the matrix of conscious sexuality. The therapist is working with their own narcissistic issues – touching their own fears and vulnerabilities beyond the 'professional' false self – in the establishment of a therapeutic dyad which could eventually allow a full and *energetically* open exchange, working towards the resolution of transference as the healing.

Towards an embodied ethical practice

There has been a sexual revolution since Freud. We need to re-think and re-feel our ways of being with sexuality and sexual material in the therapy room. Probably more significantly, within the world of psychotherapy there has been the 'countertransference revolution' (Samuels 1993: 24) permitting and encouraging therapists to be more fully themselves and to bring all aspects of themselves into the therapeutic relationship, providing they consider this to be for the client's benefit.

This is an enormous responsibility, requiring far greater discrimination and self-enquiry and a more flexible self-boundary. Psychotherapists today argu-ably need to have a more bodily-based identity from which to work, because they can rely less and less on 'outer' forms and norms: ideas and theories, cultural or societal ethos, custom and tradition.

I have talked in this chapter about boundaries and differentiation and the use of touch in the therapeutic sense as an elucidation of the transference: touch is symbolic as well as literal, as is the body itself.

Arguments against the use of touch in psychotherapy often include refer-ence to maintenance of professionalism and ethics. The intimacy of the set-ting with a client is a danger to the maintenance of professionalism. But rarely do we discuss the ways in which we fail by *not* touching or reaching our clients; in our attempts to protect ourselves from risk, many of us err on the side of distance. Clients may leave feeling disappointed, isolated or abandoned by us, but they will never make an official complaint.

Although the UKCP presently keeps no records that monitor complaints specifically of sexual misconduct, there has been increasing research into the subject: Jehu (1994) has found that something under ten percent of therapists have had sexual contact with their clients, and *this is regardless of the therap-ist's theoretical orientation* (Mann 1997: 17). There is no evidence to suggest that touch or physical contact with clients increase the likelihood of acting out sexually, nor that distance or analytic rigour prevent it.

I would argue to the contrary. If the analytic frame of abstinence and distance was designed to increase the transference – including the erotic – then it follows that a more natural ease of relationship which focusses aware-ness on the bodily reality will decrease or defuse the erotic charge, bringing the client into a more 'related' state with regard to their body: the body does not equal the erotic, but includes it.

The relational use of touch and the inclusion of the body necessarily increases the therapist's awareness of sexual dynamics, and brings it to con-sciousness in the client. The body psychotherapy supervisor is alerted to an absence or avoidance of touch or bodywork with a particular client, and this may focus on the fear around erotic 'charge', whereas avoidance of the body and contact as a *rule* precludes discussion.

> Freud's 1915 moral and theoretical strictures, far from curtailing professional sexual relationships, merely drove them underground and has intimidated analysts from healthy disclosure to colleagues and supervisors which might have gone further in stopping the abuse of the therapeutic relationship.
>
> Mann 1997: 51

So how can we strike a balance, the right use of touch, the appropriate level of contact for each therapeutic encounter? To develop a relationship of integrity with our erotic and sexual selves as therapists we must embrace an embodied sense of morality and ethics, not a rule imposed from the outside, or a prohibition, but an inner knowing and felt sense. This naturally implies an embodied sense of self.

Whilst to transgress is to breach our own inner boundary, thereby betraying ourselves as much as betraying the other, we know that the transgressive always represents a lost part of the self, and something precious is lost when we act out *either* by denying the erotic *or* by literalising it. It is rich material for the work. We must re-learn to trust what is under our skin, the knowledge in our bones, the feeling in our guts. And develop a deep respect for the power of the erotic.

> Desire is a living stream. If we gave free rein, or a free course to our living flow of desire, we shouldn't go far wrong. It's quite different from giving free rein to an itching, prurient imagination. The living stream of sexual desire itself does not often, in any man, find its object, its confluent, the stream of desire in a woman into which it can flow.
>
> The two streams flow together, not often, in the life of any man or woman. Mostly, men and women alike rush into a sort of prostitution, because our idiotic civilisation has never learned to hold in reverence the true desire-stream. We force our desire from our ego: and this is deadly.
>
> D.H. Lawrence: from *Reflections on the Death of a Porcupine and Other Essays*

References

Boyesen, G. *Collected Papers of Biodynamic Psychology, Vols 1–3*. Biodynamic Psychology Publications 1980. Printed originally in *Energy and Character – Journal of Bioenergetic Research* edited by David Boadella (1972–1982). Also see *Journal of Biodynamic Psychology* (Summer 1981) *Vol 1*, (Winter 1982) *Vol 3*, (and Spring 1998) *Vol 2*. Calvert's North Star Press Ltd

Berliner, Jaques. Quoted from the clinical supervision programme of the then British Association of Analytical Body-Psychotherapy London, 1993–1994

Horrocks, R. *An Introduction to the Study of Sexuality*. Macmillan Press Ltd 1997

Jehu, D. *Patients as Victims: Sexual Abuse in Psychotherapy and Counselling*. London: John Wiley & Sons 1994

Jung, C. G. 'Psychological Factors in Human Behaviour'. In: *Collected Works 8*. New York: Pantheon 1960

Jung, C. G. *Memories, Dreams, Reflections*. Fontana Press 1995

Jung, C. G. *A Biography, Carl Gustav Jung*. Black Swan 1997

LeShan, D. *Cancer as a Turning Point*. Bath: Gateway Books 1989

Lewis, C. S. *The Four Loves*. Cox and Wyman Ltd 1960

Lowen, A. *The Way to Vibrant Health*. Harper and Row 1977

Mann, D. *Psychotherapy: An Erotic Relationship*. Routledge 1997
May, R. *Love & Will*. New York: Norton, 1969; Fontana Library 1974
Pierrakos, J. *Core Energetics*. Mendocino, CA: Life Rhythms 1987
Rosenberg, J. L. *Body, Self & Soul, Sustaining Integration*. Humanics Ltd 1985
Samuels, A. *The Political Psyche*. London: Routledge 1993
Stein R. *The Betrayal of the Soul in Psychotherapy*. Spring Publications Inc 1984

Biodynamic massage in psychotherapy: re-integrating, re-owning and re-associating through the body

Roz Carroll

> The body is both a representation and a reality, a manifestation of life, and life itself, what we are and something we have, that through which we live and in which we live: it is raw material, tool and crucible. The body has a language with which it responds to life, and is itself a language constituted by the language it carries, which speaks through us and ultimately speaks us.
>
> Gvirtzman 1990: 29

Introduction

Biodynamic massage is an intentional and attentional use of touch which can facilitate a very immediate and evocative quickening (i.e. bringing to life) of parts of the self that have been numbed, buried, deadened. It directly affects the autonomic nervous system, known in body psychotherapy by the more archaic term 'vegetative', a word derived from the Latin *vegetare* which means to quicken, animate, or bring to life. A smell can rapidly re-awaken a deep bodily sense of oneself and a set of feelings and memories. In a similar way touch has the capacity to ground an individual in their body, deepen self-awareness, and evoke a whole range of associations. Using biodynamic massage in psychotherapy creates the potential – and the attendant challenges – of enhancing the client's embodied sense of themselves in relationship to others and the world.

The four case histories presented in this chapter unfold the levels of complexity of this process. The stories illustrate the simple value of a nurturing touch that provides holding, containment and relief from internal pressure. Other stories show how ambivalent feelings about touch are explored. Some of the difficulties and intricacies of integrating massage as an intervention are discussed, especially the way in which indicators of fragmentation and splitting in the client indicate the need for further attention to the transference.

Biodynamic massage as bodywork

I began my training in biodynamic massage with Gill Westland 14 years ago in Cambridge whilst also working on my PhD. I was attracted to the course because of its psychological approach to massage, a development out of Gerda Boyesen's knowledge and experience of psychology, physiotherapy and Reichian vegetotherapy. Two particular experiences of receiving massage stand out: both took me to new realms of experience, and set the frame for my bodily sense of biodynamic work. One of these massages consisted of a rhythmical structured sequence of long strokes down the body. As the massage therapist worked, I began to have a sense that someone was sloughing off a layer of me, like a snake invited to shed a skin. And then it felt as if I was becoming the sea; my body was one with the rhythm of the waves. I felt as huge and fluid as the ocean. It changed again. I both sensed and saw an image of a ribbon of light down my body, from my head to my toes. In her essay on energy distribution (the massage that I received) Robyn Lee offers a possible explanation for my experience:

> These varieties of spiritual experience appear to emerge from the refining and focussing of energies of the body, and appear at those points when the organism can tolerate without fear a higher and higher frequency vibration of its own energy, and that of the energy field around it.
>
> Lee 1977: 122

This experience of the energy distribution massage was followed by a visit from the guest trainer Bernd Eiden, who worked on the muscular armour around my legs and throat. He plucked specific muscles, noting my breathing response and encouraging the expression of anger which was locked in the tense muscles. His insight into my history astonished me. His questions and comments, gently given, struck right to the heart of my childhood dilemmas and current conflicts. Whereas the first massage had opened the door to a more expanded sense of myself, the second experience, with Bernd Eiden, was a more painful coming home. It gave me both an embodied realisation of my own limits, losses and inhibition, and via the sounds and movements that I allowed to emerge from me, a taste of other ways of being.

Looking back on those experiences, I understand them as powerful catalysts which initiated my fascination with bodywork as part of a therapeutic process. My characterological defence against early pain had been to immerse myself in intellectual pursuits. Being on the biodynamic massage course – working directly with the body, sharing and exploring feelings in the group – was revolutionary for me. The intensity of those experiences resulted from feeling safe, and yet being very provoked and opened by the touch.

These two massage experiences represent two poles of a spectrum of possibilities within bodywork. One is for making conscious connections: to memories and deeper layers of feeling; to oneself and the therapist, increasing awareness internally and in relationship. The other, closely related, aspect is to support an inner process characterised by spontaneous change, flow and reorganisation on a vegetative (unconscious) level, e.g. in breathing, muscle tone or digestion. This is akin to dreaming (also a vegetative process) which can be healing in and of itself, prior to and apart from the unfolding and exploring of what it 'means'.

Startle reflexes are a characteristic vegetative event which biodynamic theory recognises as therapeutic. The startle reflex is triggered by falling anxiety, shock, or situations where there is a strong sensory-emotional stimulus. The complete reflex, which involves a sudden bodily contraction, followed by expansion and action/expression, is a self-regulating response. When it is repeatedly inhibited – a form of repression when the environment is perceived as 'unsafe' – it becomes the basis for tension in the muscles, the joints and the diaphragm. During biodynamic massage startle reflexes may occur spontaneously as the client begins to unwind, or symptoms of incomplete startle reflexes may be gradually released. This also happens during dreaming. The dreamer is re-orienting, whether they remember the dream when they wake up or not. The startle is an especially strong orientation response (Hunt 1989: 29).

Biodynamic massage sits alongside many other forms of bodywork that have flourished and developed over the last century (though often their roots are in more ancient healing arts), such as polarity therapy, zero-balancing, cranio-sacral work, shento, shiatsu, rolfing, Alexander, Feldenkrais, Trager work, Hellerwork, and many others. These forms of bodywork – often incorporating the significant word 'work' – differ from most forms of massage, which aim more simply at increasing relaxation and wellbeing. Even in the bodywork practices listed above, there is enormous variation in the degree to which the practitioners integrate a psychological process as part of the overall scope of the work.

However, in this chapter I want to make a further distinction between biodynamic bodywork as a treatment in its own right and biodynamic massage as an intervention in body psychotherapy. Bodywork on its own can be a form of healing that deepens the client's relationship to themselves and enhances the capacity for self-awareness, spontaneity, and wellbeing. Its use in psychotherapy requires a shift of emphasis from the therapeutic relationship as providing necessary safety and emotional holding, to a therapeutic relationship grounded in and guided by an understanding of transference dynamics as an essential part of the work.

In this context, biodynamic massage has a wide variety of effects, and whilst it can at times be the main modality of working, it may also be used sparingly as a very concentrated therapeutic experience which may need time, space, and reflection to be assimilated fully. The examples I described from my own experience of massage were highly-charged moments of inspiration as my in-breath was, quite literally, deepened. They took place in a training context where there was emotional holding, but the experiences in the massage were not in themselves psychotherapy. Rather, they were catalysts.

They opened a door, starting a process that flowered in my experience of group and individual movement psychotherapy and body psychotherapy a few years later. Subsequently, the layer upon layer of consequence, effect, shift and regression emerging from a body process have, in my case, been largely worked through individual psychoanalytic psychotherapy. Bringing together my appreciation of bodywork and my respect for object relations theory has been fundamental to the development of the thinking set out in this chapter.

Biodynamic massage is sometimes used as an adjunct to the psychotherapy process, where the massage therapist works on the vegetative level to support the work of the psychotherapist. Whilst there is a risk of splitting and collusion provoked by this triangular set-up, it can be mitigated by the massage therapist's awareness of transference issues and an ethical stance. Whatever the reason for the referral from the psychotherapist (and sometimes there are unconscious as well as conscious intentions at work), the massage therapist must respect the boundaries of the psychotherapy, and encourage the client to take their process back to their psychotherapist.

In other cases biodynamic massage may be used as an adjunct to a medical or complementary therapy, where the massage therapist focuses more on integrating the psychological material provoked by illness. Biodynamic massage can provide a context for both exploring and relieving psychosomatic symptoms, through supporting self-regulation, expression and embodied self-awareness. (Boyesen 1981; Carroll 1998a) It is a reflection of the broad scope of biodynamic massage that it can employed with an emphasis which shifts between the energetic/physical and the psychological/psychodynamic.

What makes the difference between biodynamic massage as a treatment and psychotherapy which includes biodynamic massage as an intervention is not the quality or the intensity of the experience. It is not the memories or insights generated, nor the cathartic responses, nor the amount of verbal reflection. It is the boundaries and the contract to work psychotherapeutically. Massage clients will nearly always receive a massage, though occasionally they just talk. For psychotherapy clients, massage is a part of a process, not a given. This means that the issues involved in using massage, the conscious and unconscious fantasies around it, the effects of shifts between chair, mattress and massage table, the client remaining clothed or not, are a fundamental part of the material of the therapy.

To clarify the role of biodynamic massage in psychotherapy, I will give a historical overview of its development by Gerda Boyesen and its modifications at Chiron. Throughout, I aim to illustrate that massage has a role to play in assisting re-integration, re-association to and re-owning of the body, i.e. increasing the clients' embodied sense of themselves. It is a fundamental premise of body psychotherapy – now being thoroughly substantiated by developments in neuroscience – that an experience of the body is vital to a robust and differentiated sense of self (Damasio 1994, 1999).

Biodynamic massage: from physiotherapy to psychotherapy

The way in which we perceive the world and interact with it depends fundamentally on the quality of aliveness of the tissue (Keleman 1981: 34).

> Discovering the natural rhythms of breathing, becoming aware of and respecting the defences against full respiration [is] a different kind of revelation . . . Witnessing this, people come to a new understanding of how their emotional life is lived in their body, and the impossibility to attempting to deceive, deny or disown the body.
>
> Lee 1977: 118

Although Gerda Boyesen has emphasised her own independent discoveries in connection with bodywork, nevertheless Wilhelm Reich was indirectly a key figure in the development of her ideas. Reich, influenced by Freud and Ferenczi, was a pioneer in the articulation of a holistic paradigm for psychotherapy. He situated bodily experience within a frame that coordinated physiology, mental representation, unconscious communication including transference and the impact of society on an individual. In particular, he focussed on muscular armour in its function of inhibiting impulses, numbing sensation and binding excitation. The musculature embodied the ego, he concluded, and every muscular rigidity contains the history and meaning of its origin (Reich 1947: 300). In his psychoanalytic work, he combined interpretation with systematic pressing and squeezing of muscle and with mimicry of and verbal description of the patient's manner, body language and gesture. He perceived his patients' bodily structure and their physical symptoms as acquired vegetative behaviour, directly reflecting and enacting their characterological conflicts (Reich 1947: 301).

Trygve Braatoy, a student of Reich and a psychiatrist in Norway, introduced his techniques for working with muscle to the physiotherapist Aadel Bulow-Hansen. It was at the Ulleval Clinic where they worked that Gerda Boyesen was trained in the technique of psycho-motor (i.e. neuro-muscular) therapy in the 1950s. Whilst Bulow-Hansen refined the technique of releasing the patient's restricted breathing via massage, she was not interested in the process material or the theory (this was taken to the psychiatrist). But Boyesen, who had undergone vegetotherapy (Reichian analysis) with Ola Raknes, had a degree in psychology and a physiotherapy training, was fascinated by the theoretical and clinical implications of what she saw. Although she later combined massage and psychotherapy, as a physiotherapist the exclusive emphasis was on observation of the vegetative (i.e. autonomic) aspects of the patient's reactions, and how both to stimulate and modify them.

Boyesen broadened Reich's idea of muscle armour and autonomic imbalances to include all other layers of psychosomatic organisation, including connective tissue, bone, skin, viscera and aura. At every level, she hypothesised, encapsulations occurred, preventing the dynamic flow of feeling/information in order to limit emotional pain: just as the musculature and the viscera have barriers to hold repression intact and prevent spontaneity, so the tissue has an infiltration, a tissue-armour, which desensitises and disturbs normal circulation and homeostasis, physical, mental and spiritual (Boyesen 1980: 70). One of her major contributions to body psychotherapy was to grasp the systemic consequences of sustained repression and deprivation, which she called the somatic compromise (Boyesen 1980). She was sensitive to the layers of hyper- and hypotonic muscle, different kinds of tissue disturbance, tension in internal organs and in joints, and variation in skin capacities.

In particular, Boyesen focussed on the way that the quality of the connective tissue – its colour, degree of sensitivity, elasticity, density or looseness, and chemostasis (toxicity) – was an immediate indicator of both chronic and acute emotional states. Through palpation of tissue she perceived the specific quality of the client's membrane (tissue) and the nature of the structure/containment it provided. She began to formulate how the vasomotoric (i.e. blood circulation) cycle was related to stages in an emotional cycle. The vasomotoric cycle is an holistic concept: the degree of permeability of tissue, the charge or absence of charge in the fluid are seen as important indicators as to how ripe feelings are for release, expression, assimilation and/or formulation. (Charge is literally manifest as increased colour, warmth and swelling in the tissue.) The combination of therapeutic presence and the use of appropriate massage techniques help the body regulate and assimilate on an autonomic level. This in effect also facilitates transitions in psychological states, whether explored verbally or not.

Feelings are regarded as spontaneous vegetative processes, which may be inhibited for any reason (conscious or unconscious) by muscular contraction (the motoric ego). Boyesen was interested in the relationship between the autonomic nervous system (broadly identified with the id) and the central nervous system (identified with the ego). The optimal cooperation between the two systems, she proposed, was converted into temporary or chronic opposition where environmental failure did not support recovery from distress (Boyesen 1980: 58–60). She suggests that the unresolved internal conflict is maintained as a latent visceral pressure, which when re-stimulated becomes a more urgent experience of psychological (mind) and physiological (body) pressure in the client.[1]

Boyesen's techniques are directed towards gradually melting visceral, tissue and muscle armour, allowing what has been repressed to re-emerge and be expressed and assimilated. The aim is a steady titration, with the awareness that at any moment the cumulative effects of dissolving tension may lead to a spontaneous emotional abreaction or vegetative reaction (sweating, nausea, startles, a rash, etc) (Boyesen 1980). In contradistinction to psychoanalytic therapy where symptoms may be perceived as acting out, vegetative reactions are seen as a kind of clearing house for completing emotional cycles.

One of Boyesen's important discoveries was that by listening through a stethoscope to the peristaltic sounds (rumblings in the gut), she could track the body's unconscious response to touch. Peristalsis is an indicator of para-sympathetic activity, and therefore relaxation, which happens when conditions of emotional safety are sufficient. But, more than that, peristalsis, she noticed, was affected by the precise location and pressure of touch, and was particularly strong where there were areas of fluid accumulation. She hypothesised that the peristalsis, a sign that the abdominal digestive process was open, actually helped digest the remnants (hormonal-psychological) of stress in the body. The converse, in neurosis, is described as abdominal closure, and is often accompanied by gastrointestinal symptoms and difficulties with processing feelings. She conceived of psycho-peristalsis as an important mechanism for discharging excess pressure/stimulation, akin to but much subtler than Reich's orgasm reflex. This intestinal function can be nurtured by massage over a period of time, so that it increasingly comes into operation spontaneously, independent of touch. In this way, biodynamic massage can help restore the optimal functioning of the gut and enhance the individual's capacity for psychological containment and self-regulation (Boyesen 1980).

Working on a wide range of psychiatric patients taught Boyesen how to moderate as well as stimulate dynamic processes in the body. Whereas challenging techniques to undo the diaphragmatic defence against breathing were suitable for some clients, for ego-weak clients following the peristalsis (so that internal pressure is consistently modified) was more effective. In addition, she started in her own private practice to combine modalities, and biodynamic psychotherapy became built around the triad of chairs, mattress (for vegeto-therapy) and massage table (see Chapter 2). In the following case history, I focus particularly on the classical biodynamic approach of melting tissue and visceral armour through gentle work on the connective tissue and psychological holding.

Case study: Sarah – a grief on hold

Sarah came to me for massage five years after her second miscarriage. She reported being alright except for ongoing headaches and back pain. Both shoulders and neck muscles were very taut. Her legs were stiff and feet icy. This rigidity in the body indicated both chronic (i.e. originating developmentally) and acute defences against collapse into need and grief. The skin on her face was puffy with red blotches, indicating feelings close to the surface (distension pressure). The tissue on the neck was denser, thickish, and disconnected from the muscle (transudation tissue), suggesting a longer-term process of holding back feelings by tensing the neck. I decided to work initially with massage to help Sarah come into the layers of grief in her body. In my experience, although bereavement always involves complex issues from early relationships which need to be addressed, biodynamic massage can give immediate support to assimilating the deep wells of grief being held back in the body.

I tailored the massage to the peristaltic sounds, working gently on a tissue level, to find areas which were ripe for release. Sarah had very little peristalsis, a sign the abdominal discharge mechanism was almost closed. Gradually, as my fingers searched out pockets of fluid, there were trickling sounds. These changed to periods of explosive popping sounds as the grief became acute again. She cried a lot during this time, which she had been unable to do in recent years. Deep crying also stimulates the parasympathetic system because it is a letting go, and tears, like other fluids that leave the body, carry with them hormonal remnants.

Following basic biodynamic principles, I also focussed on bringing energy down the body, with long strokes over her torso onto her legs, stretching her legs, and holding her feet. After several months there was a marked change in her ability to breathe with the stretches, and then to breathe occasional deeper spontaneous breaths. This helped put Sarah in touch with anger associated with her losses, and the deeply repressed protest against injustice and pain. This in turn brought up feelings about the inadequate mothering that she had received, which entered our relationship gradually in the form of her complaints and criticisms towards me.

Gradually, Sarah's face began to lose its blotchy look and the puffiness reduced. After a few weeks of intermittent diarrhoea her headaches reduced in frequency. Subsequently, parts of her body became unbearably ticklish and sensitive, as a last holding point against a fuller breath and the sensation of pleasure in the skin contact. By the time we finished, the layers of skin, tissue and muscle had begun to feel both more differentiated and more connected. Her peristalsis gurgled more frequently, and in between waves of grieving came a renewed sense of the joy of living.

Sarah decided to end when she felt that a substantial step had been made towards coming to terms with her losses. She had been offered a new job and wanted to get on with life. I supported her decision because I felt we had reached the end of a cycle. We did, however, discuss what might have come next in the therapy if she had continued. It would have meant, probably, stopping massage and allowing the negative transference more space.

In the Reichian tradition there has tended to be an emphasis on undoing patterns of muscle tension to release repressed feelings. This case illustrates an important aspect of biodynamic massage: its transmutative role on a tissue/visceral layer which complements more muscle focussed work. The connective tissue plays a key part in assimilation, integration and containment of fluids (blood, lymph and other intra- and extra-cellular fluids), which regulate wellbeing via hormones, peptides, antibodies, etc. The psychological corollary of this is a reorganisation of mood or feeling. The touch invites a vegetative free association within the body, and its effects are far-reaching and unpredictable. In this sense the client is far from passive on the table; the body's responses are part of a dialogue with the therapist.

The biodynamic massage framework is founded on perceiving and relating to these changes in the client, at multiple levels, from tissue change to breathing to subtle movements as well as verbal expression and content. Observation of subtle physiological signs forms part of the psychotherapist's intuitive sense of where the client is in an emotional cycle, and offers cues and clues for verbal processing. These observations are assimilated in an experienced body psychotherapist at a body level; it requires relaxation and openness in the therapist to keep receiving and responding to this process and this in itself is therapeutic for the client. The therapist's feedback via touch, words and presence communicates to the client a deep embodied attention (Carroll 1998).

Biodynamic massage is directly aimed at stabilising the physiological internal environment and enhancing the assimilative functions (psycho-physiological digestion). Lavinia Gomez has aptly compared this function of bodywork with Winnicott's concept of the environmental mother, whose role is to mitigate impingements on the baby's inner world by providing good physical-emotional care.[2] If biodynamic massage has been central in the early stages of psychotherapy, the process of giving it up and facing aspects of the therapeutic relationship from a new angle is often a significant process in its own right. Some clients consciously or unconsciously want to foreclose this process, keeping the psychotherapist as 'the one who can understand me through touch'. But if this transition is worked through, the memory of the massage phase can prove very rooting for the client as they struggle with more difficult transference feelings later on.

Re-owning, re-associating, and re-integrating through and in the body

Gerda Boyesen's approach to psychotherapy, which holds out for the potential of healing through the body, is powerful and compelling but it also avoids confronting the trickier aspects of the therapeutic relationship. The complexity of transference is flattened in biodynamic psychology, and the value of frustration and challenge as precipitators of change is underplayed. The founders of the Chiron Centre for Body Psychotherapy – Bernd Eiden, Jochen Lude and Rainer Pervoltz – trained with Gerda Boyesen in London. They were inspired by the teaching but also recognised the limitations of this approach, and set up their own body psychotherapy training in 1983. They turned to Gestalt, bioenergetics and analytical psychology for more structure and flexibility of intervention. From Gestalt, they took the explicit focus on awareness of sensation, contact and boundaries, and an attitude of inviting the client to have an adult role in the process. Owning parts of the self which have been projected, and recognising what has been introjected, offered a broader therapeutic base for client and therapist to explore the client's past and present relationships.

In a more recent phase of Chiron's development there has been a further stage of revising and integrating the basic premise of body psychotherapy. In particular, attention to the therapeutic relationship has been developed, with the integration of an object-relational perspective and a deepening under-standing of the transference/countertransference and its manifestation in the body. The implicit idealisation of the body and bodywork in the body psy-chotherapy tradition has been more thoroughly digested. The consequence of this has been to encourage more thoughtful and subtle use of bodywork, and with that a re-embrace of its potential (Soth 2000). (See 'Spontaneity as Integration' and 'Complexity, Complications and Contraindications' below).

The evolution of the use of massage in psychotherapy at Chiron has been influenced by the different styles of the acknowledged father of body psycho-therapy, Wilhelm Reich, and the less well-known figure of Gerda Boyesen, arguably the mother of body psychotherapy. Reich was very much a psycho-analyst: his style was rigorous to the point of being puritanical; the stern father, he challenged through interpretation and in his direct work on muscu-lar armour. Boyesen, by contrast, is more identified with the environmental mother, who merges and attunes to the bodily detail of viscera, bone, tissue, muscle and aura with exquisite precision and sensitivity, generating a wonderful invitation to expansion and flow.

Reich had an acute perception of conflict in the body as a manifestation of introjects and negative transference. In effect, he was always driving at getting the client to re-own their defences, needs and habits. He mirrored the patient's bodily attitudes by mimicking and through verbal description. Reich's analy-sis of the transference formed the basis for strategic interventions. Boyesen, on the other hand, looked for immediate signs of ripeness in the connective tissue, delicate and unformed and unfocussed stirrings to guide her work to strengthen the person so these things will go on cooking (i.e. moving towards consciousness) (Southwell 1999). Her therapeutic stance is more akin to humanistic therapies like co-counselling or person-centred work, which emphasise the self-regulative capacity of the individual.

As body psychotherapists, both Reich and Boyesen encouraged the client to lie down and surrender to the internal flow. But Boyesen's style was in general more inviting and the massage includes a broad array of techniques to give gentle and active support to letting go. Although she used certain massage techniques to challenge defences – particularly holding patterns in the diaphragm and in the muscles – the biodynamic approach supports and allows expressive movements such as kicking and hitting, with minimal interpretation. Reich made explicit links between the emergence of the patient's impulse and unconscious fantasy in a classically psychoanalytic way.

Of course, I am making a somewhat artificial – and coincidentally stereotypically gendered – polarisation between these two figures, but I want to give a flavour of the history and range of styles of working with the body. Body psychotherapy has been profoundly influenced by Reich, and Boyesen's use of massage is a very distinctive and controversial contribution to the field. In my own work, I have tried to re-introduce some of the Reichian analytical rigour and attention to transference, whilst valuing the intimate, almost microscopic, detail of biodynamic work. The following case history illustrates the interplay between these approaches.

Case history: Andrew – vaulting ambition and its recoil upon the self

Andrew came to psychotherapy because he had a friend who had benefited from biodynamic massage. He was in many ways quite cut off from himself, and he clung to the idea of massage for almost a year before he was ready to broaden the work. He is a good example of a client who uses the massage defensively to get relief from anxiety despite intense ambivalence about the psychotherapy process itself. It's a common dilemma for a psychotherapist using massage that it may be demanded rather than negotiated from within the therapeutic relationship (a more vulnerable position from which to ask for massage). It is a matter of judgement whether acceding to the use of massage will pay off in the long run, as it did with Andrew, or whether it is better to insist on exploring its function first.

Quite soon after he started with me, Andrew seized a moment at work to stake a claim for an important project although the idea for it actually originated elsewhere (an immediate parallel with his unconscious appropriation of biodynamic massage). That night he slept very little, suffering from cramps in his thigh and calf muscles. He came to the session saying he could hardly put his feet on the ground. I held his feet and encouraged him to feel the spasms and breathe. I wondered aloud if he dared to feel the reality of the leap he had taken, and the new ground he was on.

Andrew's colleagues were very hostile to him, and the shock of this manifested in a stiffening of his body, particularly his chest. Beneath the mask of pride was a fear of collapse, of falling apart with the rejection and humiliation. Initially I suggested he exaggerate the puffed-up stance; this enabled him to feel the hurt and to soften. The following week I used definition work – a technique based on the muscle tensing for building ego I learned with Babette Rothschild – to help him find the degree of bodily-based tension he needed to keep going (Carroll 1999; Rothschild 2000).

A month later he was having nightmares of explosion and execution. I linked these with his fear of being punished for his actions, although he repeatedly wanted to disconnect the link between his bodily experience and what was happening in his life. I worked with emptying – a technique designed to relieve fluid pressure – around his head, heart and shoulders. In his lower back the shame and terror were palpable as a quivering, combined with clenched buttock muscles. I supported this area by placing my hands on his lower back, encouraging him to notice how he felt.

Four months after his promotion I explored with him the idea of enduring as 'making hard', in other words to sense how, as he was trying to protect himself from unbearable feelings, his muscles were narrowing and constricting. Around this time he developed a painful right shoulder, which increasingly restricted movement, a potential frozen shoulder. It was symptomatic of his crisis in so many ways. It contained his sense of being burdened, the sadness underlying his apparent independent stance, the need to square up to the situation. And most poignant of all – an interpretation that Andrew hated but eventually allowed to affect him – it was an introjection of the cold shoulder his colleagues were giving him. In body psychotherapy, kinesthetic identification is understood to be the physical corollary of introjection of an aspect of another. The pattern of muscular holding contains and underpins the repressed feeling (Carroll 2000: html/motoric).

After massaging deeply into his stiff neck, in the following session, he dreamed of a baby. A new vulnerability became apparent. I held his head for long periods; he stayed for half the session on his side in a foetal position. Several weeks later, I worked on the shoulder again, rocking it gently, and he described feeling the rhythm of safety and wildness. It was a turning point, allowing him to recapture a positive sense of risk and also to feel the vulnerability of being connected to me, to others.

Unlike Sarah, it was difficult initially for Andrew to really receive touch and allow the associations to it – physiological and psychological elaborations – to unfold. Whilst he was trying hard to direct the therapy, he could not allow it to affect him. In my experience, if the client cannot use the touch to digest experience, then it's almost as if the therapist has to help cut it into chunks through interpretation. This also reminds the client that they are not really controlling the therapist, and this can increase the trust in the process, or provide a more explicit focus for the client's negative transference.

Working to bring awareness to the body of the body as a container

Body awareness provides the bridge between cognition and emotion, and is the platform from which various impulses and associations can be integrated and metabolised. It is the place where various levels of stimulation and activation of the nervous system can be contained and digested

Bernhardt 1995: 54

In many forms of psychotherapy, abstinence from touch is seen as an essential part of containing the client's process: the therapist and client must think together to arrive at understanding. The regularity of meeting, payment and observation of other boundaries creates safety. Whilst body psychotherapy follows most of these conventions, touch – especially massage – creates a different framework.

To work with touch is to work with the most fundamental boundary we have as human beings: the body itself. Boundaries are not just embodied in the skin (the sensitive envelope); but in survival reflexes (the instinctual level of no and yes); the muscular/motoric ego (which enables agency); the bones (which give us structure and alignment); the connective tissue (in which the immune system is embedded); and in our capacity to make sense of all the bodily information which orients us towards safety, appropriate behaviour and self and other awareness. In fact, the capacity for boundary making and containment is a bodily function deriving from the complex interaction of all its systems.[3] It is an intrinsic aspect of healthy self-regulation.

Recent developments in body psychotherapy that stem from new insights into trauma and from research in neuroscience and movement therapy, have refined the practice of supporting the client's boundary-making capacity. In particular Elsbeth Marcher in Denmark has emphasised the importance of actively encouraging the development of sensory awareness, which includes finding the intentionality behind even minor movement impulses. (So also has David Boadella [Boadella 1997].)

As Nick Totton argues in *The Water in the Glass* (1998), relationship damage (neurosis) is functionally equivalent to embodiment damage. It creates a limitation to the extreme of depersonalisation in our capacity to sense/feel our own bodies. As a result of trauma, areas of sensory and perceptual awareness are wiped out, radically split off from normal awareness. Although inappropriate for some trauma clients, biodynamic massage can be used to enhance sensory-motor awareness and provide containment through touch in order to facilitate the development of an embodied identity. In the following case history I want first to illustrate how containment is a function of integrating sensory and motor awareness with emotional awareness. And second, how this involves shifting levels physiologically between muscle, connective tissue, bone, and skin to allow the systems of the body to collectively hold identity, re-membering what has been fragmented by trauma.

Case history: Judit – abandonment trauma and the bodily acquisition of boundaries

Judit is a German Jew, whose parents fled to India during the Holocaust. As well as losing members of her family to the Nazis, she suffered the isolation of growing up without a Jewish community and with restricted contact with her parents. The trauma of abandonment and loss permeated her experience of life. Sustained mainly by an unwavering sense of humour and irony, she went into analytical therapy, and after some time her therapist recommended biodynamic massage as an adjunct to the therapy.

She became very attached to her first massage therapist, who emigrated after about a year and referred Judit on to me. So she came with a very immediate loss, and we both wondered how it would be for her to accept somebody new. My impulse was simply to hold her head, and she cried for some time. For quite a few months, holding her head was predominant. The head often represents the tiny baby: the back and sides of the head can be contained by a pair of hands as the client lies prone on the massage table, and a very young baby requires support to its head.

An integral part of our work was the piecing together of Judit's story: it was a fundamental part of her coming together, trusting me with her body and with holding her deeply traumatic life story. She needed a place for her extreme vulnerability to be held and met with understanding. Physical contact gave her the safety to dissolve, to cry unrestrainedly, whilst the boundary of my body holding her provided a sense of containment. She would sometimes hold my hand to her cheek or rest her cheek against my arm, a spontaneous gesture of longing for nurture.

Then Judit watched a BBC series about the Nazis which triggered the latent post-traumatic stress. She had panic attacks and an increase in agoraphobic symptoms. I had an image of a frozen baby waking up screaming under a pile of rubble. I used definition work to enhance her sense of boundaries, encouraging her to use me as an edge against which to feel her strength. This is a modification of the more cathartic techniques for working with anger, such as hitting and kicking, which would have been too provoking. In this way she was able both to articulate her murderous rage and loathing of the Nazis and to connect to her muscularity. I also encouraged her and challenged her around setting boundaries. Her agoraphobia made sense to me because although there was a physical density to her body, energetically she was very open and easily overwhelmed. She found it hard to set boundaries and could easily feel – and become ill from being – impinged upon by others. In order to get any sense of protection she had to withdraw to her home, which stood for the boundaries she could not experience through her body, and this cost her dearly in terms of loss of contact.

As Goodison has written of working with a similarly traumatised client, it was important to 'revers[ing] the fear of invasion by helping her to recognise and articulate impulses and needs which came from inside her *out* into the world: so that the starting point was her own body rather than the initiative of another toward her' (Goodison 1990: 386). Goodison is not a biodynamic massage therapist (she trained in energy work with Bob Moore), and so her work illustrates the point that it is a therapeutic relationship with an embodied emphasis which is important rather than any particular massage techniques.

Part of my active support to Judit's sense of her body as a container came from me simply pointing out connections between events in her life and how this was reflected in a very immediate way in her body. For example, an incident with her boss left her livid and when I went to contact her legs, she had almost no sensation at all. She felt as though she didn't have a leg to stand on. For some the symbolic nature of a body part holds such powerful unconscious sway that they lose an aspect of awareness very dramatically when certain issues are triggered. The value of massage is that not only can the association be made verbally, but the experience of sensory feedback, tracked with the therapist, can have an immediate effect.

Judit's recovery or discovery of her legs is a story in itself. When she first came to me she could not bear me to touch her legs or feet. Whilst I respected these feelings, there was also a need to feel her legs and feet in order to become more rooted, to find the strength to stand her ground, and to move forward. Over the years I have proceeded patiently and steadily, holding her feet, then extending the contact to her lower leg, then the outer thigh and knee. Now she experiences contact on her legs and feet as pleasurable and reassuring.

As Judit's struggle on a deep level is with issues of loss and displacement, it occurred to me to focus on her bones. Bones can connect us to a deep sense of knowing, belonging and being part of the structure. When I asked her the question, 'Do you have any sense of your bones?', she found it hard to relate to my question. I focussed directly on her bones by putting my hands there and saying quite matter of factly, 'this is your scapula', 'this is your sacrum' etc. She knew the anatomy, but what was novel was simply recognising the experience of feeling her bones. After the first time we did that she told me the next week that she went home and slept all that night, and all the following day. She got up in the evening for an hour and went straight back to bed. She was not ill, just 'bone tired' from having not been 'in' her bones for most of her life. The support of sinking into her own skeleton allowed her a profound new level of rest and reorganisation.

In an essay on 'Bones, Self and Paradox', Daniel Gvirtzman proposes that, in general in neurotic defense the muscles protect the skeleton, and in psychotic defense the skeleton protects the muscles (Gvirtsman 1990: 39). In Judit's case the multiple abandonment trauma (personal and transgenerational) precipitated a defence at a skeletal level. In addition she may have had a lifelong unconscious fear of feeling her bones because of an identification with the skeletal images of the dying and dead in concentration camps.

After two years of massage, Judit became conscious of more ambivalent feelings towards me and towards receiving skin contact. She had needed a strong positive transference towards me during her unfreezing process. Now an impulse to separate more became evident. For a couple of weeks she felt overwhelming repulsion around touch, a sense of being ugly and feeling unsafe with me. Awareness had penetrated to skin level: feelings of rejection overwhelmed the longing for contact and manifested in a more conscious self-hatred and paranoia. It was a crucial stage: the re-enactment towards herself of rejection. Feeling her own self-hatred she could not imagine that anybody touching her would not automatically be repulsed. We had two sessions where I did not touch her and we explored these feelings and their implication for our work. She wanted to leave, but it felt precipitous to me, so I suggested reducing our sessions over several months. At the next session she curled up on the mattress and I put cushions round her, a physical and symbolic containment. After crying deeply she felt relieved and renewed. I had accepted her need to be separate, but had stayed with her and offered my presence and a physical substitute for my body.

Subsequently her anxiety around separation was substantially diminished, and there has been a gradual reduction in the frequency of session. Sometimes she goes for a facial or manicure, a new way to care for her body as a woman and to build up other resources for herself. She is thinking seriously of living in a community rather than alone. Judit's reclaiming of her body – the experience and mapping of her embodied self – paralleled and was a corollary to her increasing sense of herself in a political, religious and racial context. To put it more simply, her sense of her identity as a Jewish woman became more rooted in her body. She said to me recently, ' the massage used to feed my soul, now it feels like it's for my body'.

Spontaneity as integration

> Whenever we have difficult feelings in relation to someone, we restrict our breathing (often quite unconsciously) in order to suppress our feelings. Alternatively, in order to keep breathing, we cut off relating.
>
> Totton 1998: 13–14

> If the conflict can be held in awareness on all levels (physical/emotional/ mental, in the here and now contact), it will spontaneously re-organise itself
>
> Soth 1999

So far I have described how massage can be used to bring the client into more awareness of unconscious material and to help contain intense feelings. The case histories have illustrated how bodywork and verbal processing can go hand-in-hand, the interpretations helping to integrate a process initiated by the massage, or vice versa. The alternation of bodywork and verbal work is a characteristic of body psychotherapy and offers the flexibility and the therapeutic challenge (for client and therapist) of meeting both the flight (in)to the body and the flight to words. The demand for massage in psycho-therapy can be defensive as it was with Andrew. It is sometimes loaded with the unspoken imperative: make me feel better, take away the pain, let's not think too much. Or, in another version of avoidance, there is a kind of forced catharsis to discharge feelings often accompanied by the fantasy that this will please the therapist. (This is the flight (in)to the body: the body is identified with the good object.) On the other hand, resistance to bodywork can carry the fear of journeying into the unknown, losing the anchor of words. The gratification of word-mongering is an intellectual defence that can mask deeper pain and uncertainty.[4] Both are forms of splitting which inevitably emerge in a relationship where both words and touch can bring the client to places of pain and difficulty. Safety, for the client, may appear to reside in the modality in which they are habitually comfortable. On the other hand, the hope for change may be invested in the less familiar medium.

It is, of course, an illusion to think that any technique is the right one. However, shifting mode can catch a dynamic and crystallise it, take it by surprise almost. Though this is related to an individual's characteristic defences and expectations of the therapy, it is also connected to the cyclical nature of a process. The inkling of something new disturbing consciousness may come in the form of a word, an image, a feeling, a sensation, a fantasy. How this then unfolds and elaborates often depends on the client being able to relate it to something else in another modality or another context.

Following this through can lead to the unexpected cohering of perceptions, movement, feeling in an experience of heightened engagement with the therapist in the transference. Such experiences can be intense and often come as the armour melts whilst the client is able to maintain contact with the therapist in the here and now. Chaotic feelings, impulses, movements and out-bursts bring to the foreground latent and unconscious aspects of the relation-ship. The building of a relationship, of a language of touch, and developed sensory awareness prepares the ground for the client to be able to allow and to survive the unexpected and sometimes overwhelming intensity of such experiences, as well as much subtler moments of connection.

Case study: Mary – dare I come into this tender touch of life?

Mary is a therapist. She presents with the sophistication of an experienced client, able to tap into her own process via reflection, dreams, awareness of transference, of fantasy, etc. One day she arrived feeling frustrated, and com-plained, 'therapy feels like work – I never make it easy for myself'. 'Shall we make it easy?' I joked, and suggested she get on the massage table. I noticed a quivering in her throat, especially in the sternocleidomastoid muscle, and she reported seeing images of quicksand. Both the tremors in the muscle and the image indicated ripeness, feelings impinging on the ego. I decided not to pursue her associations to quicksand, which would mean her working. Instead, to increase the breathing and the flow of sensory information to the muscles in the throat, I put my hand under her back and twanged rapidly across the muscles either side of the spine. I worked upwards, going deep into the levator scapulae muscle, which was tight with fear. She found it painful but breathed deeply into the process. As tension dissolved on the left side of her body, she felt tingling down her legs. She became aware of a more defended right side and particularly the tightness in her jaw. She described an animal sense of wanting to bite.

I could have switched directly to focussing on this wanting to bite but I continued to twang the neck muscles deeply and firmly because it felt as though the dynamic was still building. (Part of the repertoire of a body psychotherapist is the capacity to sense the resonance of the charge in the client's body.) Suddenly the muscles became sensitised and softened, indicating that the defence against the feeling had been given up. Mary described a sense of expansion around the head. I worked gently on the skin level now around the mouth, jaw and chin. The whole area felt so porous, like the energy field around a baby. She felt a melting sensation around her mouth, and could imagine being a baby wanting to suck. She told me afterwards that she felt extremely vulnerable at that point. This was palpable, along with the sense of peace. Although we talked a bit afterwards, it is crucial at such moments for the therapist to sense whether or not words are needed to clarify the experience. I stroked the energy down over the chest and into the arms, and down over the hips to the legs to give a sense of grounding and connecting downwards. This continued and gave a concluding shape (for that session) to the wordless intensity of surrender and the sense of being met at a deep level.

Mary is a client with whom I have used massage intermittently in the psychotherapy process, like a resource to be dipped into. What this mirrors is her struggle with an omnipotent need to provide me with material, a defence which occasionally drops to reveal her deep need for holding and a very immediate kind of care from me. Her active working (even during the massage she maintains thoughtfulness) comes from a tremendous fear of receiving, of letting me be the therapist.

I could have engaged her more directly with the frustration and with the desire to bite but I felt she was more in touch with her defence than what was underneath it. First Mary was aware of frustration, then of wanting to bite and of holding that desire back. This is an *embodied insight – to feel on a muscular level the instinct and the defence against it simultaneously and to tolerate both.* (She told me after the massage that she could feel how she held her disapproval and disdain in her jaw.) The deep work on the muscles had led to an increase in breathing (raising the charge). She did not contract or dissociate on a bodily level and this was the indicator that the charge was being contained. As I continued with the softer work, she was able to let go of many layers of defence, and yield both to the desire to take in and to experience the vulnerability of that position.

This involuntary drop into a less defended place, where dependence is experienced as non-traumatic, is an enormously important marker or register to have in a therapy relationship. It is a reference point that anchors the possibility for change.[5] We did not stay on that level, or with massage for long in that phase of the therapy, but it had a deep effect. One point to make clearly here is that Mary did not reach this place because of the massage, though that did nudge her in its direction. It happened because it was ripe (her opening remark about therapy feeling like work contains the unconscious hope that the therapist might make it easy for her). If it hadn't been ripe, the deep twanging would have put her more in touch with anger or loss, or she would have defended by cutting off in some way. (As with all psychotherapy interventions, timing is critical.)

Two years later, Mary and I have started to use massage again as part of the therapy. This move has been precipitated by a major loss in her life, which has thrown her into a more self-conscious and explicit dependence on me. The loss recapitulates some of the features of her birth. Mary was a breech baby (i.e. a baby who tries to come out feet first rather than head first), who was eventually born by Caesarean while her mother was under anaesthetic. After birth, she had difficulty feeding and breathing. Whilst with many people the details of their birth story are not known nor relevant, sometimes there are clients for whom the impact of birth trauma seems significant both symbolically and in terms of the unintegrated key reflexes. Birth is the first manifestation of will on the part of the infant: the baby is usually the initiator of birth, is highly active, and the actual process of birth stimulates and integrates a number of reflexes. In Mary's story the symbolism of trying to come out feet first suggests a bold attempt at independence which is then massively thwarted by the Caesarean. Her difficulty with active initiation is bound up with a deep hopelessness and compensated for by reflection and processing. The reflexes of reaching and pushing (involved and evolved in birth and early developmental stages) are subdued.

Clearly the hopelessness needs understanding in a total relational-developmental context, not as a product of one event. This is where the exploration within the transference is fundamental and it can happen on a number of levels, including through bodywork which supports, identifies and clarifies reflexes.

To try to illustrate how bodywork and verbal interpretation can be mutually enhancing, especially when deeper processes are being strongly inhibited, I want to describe a sequence from a recent session which was quite chaotic. Mary was feeling her helplessness, loss and abandonment, and initially when I touched her head and back, she dropped into the depth of her fear. After a couple of minutes she flipped out of this into a more paranoid space. She had started to watch herself and attack her need. She expressed a sense of self-disgust. I wondered how to proceed at this point. I commented on what I imagined had triggered this insertion of something alien and objectifying into the room, which was that I had broached with her earlier the subject of using her as a case study in this chapter. After a while I continued the massage, and she described the fantasy of being on stage in a lecture theatre. The image contained her fear of exposure. When I moved to hold her feet, she felt I had abandoned her back. I suggested that she felt more in touch with being abandoned by me.

Then Mary's toes began to make urgent grasping movements towards my hands. It was as if her feet were hands they were so flexible, with the toes differentiated, reaching curling round my fingers. I took the soles of her feet in my hands, and her toes continued to reach and explore my wrists for a while. Then I started to put a bit of pressure on her feet, and she began to push back. I maintained minimal pressure, while her pushing became kicking. The kicking came from her belly and she made sounds of longing and effort. She clasped at her collarbone and arched her back. These movements were a concentrated expression on many levels – of birth reflexes, of reaching, of pushing – integrating desire and rage as an active movement out into the world (as opposed to collapsing inward into fantasy, paranoia and narcissistic defences). They belonged both to the birth scenario and to the transference with me. Through embodying impulses, rather than distancing by reflection and conceptualising, the transference is spontaneously manifest in its intensity. The movements are not just a discharge but a strong communication which integrates at the level of the nervous system *and* as a conscious insight.

Complexity, complications and contraindications

Using massage in psychotherapy has many dimensions to it, and I have structured the four case histories to illustrate a few of these different facets: the transmutative and nourishing role of touch; getting to the unconscious via interpreting the body; supporting containment via bodywork; and finally looking in more detail at the complexity of directly engaging and working through transference issues.

I have emphasised the value of massage in this chapter, but it is, of course, a very unorthodox therapeutic intervention, and one which can be complex, tricky and challenging to integrate effectively. Many of the psychotherapy clients referred to me come to Chiron because they want bodywork: this means that they have already chosen a therapeutic culture where physical contact is a normal and accepted part of a process. Naturally, using massage, the massage table and the whole process of taking clothes off still invites strong conscious and unconscious fantasy. All this can be talked about, and used as potent grist to the therapeutic mill (Carroll 1998b). For example, with Mary, re-introducing massage and allotting time for it (a second session, a longer session, half a session, etc.) focussed the Oedipal issue: conflict between the need for mother (massage) and the need for father (talking); the need to regress versus the need to expand into new challenges.

Working with massage in psychotherapy requires a client with sufficient ego-strength to appreciate the more flexible boundaries involved. The therapist has to consider whether the client can potentially take in the touch and make use of the massage process. It is best suited to those who can be open to bodywork and comfortable enough with the shifts between table, chair and mattress. It is not appropriate when there is a strong transference and a working alliance that is not well-established.

As I have tried to demonstrate, biodynamic massage is not a psychotherapeutic technique in itself, but only becomes so when used in a context which pays attention to the complex issues evoked by working within the transference. This is challenging for the therapist at the level of technique and structure. Massage is obviously less easy to interweave with other interventions, although the more relaxed the therapist is with such transitions, the easier they become. But, as a psychotherapist, if I am really paying attention to the transference, there are always avenues opening up which may be more appropriately explored in detail with the client in a less vulnerable position. Biodynamic massage does not preclude the rigorousness of sitting face-to-face with the client, who is struggling to articulate and deal with difficult, obstinate or intense feelings towards the therapist. However, the differences in the two ways of working may clash more than complement each other.

One of the dilemmas I often face in using massage has to do with the time it uses: biodynamic massage has a rhythm of its own, it works deeply and sometimes slowly at a non-verbal level. The suspension of words – though there is still plenty of verbalisation – is actually quite precious in itself. It allows the client – if they are able – to sink into and be with themselves whilst being held by the therapist.

The effect of biodynamic massage is cumulative: used occasionally, it provides markers for the client's history, for anchoring significant insights, for enhancing embodied self-awareness. Used long-term, its effects can include a profound change in the client's capacity to know through the body, to pick up the subtlest cue – the twitch of a muscle, the sense of vegetative stirring – and to let it unfold to its resolution, much as a patient in long-term analysis can allow the elaboration of a chain of associations in words.

In this way the client comes to know themselves as a subjective being, as having a richly-textured interior life, and they begin to experience themselves 'objectively' by being aware of the very source of that subjectivity, the body. Body awareness has an incontrovertible communicative value to the client about him/herself. The body is extra-ordinary territory, at once common and basic, and at the same time having an infinite range and resonance with life in all its forms.

All of the creativity and free-ranging mobility that we have come to associate with the human intellect is, in truth, an elaboration or recapitulation of a profound creativity already under way at the most immediate level of sensory perception

Abrams 1997: 49

Notes

1 Although biodynamic theory has not been incorporated into mainstream science, its formulations anticipate emerging neuroscientific principles that emphasise complex holistic functions: the concerted effect of both neural and chemical processes, functional identity of emotional and autonomic self-regulation, and the complex interplay of parts of the nervous systems developed at different evolutionary stages (Damasio 1994, 1999). In the developing field of neuro-psychoanalysis, there has been great interest in self-regulation. The balancing of sympathetic and parasympathetic functions is an aspect of psychological health deriving from secure attachment, and its antithesis is the chaotic emotionality of an individual whose autonomic nervous system is chronically disordered (Schore 1994). Although body psychotherapy theory has not been incorporated within the frame of reference of the neuro-psychoanalysts, I believe it has a valuable contribution to make as a third reference point, integrating physiology, phenomenology and psychodynamic theory.
2 In a discussion of the role of bodywork at a seminar on Object Relations given at Chiron in 1998 (Gomez 1997).
3 Body psychotherapy has always challenged the dualistic assumption that the mind operates on the body, and that containment is a mental function (Soth 2000). Now with the advent of complexity theory and its incorporation into neuroscience there is an up-do-date scientific model that is beginning to elucidate how mental capacities are derived from the totality of brain/body processes (Solms 2000; Damasio 1994, 1999; Schore 1994)
4 The phrase comes from Sue Law, my colleague at Chiron, who elucidated the distinction flight (in)to the body and flight to words. This is an important riposte to the analysts who suggest that to use touch is gratifying *per se*, and that use of language (symbolising) is less regressive psychologically.
5 The pioneering neurologist Antonio Damasio has put forward a theoretical explanation for what might otherwise be called a gut feeling. He suggests that body signals – crucially the nucleus of motor and sensory signals processed by the autonomic nervous system – forms a basic concept of self [. . .] a ground reference for whatever else happened to the organism (Damasio 1994: 240). Stored representations of body signals over a lifetime are used as a memory bank to make decisions in the present about the future; these are somatic markers that help us anticipate good or bad outcomes of situations, based on experiences that have felt similar.

References

Abrams, D. *The Spell of the Sensuous: Perception and Language in a More-than-Human World*. New York: Vintage Books 1997
Bernhardt, P., Bentzen, M. and Isaacs, J. 'Waking the Body Ego: Lisbeth Marcher's Somatic Developmental Psychology, Parts 1'. *Energy and Character* 1995; 26(1): 47–54. See also 1996; 27(1, 2)
Boadella, D. 'Awakening Sensibility, Recovering Motility. Psycho-physical Synthesis at the Foundations of Body Psychotherapy: The 100-year Legacy of Pierre Janet (1859–1947)'. *International Journal of Psychotherapy* 1997; 2(1): 45–55

Boyesen, M. L. 'Psychoperistalsis: The Abdominal Discharge of Nervous Tension'. *Collected Papers of Biodynamic Psychology, Volumes 1 and 2*. London: Biodynamics Psychology Publications 1980

Boyesen, G. and Boyesen, M. L. *Collected Papers of Biodynamic Psychology, Volumes 1 and 2*. London: Biodynamic Psychology Publications 1981, 1982. Reprinted from *Energy and Character*. Abbotsbury Publications 1969–1979.

Carroll, R. 'Psychoneuroimmunology and the Role of Massage'. *Continuum* 1995; (3): 6–9

Carroll, R. 'Hamlet and the Somatic Metaphor'. *AHBMT Journal* 1998a; (1): 5–10

Carroll, R. 'Massage in Psychotherapy: Mapping a Landscape'. *Association of Chiron Psychotherapists Newsletter*; 1998b; No. 13

Carroll, R. *Integrated Muscular Work*. http://www.thinkbody.co.uk 1999

Carroll, R. *Thinking Through the Body: Integrating Neuroscience, Psychoanalysis and Body Psychotherapy*. http://www.thinkbody.co.uk 2000

Damasio, A. *Descartes' Error: Emotion, Reason and the Human Brain*. London: Putnam 1994

Damasio, A. *The Feeling of What Happens: Body, Emotion and the Making of Consciousness*. London: William Heineman 1999

Eiden, B. 'The History of Biodynamic Massage'. *Association of Holistic Biodynamic Massage Therapists Newsletter* 1995, No. 3

Eiden, B. 'The Use of Touch in Psychotherapy'. *Self and Society* 1998; 25(2): 6–13

Goodison, L. *Moving Heaven and Earth: Sexuality, Spirituality and Social Change*. London: The Womens Press 1990

Gomez, L. *An Introduction to Object Relations*. London: Free Association Books 1997

Gvirtzman, D. 'Bones, Self and Paradox, Part 1'. *Energy and Character* 1990; 21(2): 28–45

Hunt, H. T. *The Multiplicity of Dreaming: Memory, Imagination and Consciousness*. New Haven: Yale University Press 1989

Keleman, S. *Your Body Speaks Its Mind*. Berkeley, CA: Center Press 1981

Lee, R. (1977) 'The Scope of Energy Distribution'. *Energy and Character* 1977; 8(2): 119–122

Reich, W. *The Function of the Orgasm*. Reprinted by Souvenir Press, 1983 [1947]

Reich, W. *Character Analysis*. New York: Reprinted by Farrar, Strauss & Giroux, 1990 [1972]

Rothschild, B. *The Body Remembers: The Psychophysiology of Trauma and Trauma Treatment*. London: Norton 2000

Schore, A. N. *Affect Regulation and the Origin of the Self*. Hove: Lawrence Erlbaum Associates 1994

Solms, M. and Kaplan-Solms, K. *Clinical Studies in Neuro-Psychoanalysis*. London: Karnac, 2000

Soth, M. 'The Client's Internal Conflict as a Relationship Pattern'. Chiron Training Paper (unpublished), 1999

Soth, M. 'Body/Mind Integration'. *AChP Newsletter*, 2000 nos 17, 18, 19

Southwell, C. Interviewed by Judy Cowell. Unpublished, 1999

Totton, N. *The Water in the Glass: Body and Mind in Psychoanalysis*. London: Rebus Press 1998

Winnicott, D. W. (1960) 'The Theory of the Parent-Infant Relationship. In: *The Maturational Process and the Facilitating Environment*. London: Karnac 1990

Chapter 5

Body psychotherapy without touch: applications for trauma therapy

Babette Rothschild

Introduction

Memory of traumatic events differs from memory of other events in that it is often non-verbal, somatic, implicit memory. This makes body psychotherapy a natural for helping to integrate traumatic experiences. However, many traumatised clients – especially those who have suffered at the hands of others – cannot be touched without becoming overwhelmed or going dead in their bodies. This presents a unique challenge to the psychotherapist and the body psychotherapist: how to integrate body experiences without touch? This chapter will offer both theory for understanding and techniques towards solving this dilemma.

Psychotherapists and body psychotherapists have much they can learn from each other. The bias of each group is actually its unique contribution to the field of psychotherapy. Psychotherapists tend to emphasise cognitive understanding and integration. Though some may pay attention – more or less – to the body, it is the mind that is their focus. Body psychotherapists, on the other hand, tend to be most interested in the integration of bodily reactions and emotions. Though the body psychotherapist considers cognitive aspects, it is the body that is the usual focal point.

The study of posttraumatic stress disorder (PTSD) is forcing a long overdue meeting of these two orientations. This is occurring because PTSD has become a well-known psychiatric diagnosis that has recognised somatic (most notably hyperarousal in the autonomic nervous system (ANS)) as well as cognitive components (American Psychiatric Association (APA) 1994). Inspired by the phenomenon of PTSD, body psychotherapists are being challenged to pay more attention to what is happening in the mind, increasing skills in cognitive integration. Simultaneously, the psychotherapist is being challenged to pay more attention to the body, increasing skills in mind/body integration (Rothschild 2000).

This juncture poses difficulties for all concerned. The psychotherapist may shy away from paying attention to the body for fear that touch will become an issue. The body psychotherapist who employs touch as a usual tool may find that the symptoms of some clients – particularly those who were traumatised by assault, rape or abuse – will worsen with touch. The possibility that somatic symptoms can be addressed without touch has not often been explored.

An abbreviated glossary of relevant terms

This short list of relevant terms (Rothschild 1998) should lay a useful foundation for the rest of this chapter:

The *autonomic nervous system (ANS)* is the division of the body's nervous system that regulates viscera and smooth muscles: heart and circulatory system, kidneys, lungs, bladder, bowel, pupils, etc. There are two branches:

* The *sympathetic nervous system (SNS)* is primarily aroused in states of stress, both positive and negative. Signs of SNS arousal include increased heart rate and respiration, cold and pale skin, dilated pupils, elevated blood pressure.
* The *parasympathetic nervous system (PNS)* is primarily aroused in states of rest and relaxation. Signs of PNS arousal include decreased heart rate and respiration, warm and flushed skin, normally reactive pupils, lowered blood pressure.

These two branches usually function in balance with each other: when one is activated, the other is suppressed. Persistent extreme activation in one or both branches is referred to as *hyperarousal.*

Stress can result from any emotional or physical demand (positive or negative). It was first recognised by Hans Selye (1956) through the observation of 'evidence of adrenal stimulation, shrinkage of lymphatic organs, gastro-intestinal ulcers, and loss of body weight with characteristic alterations in the chemical composition of the body.' Stress causes activation in the SNS. Generally regarded as a response to a negative experience, stress can also result from positive experiences: marriage, job change, moving, sex, etc. The most extreme form of negative stress is *traumatic stress.*

Traumatic stress is a psychobiological reaction to a *traumatic event* (i.e. war, disaster, car accident, rape, assault, torture, surgery, molestation, loss of significant other, etc.). Occurring in the face of threat to life and/or limb, traumatic stress causes hyperarousal of the ANS and elicits the survival responses of fight, flight and/or freeze. It is necessary to survival.

Posttraumatic stress (PTS) is traumatic stress that persists after (post) a traumatic incident when it has not been relieved through successful fight or flight, or other natural or therapeutic means. PTS may be characterised by periodic symptoms of hyperarousal in the ANS, flashbacks and/or dissociation. It does not disrupt general functioning.

Posttraumatic Stress Disorder (PTSD) is the result of accumulated post-traumatic stress, resulting from one or more traumatic events, that is of sufficient severity and constancy to decrease a person's ability to function in his life. PTSD is characterised, in part, by chronic symptoms of ANS hyperarousal (including sleep disturbance, lack of concentration, hypervigilance, exaggerated startle reflex) and continued activation of the survival responses of fight, flight and/or freeze. Hyperarousal indicates that the traumatic event is being repeatedly remembered in mind and/or body. In addition there will be avoidance of environmental stimuli associated with the trauma (*triggers*). PTSD is considered *acute* if the duration of symptoms is less than three months, *chronic* if the duration of symptoms is three months or more. *Delayed onset* of PTSD is recognised when symptoms arise at least six months after the traumatic event, including reactions in adulthood to an event that occurred in childhood (APA 1994).

Dissociation is a psychological state where the memory of an event is divided into parts. Recall of all of the parts as a whole is not accessible to consciousness at any one time. Instead, the event might be remembered as disjointed elements or, seemingly, not at all.

A *flashback* is a common, though not always present, symptom of PTSD. 'In rare instances, the person experiences dissociative states that last from a few seconds to several hours, or even days, during which components of the event are relived and the person behaves as though experiencing the event at that moment' (APA 1994: 424). During a flashback the ANS prepares the body for fight/flight/freeze as if the event were occurring now. Flashbacks can be visual, auditory, behavioral and/or tactile.

The extreme somatic consequences of trauma

While any emotional response to a life event affects the body, trauma does so to the utmost. During a traumatic incident the brain's limbic system uses hormones to signal an alarm to the ANS. The ANS responds to this signal by activating the SNS to its most extreme arousal: preparation for fight and/or flight. Blood flows away from the skin and viscera and into the muscles for quick movement. Heart rate, respiration and blood pressure all rise to meet the needs of muscles for more oxygen. The eyes dilate to accommodate sharper sight. All of these elements of SNS arousal are necessary to respond to the threat. When fight or flight are not possible or have not been successful, the limbic system may further signal the ANS to *simultaneously* activate the PNS. The SNS continues its extreme arousal while the action of the body freezes in place, the muscles becoming either slack like a mouse caught by a cat or stiff like a deer caught in headlights (Gallup 1977). The resulting internal strain is something similar to putting a car's accelerator to the floor while holding tight on the brake. During a freezing episode time slows down and body sensations and emotions are numbed; it is a kind of dissociation. As freezing only occurs when the threat is extreme and escape is impossible, these reactions make perfect sense. People who have survived mauling by animals or falls from great heights report that this kind of dissociation reduces the physical pain and emotional terror during such experiences.

Successful fight or flight is usually enough to discharge the arousal of the SNS. Most people experiencing traumatic events do not end up in need of psychiatric intervention. The picture with freezing can be quite different.

As a survival mechanism freezing is excellent – witness the survival of our clients in that they are able to walk into our offices. However, freezing exacts a higher price in the wake of the traumatic incident than the responses of fight and flight. As a form of dissociation, freezing during a traumatic event is a major predictor of who develops PTSD (Bremner et al. 1992; Classen, Koopman and Spiegel 1993). People who have frozen during traumatic incidents and survived appear to have a greater difficulty coming to terms with their trauma. Many are plagued by symptoms of PTS or PTSD. Somatic symptoms abound as the hyperarousal in both SNS and PNS persist chronically, or are easily set in motion by environmental triggers. It is these people who have the most difficulty with psychotherapeutic touch.

Limitations of touch when working with trauma

While clients with little or no posttraumatic stress in their bodies may respond well to touch, there can be problems with clients who have suffered greater and lesser degrees of trauma, especially when those traumas were sustained at the hands of humans. There are at least two mechanisms underlying a client's inability to work with touch. The first is dependent on the type of trauma and the possibility that touch is a direct trigger to the memory of traumatic events. This includes, but is not limited to, situations where there is danger that the touching therapist could be perceived as the/a touching (sexual, violent) perpetrator. It is to both the client's and the therapist's advantage to avoid this situation. A therapist who becomes perceived as a perpetrator is lost as an ally in the therapeutic process. Time and again clients decompensate and/or quit therapy where this confusion has occurred.

A second mechanism influencing a client's touch tolerance involves the effect of touch on the nervous system. When PTS has accumulated to the point that an individual's hyperarousal is already 'near the top', touch could send that arousal soaring over a tolerable/containable threshold. If in doubt, it is better to hold off until the client is in a calmer state. This is not to deny that sometimes touch can be calming, but it is a challenge to predict or know the difference. The best expert on whether touch is calming or not is the client. Asking the client frequently about her reaction – 'Are you feeling calmer, more present, more grounded?' or 'Are you feeling more anxious, more distant, cut off?' – should help guide both therapist and client.

Some may question whether touch must only be used when it is calming; can it also be employed in a useful manner to provoke trauma processes for working through of issues? It can be, but it is not always a wise choice. Provoking an individual with PTS or PTSD is not a good idea. It is important to regard the nervous system of such individuals as already highly provoked, actually over-provoked. As such it is more practical to work to *reduce* the provocation in the system rather than to increase it.

> A useful analogy is to liken the person with PTSD to a pressure cooker. The unresolved trauma creates a tremendous amount of pressure both in the body and in the mind in the form of ANS hyperarousal. With the modern pressure cooker, once the pressure is built up, it becomes impossible to open it, but if you could it would explode. You must first slowly relieve the pressure, a little 'pft' at a time. Then, and only then, can you open any pressure cooker safely.
>
> Rothschild 2000

What is body memory?

There are basically two categories of memory: explicit and implicit. Explicit memory is conscious and requires language. It is comprised of concepts, facts, events, descriptions and thoughts. Implicit memory, on the other hand, is unconscious. It is made up of emotions, sensations, movements and automatic procedures. The terms 'body memory' and 'somatic memory' suggest the implicit.

The concept of body memory is easily misunderstood. Actually, it is not the body, *per se*, that holds a memory itself. It is the brain that stores memory. What is meant by body memory is, more precisely, an intercommunication between the brain and the body's nervous systems: autonomic, sensory and somatic. When, for example, you remember how to ride a bicycle, it is not your muscles that remember the movement, though they are a crucial part of the process. This memory was laid down when you learned to ride. At that time the sensory and somatic nerves in your leg's muscles and connective tissues communicated new patterns of movement (getting on and riding, how to balance, etc.) to your brain. It is there that those patterns were recorded and stored. Now, when it is time for you to hop on a bike, the same patterns are recalled from the brain which sends messages back to those same tissues in your legs to replicate the same movements. Body memory is unconscious, implicit, memory. That is, it is automatic, you don't have to think about it. That is why once you learn to ride a bicycle, type, swim, etc., you (usually) don't have to learn it ever again. Those patterns of movement are stored forever in the brain.

The body also remembers traumatic events. The body sensations that constitute emotions (i.e. terror) and physical states (i.e. pain or ANS arousal) and the patterns that comprise movements (i.e. fight, flight, freeze) are all recorded in the brain. Sometimes the corresponding explicit elements – the facts of the situation, a description of the events, etc. – are simultaneously recorded, sometimes they are not (Rothschild 2000).

Traumatic memory versus memory of other events

The amygdala and hippocampus

Within the *limbic system* of the brain are two related areas that are central in memory storage: the *hippocampus* and the *amygdala*. The last few years have produced a growing body of research which indicates that these two parts of the brain are essentially involved in response to, and memory of, traumatic events (van der Kolk 1994; Nadel and Jacobs 1996). It is believed that the amygdala's job is to register highly-charged emotions, such as terror and horror, along with the body sensations that identify them. The amygdala becomes very active when there is a traumatic threat. This is the part of the brain that signals the survival alarm which eventually leads to the ANS preparing the body for fight and/or flight. Memories of terror and horror are not stored in the amygdala but must be processed through the amygdala for them to be recorded in the brain's cortex.

The hippocampus, on the other hand, is necessary to the eventual storage of information that helps us make cognitive sense of our memories, for example the context of time and space: the hippocampus helps to put our memories into their proper perspective and slot in our life's time line. As with the amygdala, memory is not stored in the hippocampus, but the information must be processed through it before being recorded on the cortex.

Understanding the importance of the hippocampus becomes clearer when looking at what can happen to memory during a traumatic threat. When the arousal in the ANS becomes very high, the activity of the hippocampus becomes suppressed by the wealth of stress hormones that are released. When that happens, its usual function of lending context to a memory is not possible. The result may be that the traumatic event is prevented from becoming a 'memory' in the normal sense of the word – a piece of information about oneself that lies clearly in the past. What can occur instead is that the 'memory', unanchored in time, seems to float freely, often invading the present. It is this mechanism that is behind the PTSD symptom of 'flashback' – episodes of reliving the trauma as if it is happening now.

Dissociated elements of experience

Memory of any event is made up of the components of that experience. Peter Levine's SIBAM model (1992) is a useful way to conceptualise this. This model was developed in an effort to understand dissociation of memory and is useful for understanding memory in general. Levine has identified five major elements – sensations, images, behaviours, affects and meanings – common to any experience. Usual memories of non-traumatic events hold all of these elements intact. Recall triggered by one of the elements usually elicits the others. This is a common experience: remember the last time you were reminded of a pleasant time in your life by the smell from a bakery or a particular song. This kind of memory recall happens from time to time to nearly everyone.

Memory of traumatic events, however, can be different. Though sometimes a traumatic event is remembered in its entirety, it is more common – particularly for those with PTS or PTSD – for such events to be remembered piecemeal, dissociated. That is, some of the elements appear to be missing. One client might have visual flashbacks of an event indicating that she remembers images and has emotional reactions to them (terror), but lacks body sensations and the narrative (meaning) that can make sense of the flashbacks. A child might reenact his trauma during play indicating that behaviours are remembered, but have no recall in images or of facts that could tell where or why his behaviours originated.

The most troublesome traumatic memories are those that involve body sensations and little else. Individuals plagued with anxiety and panic attacks are examples of this. In such cases, the body sensations associated to the traumatic memory are intact, but the other elements, particularly the cognitive aspects (facts, narrative, time and space context) that could help the individual to make sense of the memories appear lost. Working with implicit, trauma-based sensations in the absence of a trauma narrative can be difficult. The explicit memory may or may not emerge. In such cases it will sometimes be necessary to find ways to ease the symptoms and/or increase their containment as the origin might never be known.

Using the body to integrate traumatic experience

Within the confines of this chapter it is not possible to describe all possible techniques for non-touch body work with trauma. What follows is a selection of those which are the most usefully adaptable within any framework of psychotherapy or body psychotherapy. What is important to remember, though, is not to depend too heavily on any one tool or technique. The safest trauma therapy is that which is adapted to the individual needs of the client. Never expect the same technique to have the same result with two clients. Having several tools – body oriented as well as cognitive – at your disposal is the best way to assure your clients of productive therapy (Rothschild 2000).

This section includes three case example excerpts from *The Body Remembers: The Psychophysiology of Trauma and Trauma Treatment* (Rothschild 2000). They will help to illustrate applications of non-touch body techniques with trauma work. In addition, a complete session transcript, not previously published, follows at the end of this section. For the sake of protecting privacy and confidentiality, the cases presented are actually composites of several cases. In each instance the basic principles and thrust of the therapy being presented has been maintained.

Body awareness

Simple body awareness is the single best foundation for non-touch body work with PTS and PTSD. The use of body awareness as a means to health and enlightenment has roots that reach all the way back to the Eastern practices of yoga and meditation. The first use of body awareness as a tool in Western psychotherapy comes from the early days of Gestalt therapy (Perls 1942). For the purposes of this chapter, body awareness is defined as 'the precise, subjective consciousness of body sensations arising from stimuli that originate both outside and inside the body' (Rothschild 2000). In trauma therapy, the client's ability to identify and name somatic sensations will help the process immensely. This is not to say that individuals with no sense of their bodies will be unable to come to grips with a traumatic past. However, having or developing body awareness will facilitate the task.

Body awareness furthers trauma therapy in many ways. First, it supplies a much needed gauge to evaluate how the client is handling the therapy overall, and each intervention in particular. Second, body awareness points the way to troublesome body sensations that may have roots in the traumatic incident being addressed. Third, focusing on body sensations provides a necessary link to the present: body awareness is a current-time activity. Body sensations can be remembered or imagined from the past, but they can only be *felt* in the present. As such, body awareness can also be called upon as a tool of containment.

Angie

Angie was trying to stay away from her abusive husband. Sometimes he would show up where she was staying and she would go with him. It wasn't until later that she realised she had made a mistake. For her it was as though she entered an altered state. The fact that she couldn't control her behaviour, let alone describe what that state felt like, disturbed her immensely; she felt stupid and ashamed. Body awareness was difficult, generally, for Angie, but despite some anxiety, she was willing to try. I decided not to ask her about her body specifically, as she could quickly become frustrated when she did not produce the 'right' answer. Instead I asked, 'Can you feel the chair under your buttocks?' That she could feel. I ventured, 'What does it feel like?' She was able to describe how the consistency of the cushion felt, as well as that the chair was unsteady because one leg was slightly shorter than the others. 'Do you feel more anxious, less anxious, or the same as when you arrived?' She felt slightly less anxious. So far, so good; I could dare a bit more. 'You can feel the chair under you now. Do you think that when your husband is around, you would be able to feel the chair?' Her interest increased as she answered the question, 'No, I don't think I could. Actually, I don't think I can feel anything when I get around him.' For the first time she could describe an aspect of her altered state: the absence of sensation. Already, via this short introduction to her body, it began to make sense to Angie that if she couldn't feel anything in the presence of her husband she would easily acquiesce. This was a microstep on the road to helping her gain control over her life (Rothschild 2000: 104).

Working with touch with Angie is not possible as she has been so traumatised by it. Body awareness was the primary tool for helping her to identify her dissociation. Some of the additional steps will involve increasing her body awareness and her muscle tone (see below). Angie will need to feel her body as strong in order to be able to eventually say 'no' to her husband. At a future point, becoming trained in self-defense will be a good idea.

Working with movement

Movement can also be a useful non-touch tool for resolving traumatic memories. It should be used with caution as its use can quickly accelerate contact with traumatic memories – sometimes overwhelming the client. Nevertheless, when it is timely, working with movement – particularly defensive movement – can greatly facilitate the process. Slow replication of movements that were used for protection during the traumatic incident (cowering, crouching, hiding, rolling) as well as training of movements that might have been more useful (running, pushing, kicking) can be very powerful. Work with movement must be done with particular caution. Careful attention with an eye to gauging the client's reaction (ANS arousal) is necessary each step of the way. If taken prematurely, too quickly, or in too big bites there is the risk of overwhelming the client or triggering an unproductive flashback.

Daniel

Daniel had suffered anxiety since surviving a big earthquake. He was hypervigilant, sleeping poorly and even having trouble bathing. He felt he must be always at the ready for the next quake. As he talked I noticed a dissonance in his posture. He appeared to be leaning back comfortably in his chair, but his feet were placed on the floor in a manner suggestive that he was preparing to bolt. When I pointed this out to him he agreed that he was not able to relax at any time; he was always preparing to dive under the nearest table or run to the nearest doorway for protection. In addition, right at that moment, his heart rate was elevated and his hands were sweaty. I asked him if he had practised any of these defensive manoeuvers. He had not. I suggested that he do so now, following the impulse in his already defensively positioned feet. He did, bolting toward my office door. He opened it and crouched in the doorway. I encouraged him to repeat that movement several times – chair to doorway to crouch. After three practices I inquired as to his heart rate and hand mois-ture. Both were normalised. I encouraged Daniel to continue practising at home and at work, finding the best routes to safety. By the next week his constant vigilance had eased considerably, as he had by then anchored in his body the defensive moves necessary to reach protection during an earthquake (Rothschild 2000: 89).

Using simple body awareness and following behavioral impulses helped Daniel to develop protective movements that he was unable to use during the quake. Developing new modes of protection reduced the traumatic afteref-fects of the remembered earthquake. Moreover, it helped Daniel to feel pre-pared for the next one – an inevitability in the area where he lived. There is no doubt that when the next quake comes he will be able to move to safety effectively.

Donna

Sixty-year-old Donna was still mourning the death, five years earlier, of her husband of 35 years. It had been a shocking blow. He had a heart attack while a passenger in the car she was driving. She had driven like a maniac in an attempt to get him to an emergency room before he died. Of course we spent a lot of time processing the incident and her grief. She also suffered a persistent right hip problem, which caused chronic pain. The condition had emerged about one year after her husband's death. A series of orthopaedists, chiropractors, and acupuncturists had helped a little, but the pain persisted. She decided she wanted to see if I could help with that, too. I had her focus on the hip, describing the sensations and being as specific as she could about the pain – its type, location, if it was steady or throbbing, etc. Inspired by Levine's SIBAM model, I investigated other aspects of her consciousness. While she stayed focused on the hip pain, I asked about other sensations in her body. It seemed that the more she focused on the pain, the faster her heart beat. I also asked her to notice what emotions she was feeling. She was scared. I had her stay with those sensations for a few minutes: pain, heart rate, fear. As she persisted her right foot dug deeper and deeper into my carpet. It wasn't long before she took a huge breath and began to sob, 'I drove as fast as I could. I floored the accelerator. It was an old car and I just couldn't get it to go faster!' It became very clear that a significant part of her hip problem was this memory of bearing down on the accelerator. This work didn't cure her physical problem completely, as she had been holding that leg tension for four years. But the pain eased and medical treatment became more effective. The session also facilitated her mourning process. She was able to release some of the guilt she had harboured for not making it to the hospital soon enough (Rothschild 2000: 117–118).

Donna had remembered the trip to the hospital, but had never realised that the pressure she put on her leg was the root of her current hip pain. She knew she felt guilty, but hadn't remembered how hard she had tried to get there as fast as possible. Beginning with body awareness and then bringing in the elements of emotion and movement helped to clear her memory of the events and forgive herself for not being able to save her husband's life.

Muscle toning

Another very useful application of non-touch body work with trauma is increasing muscle tone in the client's body. This might seem a contradiction, especially to the body psychotherapist. It is more common to increase relaxation in our clients. However, there are some individuals who actually become more anxious with relaxation exercises, yoga, etc. (Heide and Borkovec 1983; Lehrer and Woolfolk 1993). With such clients – usually individuals with high levels of PTS or PTSD – muscle tensing will actually work to create more calm than relaxation. Weight training, walking, stairmaster, pushups, situps and so on can all be useful tools for increasing muscle tone and thereby calming for those suffering the effects of trauma. The best way to know if a muscle toning exercise is useful for your client is to ask: 'Does this make you feel more calm, more present, more clear headed, etc.? Does this make you feel nauseous, spacy, anxious?' The answer to those questions should help you and your client to decide if a particular toning exercise is useful or should be discarded.

A sample session transcript

K is a single man in his mid-thirties. He has been T's client for two months. This session is the first of several addressing this particular incident. Two major interventions are illustrated: 1) a body-oriented model for setting up the therapy situation, 2) the beginning use of non-touch techniques to integrate a major aspect of the trauma being addressed – in this case, isolation.

T: How are we sitting – this distance and positioning?
K: It's fine.
T: What's happening in your body?

Using body awareness as a guide to setting up the therapeutic space. This is also a good way to begin training body awareness.

K: A little excitement.

T: What are the body sensations?

K: My heart's beating faster and I'm shaking a little.

T: I suggest you experiment with the distance between us.
      K moves his chair back from T about 25cm.

T: What happens to your heartbeat and shaking when you move your chair back?

K: Better now. Both are less.

T: What does that tell you?
      Making sense of the change in sensations: mind/body integration.

K: I was sitting too close to you. I'm more comfortable now.

T: OK. Tell me just the title of what you want to work on.
      This is a strategy for pacing entry into work with the trauma. We go in a step at a time instead of jumping in with both feet.

K: 'A close call – too close!'

T: What happens in your body when you say that?

K: It becomes more tense.
      Just naming the title has already been activating. This is not uncommon and helps to alert both client and therapist to the importance of pacing.

T: All over, or somewhere particular?

K: Especially in my chest. It is hard to breathe.

T: Is there anywhere that doesn't feel tense?

K: I feel weak in my legs.
      Trauma often gives a feeling of being 'weak in the knees'.

T: Try pressing your feet into the floor so that your thighs tense up. Can you do that?

K: Yes.

T: What happens in your chest when you tense up in your thighs?

K: My chest relaxes a little and I can breathe easier.
      This is an example of using muscle tensing to mediate negative reactions. Bringing more strength to the legs made it possible for the overly-tense chest to relax a little.

T: Would you like to talk about what happened? Just the outline, first – the headings.
      Again, pacing the telling of his story so that he can digest the pieces.

K: Three years ago I was shot at by a sniper. I was driving in my car, he was on an overpass. I wasn't hurt, he just shot out my rear windshield. I called the police, but as no one had seen the sniper and he left no evidence, they couldn't do anything.

T: What's happening in your body?

K: Only a little tension.

It appears to be OK to go on.

T: OK. What were the next steps?

K: I stopped going out so much.
     K cries deeply. A central issue has emerged.

T: I see you are crying. Can you tell me what's happening; what you are feeling while you are crying?
     I want my client to be able to think and feel at the same time – the goal of mind/body integration.

K: All mixed up.

T: What feelings are mixed up?

K: Being by myself. No one could help me. No one knew who it was. I didn't know if it could happen again.

T: And so you are feeling?

K: Like lost, completely lost.

T: What are the sensations in your body?

K: Like I am covered with a film.

T: How do you experience that?

K: I feel a bit numb. And you are a little blurry.
     Slight dissociation.

T: Have you ever told anyone about what happened?

K: My wife, but it scared her so much I never mentioned it again. And the police, but they couldn't do anything, so I gave up.

T: It sounds as though you were quite isolated during that time.

K: *Eyes watering.* I didn't know who to talk to. The police couldn't help me. I didn't want to scare my wife more. Because she got so scared, I was afraid to tell – and scare – anyone else. I didn't want to make a big deal out of nothing.

T: What were your feelings then?

K: I felt really scared.
     K begins to cry.

T: Say that again.

K: I was really scared.
     K cries more deeply. The sobs subside after a while.

T: How are the feelings of being scared then, and being scared now different?

K: *Takes a deep breath.* Right now I can relax. Then I was just always wound up.

T: Can you feel that difference in your body now?

K: Yes. I can breathe!

T: You never told anyone how scared you were?

K: No, not really.

T: Can you tell me?

K: I was really scared.
     K trembles a little.

T: I see you are trembling. See if it can be OK to just let that happen.
     K continues to tremble for about 30 seconds.
T: How do you feel?
K: I feel more relaxed in my chest.
     Something changes in K's eyes.
T: What is happening to your vision?
K: I can see you more clearly.
T: And the numbness?
K: A little less.
T: What do you think that means?
K: That I am a little less scared.
T: Can you say more about that?
K: After shaking and crying I can see you more clearly. I am relieved to
     have finally told someone.
T: Do you think you could tell someone else?
     *It is important to help make a bridge out to K's daily life, to decrease his
     sense of isolation there.*
K: That isn't easy for me.
T: Do you know why?
K: I'm sort of embarrassed to still be scared about something that hap-
     pened three years ago.
T: Is there anyone who might understand that?
K: Probably my brother.
T: How do you think he would respond to hearing your story?
K: I think he would be empathetic. But he might also be irritated I never
     told him before.
T: Do you think you could handle that?
K: Yes.
T: How might it feel to tell him?
K: It might be a relief.
T: Can you imagine telling him?
K: Yes. I'm doing that.
T: What happens when you tell him? *K exhales deeply.* Can you feel how
     much you are exhaling?
K: It's reducing the pressure inside. I was so confused. I didn't want to scare
     anyone. I was so alone. *K cries again.* Someone should have seen how
     scared I was.
T: How do you feel when you say that?
K: I feel angry. I was protecting everyone when I was needing support.
T: What do you think about that now?
K: I think it's about time I told someone.
T: When?
K: I'll call my brother tonight.
T: How are you feeling in your body?

K: Lighter. Relaxed. Relieved.

In subsequent sessions K was helped to talk with his wife and repair the rift that occurred at that time. Eventually he was able to address his somatic response to having been shot at, releasing that anxiety from his mind and body.

References

American Psychiatric Association. *Diagnostic and Statistical Manual of Mental disorders* (4th ed.). Washington, DC: APA 1994

Bremner, J. D., Southwick, S., Brett, E., Fontana, A., Rosenheck, R., and Charney, D. S. 'Dissociation and Posttraumatic Stress Disorder in Vietnam Combat Veterans'. *American Journal of Psychiatry* 1992; 149: 328–332

Classen, C., Koopman, C., and Spiegel, D. 'Trauma and Dissociation'. *Bulletin of the Menninger Clinic* 1993; 57(2): 178–194

Gallup, G. G., and Maser, J. D. 'Tonic Immobility: Evolutionary Underpinnings of Human Catalepsy and Catatonia'. In Seligman, M. E. P. and Masser, J. D. (Eds) *Psychopathology: Experimental Models*. San Francisco: W.H. Freeman and Company 1977: 334–357

Heide, F. J. and Borkovec, T. D. 'Relaxation-induced Anxiety: Paradoxical Anxiety Enhancement Due to Relaxation Training'. *Journal of Consulting and Clinical Psychology* 1983; 51(2): 171–182

Lehrer, P. M. and Woolfolk, R. L. 'Specific Effects of Stress Management Techniques'. In Lehrer, P. M. and Woolfolk, R. L. (Eds) *Principles and Practice of Stress Management*. New York: Guilford 1993: 481–520

Levine, P. *The Body as Healer: Transforming Trauma and Anxiety*. Lyons, CO: 1992

Nadel, L. and Jacobs, W. J. 'The Role of the Hippocampus in PTSD, Panic, and Phobia'. In Kato, N. (Ed.) *Hippocampus: Functions and Clinical Relevance*. Amsterdam: Elsevier Science, 1996: 455–463

Perls, F. *Ego, Hunger and Aggression*. Durban, South Africa: Knox Publishing 1942

Rothschild, B. *A Trauma Glossary*. unpublished manuscript 1998

Rothschild, B. *The Body Remembers: The Psychophysiology of Trauma and Trauma Treatment*. New York: W.W. Norton 2000

Selye, H. *The Stress of Life*. New York: McGraw-Hill 1984

van der Kolk, B. 'The Body Keeps the Score'. *Harvard Psychiatric Review* 1994; 1

Chapter 6

The use of imagery in body-oriented psychotherapy

Margaret Landale

> Where do these wise and creative things come from? The answer is the apparent chaos of the depth self. The music of essence plays over this chaos, pulling patterns up from the depth.
>
> Jean Houston, *A Mythic Life*, 1996: 130

Introduction

This chapter is about imagery, in particular those forms of imagery which arise spontaneously and directly from the depths of the unconscious. I will be focussing specifically on the interrelationship between the body and imagery, the interface between physical, emotional and imaginative processes and I will highlight some of the clinical applications of the use of imagery in body-oriented psychotherapy.

Imagery has been of great influence and consequence in my clinical work. I consider it one of the most vital tools for the release of unconscious hidden patterns and experiences. So often I have been stunned by the sudden emergence of a symbolic image, which when caught and acknowledged in time has led to the spontaneous unfolding of a deeper understanding.

We all know about the symbolic power of imagery. In fact most of us will have experienced how certain symbols engage our imagination intensely. Some dream images, scenes or pieces of art will leave a lasting impression more clearly than many other events or experiences. There seems to be a radiance or 'charge' to certain images, which at times can become palpable even to others. For example, I remember a client who, as she became increasingly aware of how much rage she felt inside, saw herself as a volcano. As she let images of the volcano's eruption spew forth from her unconscious I could literally feel the room and myself heating up. Whether this was the power of her or my own imagination, what matters is the realisation that our imagination is a powerful force deep within which can make us well or unwell.

Imagery becomes particularly potent when it is being embodied, in other words when it is being experienced physically and emotionally. Imagery is seen here as a mediating force between conscious thought process and unconscious psychological and biological dynamics and patterns. I call this *innate imagery* in order to distinguish it from the large spectrum of imagery and visualisation techniques which have a more general application and have been written about widely in Humanistic and transpersonal settings. I will define innate imaging as a form of *free association with distinct physical properties*. Traditionally body psychotherapists have viewed the body as the container of unconscious material and conflict and have aimed at surfacing or carthartically releasing this material. I believe that innate imaging provides a less challenging and thus less resisted approach, as it works more indirectly with the body.

In this context I will illustrate some of the imaging techniques that help to create a communicative link between mind, feelings and body and which can give the body a voice to express its hidden insights and medicine. I will be looking, for example, at how to involve the body more actively within the psychotherapeutic process, and how to overcome some of the typical mind-body dissociations experienced by most people. These dissociations may frequently result in psychosomatic symptoms, and I will therefore also be focussing on how to work more directly with physical sensations and symptoms.

Another question I will be exploring in this chapter is how imagery can provide access to early memory and be used as a tool to facilitate regression, thus making sense of early manifested relational responses and patterns. I have been deeply influenced here by the work of Winnicott and Stern, both of whom have brought greater insight into early developmental states and the impact of the environment on the growing self. I will draw particularly on Winnicott's concept of true and false self.

In this context I will also consider how imagery can help us to understand the dynamics of the psychotherapeutic relationship and how it allows the therapist to engage with a client on an inter-affective and/or pre-verbal level, bringing deeply-rooted relational patterns to the surface.

Imagery as ongoing mental activity

Imagery has been developed and applied in a number of forms throughout the history of psychotherapy. It is commonly identified with forms of guided visualisation and hypnosis techniques. All of these techniques involve the body initially and make use of relaxation to facilitate visual images. In fact, hypnosis was an inspiration to medical professionals in the late nineteenth century and had a significant influence on the development of psycho-analysis. Both Breuer and Freud initially experimented with hypnotic techniques and Freud's concept of free association was conceived from these experiments. Freud saw images as arising out of primary process thinking or as a way of surfacing or releasing unconscious early memory, which could then be interpreted by the analyst.

Jung was fascinated by the symbolic content of the unconscious and the psyche's creative forms and expression. His concept of active imagination acknowledged the key role that imagery plays in assisting the unfolding of meaning in relation to personal experience. Based on his own experience he was keen to promote an inward reflection in his patients, and he believed that the study of their own active imaginative processes would help integrate unresolved or unconscious material. Describing active imagination he writes:

> One concentrates one's attention on some impressive but unintelligible dream image, or on a spontaneous visual impression, and observes the changes taking place in it. Meanwhile of course all criticism must be suspended and the happenings observed and noted with absolute objectivity.
>
> Jung 1941: 190

Jung firmly believed in an alliance between patient and analyst and introduced the notion of self-reflective processes into the analytic framework. He influenced the Humanistic and transpersonal traditions, which all rely heavily on the self-reflecting capacities in their clients and have continued to develop the use of imagery as a form of self-exploration and discovery.

Roberto Assagioli was inspired by Jung's work and, in developing his psychosynthesis approach, has probably done most to highlight the practical applications of imagery in psychotherapy. Importantly Assagioli emphasises that imagery is not only visual, but includes all our sensory perceptions.

> Imaging is a function which in itself is to some extent synthetic, since imagination can operate at several levels concurrently: those of sensation, feeling, thinking, and intuition. It includes all the various types of imagination, such as visualisation – the evocation of visual images – auditory imagination, tactile, kinesthetic imagination and so on.
>
> Assagioli 1990: 143

It is important to remember that many people do not have visual images, but a very active imagination triggered by and experienced through other senses.

In this context I would define imagery as *an ongoing mental activity which underlies or evokes conscious thinking processes*. It is distinct from thinking because it always includes a sensory component. However, thinking and imaging overlap and tend to be interwoven. Images are experienced consciously or unconsciously on a physical level. In other words, *the body is actively and continuously involved in any imaging process*. For example, we can think about an oak tree and its relevant data but as soon as we imagine the oak tree, some sensory functions will be evoked. An image of a particular oak might come to mind, a memory of walking past it, or touching it, resting under its shade, or hearing the leaves rustling above. These mental associations might not even be registered by the conscious mind but will evoke some form of physical response such as relaxation. This has been applied and adapted by various healing traditions, notably with terminally-ill patients. Jean Houston, a leading voice in the world of Humanistic psychology, has emphasised throughout her work the potent interrelatedness between body and mind. She writes:

> Numerous studies have confirmed the fact that vividly experienced imagery, imagery that is both seen and felt, can substantially affect brain waves, blood flow, heart rate, skin temperature, gastric secretion, and immune response – in fact the total physiology.
>
> Houston 1982: 11

Imaging processes in body psychotherapy

All forms of body psychotherapy developed since Reich are based on the key assumption that, from birth onwards, experience is being embodied, resulting in a complex structure of physical, emotional, mental and relational patterns and dynamics. Recent neuro-scientific research supports this assumption; notably, Antonio Damasio's investigation of the interplay between body-mind-emotions highlights the important role the body plays in psychotherapy (Damasio 1996). The aim of body psychotherapy is to surface and release embodied experiences and memories.

This can occur through symptoms, sensations or involuntary motoric or cathartic processes. However, what has at times been lost or not sufficiently acknowledged is that these spontaneous body processes are inextricably linked with imaging processes and/or flashbacks. In the past, body psychotherapy placed great emphasis on the physical discharge of blocks and tensions with the aim of motivating spontaneous cathartic processes. The idea was to shake up the embodied psychological structures, to aim at a form of physical breakdown so that a new structure could emerge with the help of vegetative process. The criticism laid at the door of the more radical body approaches was that, although something was certainly triggered through physical catharsis, it could be difficult, if not impossible, for a client to understand this experience. As a result they might be left feeling disturbed or overwhelmed.

Images can bridge the gap between overwhelming physical-emotional sensations and conscious recognition. They offer symbolic meaning and thus containment to an otherwise overwhelming experience. Given the above definition of imaging as mental processes with sensory qualities, it follows that we can expect a strong imaging dimension in all body-induced awareness processes. In fact, it is through imagery or metaphor that we can consciously recognise or describe physical or vegetative process.

As Stern's work has shown (1998) the newborn baby immediately begins to organise her initial world of sensations into recognisable structures. Imaging is the earliest form of mental activity. Vision as a sense is fully developed at birth, and babies quickly respond affectively to shades and forms. Furthermore, tests with young babies show that they are able to recognise visually the form of a nipple which they have suckled but not actually seen. This confirms that sensory perception is interwoven with mental and imaginative activities.

The baby experiences himself and his environment through the senses and thus first develops his sense of embodied self (body self). Experience is being internalised and formed into mental representations. In this way, memory – as well as interpersonal patterns and beliefs and most importantly unconscious fantasies – is being developed and stored. Body experience and imaging processes are thus interactive right from the start. Unresolved experiences remain alive and penetrate a person's existence in many ways. Memories can surface in the psychotherapeutic environment either within the psychotherapeutic relationship (transference/countertransference), or through symptoms or innate imagery.

Imaging continues to serve as a major mental activity throughout our lives, and we can assume it serves continuously as a bridge between our physical and mental experiences and activities.

Body communication

We have already explored the sensory qualities of imaging and viewed imagery as a form of communication in which physically-held experience or memory can be revealed. We now need to look at how to help the body release this hidden information, and how to prepare the ground for imaging processes within the therapeutic experience.

Whilst we may perceive the body to be central to the psychotherapeutic process, it is worth remembering that clients often have an extremely uneasy and alienated relationship with their body. This requires us to find subtle ways of including the body and to foster ways in which the client can integrate sensual perception alongside their growing psychological self-awareness.

Creating a space for the body in the psychotherapeutic environment starts with an ongoing observation of the client's body language: how they hold themselves, the way they speak, the texture of their skin, the clothes they wear and the mannerisms they use. Most people have complicated relationships with their own bodies. Embarrassment, shame and fear of the body and its involuntary processes are common. For many clients the concept that their body represents a part of who they are is incomprehensible. If clients have a sense of self-image through their body it may well be glorified (Narcissistic) or expressed though negative identification, e.g. 'Nobody loves me because my nose is too big'. Attempting to communicate to a client through their body image is a charged affair and can easily be misinterpreted. So how can we use this unconscious language and communication which is being broadcast by our client and that we believe can hold such useful material in the search for identity and meaning?

The principle here is to remember that the body's reality is immediate and simple. The language a therapist uses when engaging with the body's communication thus has to aim at getting the client into *experiencing* their body rather than *thinking* about it. Engaging the body in the psychotherapeutic process starts simply with 'what is' statements such as, 'you look sad' or 'you seem restless'. This emphasises the non-verbal levels of communication and reflects our interest in the body's language.

A client who is stuck with a seemingly intractable problem can sometimes relate to it differently and more deeply when her attention is drawn to its physical components such as short breath, tight chest or involuntary movements. As therapists we can be aware of these physical signs of distress and respond and acknowledge them accordingly. We can also comment on changes of posture or gestures which seem related to the lines of thought in which the client is engaged. All these interventions will be registered by the client and will validate the body as a valuable part of the psychotherapeutic process.

The building of rapport in this area is both sensitive and extremely valuable. Most people will feel self-conscious or embarrassed when their physical expression is commented on. Such close observations can feel like an intrusion. However, they also provide ground for the exploration of transferrential dynamics and allow the therapist to develop forms of communication which are tuned into the client's internal experience. So, for example, if a client is rubbing her knees as she recounts an argument with her mother, the therapist's comment, 'I see you are rubbing your knees' might be taken as lack of attention to what the client was saying, or make her feel self-conscious. Whatever the reaction to the therapist's intervention, it provides ground for exploration and can only be useful. 'What is' statements or observations are advisable when working with clients who have a sensitive relationship with their body or who find it hard to accept the psychological dimension of their body. This can also be seen as an active way of working with resistance.

When working with a client who has more tolerance for his psychosomatic reality, we might choose to encourage the insight into his own bodily perception of a situation by saying things like, 'Just notice how you feel in your body as you recount the argument with your mother,' or 'Close your eyes for a moment and let yourself feel your legs and hands', or 'Perhaps your legs and hands would like to say something to your mother that you haven't dared say with words'.

Alternatively we might open our own awareness to the movement and contemplate it in the context of the material presented. Thus the rubbing might seem a way of holding her knees still, perhaps keeping them from kicking? Or as a way of comforting herself at a time of distress? We might then use these intuitive impressions to formulate an interpretation or speculate with the client what such rubbing might represent.

The body remembers

Clients may bring a traumatic event to therapy and be unable to access their emotional responses to the event. When a client's relationship with her partner ended because he had started a relationship with one of her friends, she found it impossible to feel anything; her only response was numbness. Though she kept recollecting the moment he had told her, she was unable to feel any affect as she spoke. This is a common feature of traumatic material. In order to help her engage with the physical memory of the experience, I began to ask specific questions regarding the details of the exchange such as where they'd met, which words he'd used, what his face looked like as he broke the news. She told me how he had looked guilty and had held her hand, saying how sorry he was. I encouraged her to tell me how he had held her hand, was it firm or gentle, her hand in his, or his hand on hers. I engaged with the image of his holding her hand because I had noticed that she had been wringing her hands for most of the session and it seemed to me that some of her unfelt emotion was being held in her hands. She said, her voice breaking: 'He is holding my hand only to push me away!' and then she cried for a long time. This opened the door to an emotional process that over time helped her to integrate the experience. By focussing on the descriptive details of a situation we can engage the senses and, with that, the body's stored memory. This helps in the reliving of a situation, and consequently encourages an affective expression and release.

The ways of welcoming the body into the psychotherapeutic space are manifold. Yet it is the simple acknowledgement of the client's physical reality that forms the interactive ground for experiential process. One approach with which most body psychotherapists are familiar is introducing the horizontal position as a way of engaging the client with their inner reality.

In my own practice I will encourage clients, when it seems appropriate, to lie on the couch – especially when working with imagery. Lying down puts into operation some important mechanisms. The client physically relaxes and their body experiences a feeling of being held. As in early infancy the head and whole body are being supported, and this can activate and support regressive processes and inner reflection. The client does not have to keep eye contact or face me, which means I am being experienced as less intrusive. Energy that is bound up in maintaining the superficial layer of relationship with the therapist may be released into free associations or inner-awareness processes. Most of all, by encouraging the client to lie down, whether on the couch or a mattress, I am signalling again that there is a space in the process for the body. The following vignette illustrates this and also highlights the importance of following the client's process even when offering a directive.

Sally was a woman in her 50s who came into therapy because she felt unable to cope with her stressful workload and was frightened she would lose her job. She presented as anxious and upset, and reported that she had problems sleeping because she kept worrying about things that had happened during the day.

Sally spent the first few sessions sitting on the edge of her chair. She was agitated and visibly tense. She was overtly critical of herself and complaining tearfully about her workload. I put it to her that despite thinking hard about her problems she always seemed to return to the same dilemma. I suggested that she might need to stop thinking so much and allow herself to rest and look within for an understanding of why and how she had ended up in this position. I then asked her if she would consider lying down, as a way of physically shifting her position.

As often happens, Sally found the idea of lying down awkward and embarrassing. I therefore asked her to simply imagine herself lying down and to then describe what she saw. She immediately said, 'It would make me feel like I am an ill child'. I noticed how spontaneously she had slumped into her chair, her attention drawn inwards. I asked her to tell me a bit more about the ill child. 'She is all alone in a dark room, she's got the measles, like when I was five. My Mum is busy and the others are at school or out playing. I hated being sick,' she added, 'and everybody says that I got better amazingly quickly.' I encouraged Sally to become aware of how she felt in her body. She was silent for a moment and than said: 'I feel heavy and tired. If I lie down I fear I would never get up.' Before I could respond she quickly opened her eyes and, sitting upright on the edge of the chair, commented: 'I just can't afford to get tired. I have so much on, I need to keep my wits about me.'

This vignette makes several important points. By asking Sally to lie down I introduced the reality of her physical body and how it might be involved in her search for answers to her problems. I had the impression that Sally needed to slow down and that her inability to rest was exacerbating her problems. I chose to respond to her embarrassment only by not insisting on her physical lying down but, meeting her in the middle, I invited her to image the situation. It quickly transpired that Sally could clearly imagine herself lying down, otherwise she would not have shown such a strong response. This then allowed her body to release a small fragment of memory, which provided an important clue to her current situation. Even though Sally snapped out of the imagery quickly, this memory – and indeed her statement that she could not afford to get tired – became an important narrative in helping her to understand her habitual anxiety and her inability to find rest.

Finally, it is worth emphasising the importance of responding intuitively and immediately to those moments of inward energy or reflection. Such moments are often found in the brief instances where habitual or comfort states are being challenged or, indeed, when the body is being acknowledged.

Imagery, body sensations and symptoms

In order to work with body sensations or symptoms, a client is typically taken by surprise or feels relaxed and trusting enough to drop her mental defenses and engage directly with the present experience as process. Spontaneous body-led process can be evoked by encouraging the client to identify with a sensation or sometimes just by looking within. It is important to get the timing right when introducing imagery and to intuit the client's readiness for it. The instructions I give are simple; I believe it is unhelpful to suddenly to develop a 'misty sotto voce'; being oneself and using one's normal voice help to make imagery a natural part of the interaction. The sort of instruction I might give would be as follows: 'Close your eyes and notice how you feel in your body/chest/legs right now. You talk about your back aching so let your attention go there, see whether there is an image coming to you from your back. Notice what comes up and try not to censor anything'.

Introducing imagery requires confidence and good timing. It also requires that the psychotherapeutic relationship is safely established and that the therapist is experienced as containing and holding. Transferential dynamics often have to be explored and understood before the client will allow her conscious defenses to drop in order to allow a spontaneous physical emotional process or free association. Body-led imagery often happens in the form of free association. The spontaneous flow of image and association indicates that the defenses are momentarily relaxed. Herein lies a distinction between what we might call *conscious imagery* and *innate imagery*. Conscious imagery has an order to it, it is easily accessible in its meaning and is often clichéd. The client tends to observe it and talk about it rather than becoming fully submerged in it. It might also be described as a kind of voluntary daydreaming. Innate imaging means that defense organisations have momentarily been surrendered to a spontaneous flow of emerging associations, which tend to come across as somewhat chaotic and unstructured. Like dreams, they appear to operate under a secret code that cannot immediately be deciphered. Winnicott reflects on this when he writes:

> I am trying to refer to the essentials that make relaxation possible. In terms of free association this means that the patient on the couch, or the child among toys on the floor, must be allowed to communicate a succession of ideas, thoughts, impulses, sensations that are not linked except in some way that is neurological or physiological and perhaps beyond detection.
>
> Winnicott 1997: 55

As body-oriented psychotherapists we can apply this directly to sensation or symptoms. Sensations or symptoms already carry a certain emotional charge, since they are linked with the unconscious through biological process (i.e.

embodied memory, somatic markers). Thus the physical symptom can function either as a symbol for, or catalyst of, spontaneous body process, or give rise to free association and imagery.

Sensation, imagery and free association interlink to form a dynamic triangle. It is essential, however, for both therapist and client to give up control momentarily and surrender to the unfolding process, which can be felt as chaotic. Again, to quote Winnicott:

> . . . free association that reveals a coherent theme is already affected by anxiety, and the cohesion of ideas is a defense organisation . . . organised nonsense is already a defense, just as organised chaos is denial of chaos.
> Winnicot 1997: 56

Symbols and images are containers of process and allow a seemingly chaotic sharing of unstructured process. Sustaining rapport through this apparent chaos of free associative mental or physical emotional process builds instinctive trust and tends to have a transformative quality. If the therapist remains in the role of observer or commentator and tries to control the situation then the involuntary and organic process is restricted or non-existent.

One client, whom I shall call Nick, entered a spontaneous free association when actively identifying with his headache. It went as follows.

'My head aches . . . pain and ache . . . my body is light . . . my head is heavy . . . a heavy blackness, heavy and black as the night . . . no features . . . just heavy blackness . . . my body is so light it loses air . . . the blackness sucks out the air . . . I'm being squashed . . . can't see . . . no features . . . can't get away.'

Nick fell silent at this point, a heavy silence which became palpable in the room. My instinct was to let the silence happen, both because he seemed deeply engaged in the experience of heaviness and also because this behaviour differed dramatically from his usually verbally active and rational manner. I used my countertransferrential experience of heaviness to stay engaged, and it was from within this shared state that I ventured: 'Heavy and silent'.

With a voice deeper than his usual, he responded: 'Silent as the grave, I'm buried . . . they've buried me alive . . .' *deep heavy inbreath, shaky, rattling outbreath, signals of distress.*

'They have buried you alive,' I repeat, slightly emphasising 'they'.

'People in black, all are wearing black, staring down at me as the coffin goes down . . . I have to stay with him . . . he is taking me with him! . . .' *short, panting breathing, distress.*

Being careful not to interrupt what had become a deep involuntary process, I chose to assure Nick indirectly of my presence by echoing his last comments: 'Have to stay with him, he is taking me with him . . .'.

And with greater distress in his voice, almost shouting, with a childlike quality: 'But he is gone, he's just left me, I'm here all alone and the darkness is so heavy, so alone . . .' and he sobbed heavily and uncontrollably.

Nick's father had died in an accident and the news had arrived at night, ripping him and his mother out of their sleep. His mother had been unable to cope with this sudden loss and had started to drink heavily and regularly brought different men home at night. Nick remembered lying awake at night, listening to the noisy sexual activity that went on in his mother's bedroom.

This was the first time he had been able to release the grief and despair he had felt in the years after his father's death. He began to understand that a part of him had been buried with his father and that the active and happy little boy he had been had also died at that time. Over the coming months he grieved for this loss and began to understand how this experience had affected his life and relationships.

This example illustrates how surrendering into a sensation can trigger strong affective memory, how the body releases its stored and unresolved experience and allows an identification with old pain which can bring meaning to unconscious reactive patterns. It was crucial for me to follow Nick's emerging process closely, echoing his words and allowing my own instinctive perception of what was unfolding before me, but most of all trusting his body and imagination to navigate us through the material.

These types of sensations and images are always personal and unique and it is important to stay open to the underlying story. As it unravels it will release its individual and innate meaning which can then be integrated in the context of past or present experience. Sensations can trigger deep process because clients are unsuspecting about the experience stored in their bodies. When Nick started to talk about his headache he had no inkling that such a revelation would emerge.

When working with more severe psychosomatic states we cannot expect such spontaneous process to occur. In such cases, symptoms are often part of a deeply-held anxiety and an internal disorder, the exploration of which will be fiercely resisted for fear of being overwhelmed. Yet there will still be vivid images, stories or metaphors surrounding the psychosomatic symptoms and their careful exploration through free association, detailed body awareness and other creative techniques can prove meaningful.

Imagery techniques that I find helpful in this context include drawing, working with objects and dialoguing with the symptom (i.e. objectifying it). I would include these techniques as part of imaging work because they trigger a person's imagination. Working with objects I have found to be particularly helpful, because most clients experience it as playful and creative. I have a collection of small toys and oddments which I sometimes introduce into sessions. I ask clients to choose one of these objects to represent the situation or person with whom they have been grappling. My intention in using this technique is that I will be both engaging the client's playful and inquisitive nature and bypassing their more entrenched defenses. When clients go along with the suggestion, they often find it easy to make meaningful associations from their chosen object and gain considerable insights into the history or nature of their issue.

Drawing is another powerful technique that accesses the images of a client's inner world. A female client suffering from bulimia was asked to draw an image of herself in front of the fridge in the middle of the night (the typical scene of her bingeing). She drew a mouse with a hole in its belly which was stuffed up with old teddybear straw. Asked what came to mind about teddybear straw, she remembered her old teddybear, which she had operated on as a four-year-old, cutting open its belly in order 'to take out what made his belly hurt'. In tears the client then remembered how her mother had thrown the teddy into the bin. Yet the teddy had helped her go to sleep and she remembered lying awake at night, feeling frightened without it. The image of her teddy and explorations around tummy aches provided the first fragments of meaningful explanation to what drove her to binge in the middle of the night.

Core images in a client's life story

Another way of thinking about imagery in psychotherapy is as a creative and facilitated process for the re-discovery of self. I draw here again on Winnicott, and explore his concept of the true and false self. Winnicott, as we know, was particularly interested in observing the unfolding development of infants and young children. He came to believe that we enter life with an inborn sense of self, following an individual and natural blueprint. He argued that when the environment is friendly and receptive enough to our unfolding, we can develop naturally from within, gradually waking up to the world around us and integrating outer influences into a congruent self experience. We can go on being ourselves. Or as Josephine Klein put it:

> The true self appears as soon as there is any mental organisation of the individual at all, and it means little more than the summary of sensory-motor aliveness ... The true self is firmly associated with all things bodily, including the homunculus core of the self, where all perceptions, all movements, all reactions are mapped. The fortunate infant develops self-structures whose core is homunculus based. The *me-to-whom-things-happen* and the *I-who-do-things* are homunculus based. Winnicott calls this fortunate state *indwelling*: 'I dwell in my body and my body is very much "me", – I have the sense that my body and mind are integrated and not isolated each from the other'.
>
> Klein 1997: 234

As experience is processed on an organic-physical and primitive emotional level, these early influences become personal memory, which is stored on a somatic and largely unconscious level. Winnicott calls these *self-organising processes* and they continue throughout childhood, giving rise to our mental processes and conscious forms of identity from within the embodied experiences of our early years. Thus they shape the complex structures of our ego and personality. However, when this natural process of self-development and integration is disrupted, the inborn sense of self will be arrested or supressed, which in turn gives rise to the development of a false self, a self which is being constructed as a response to environmental pressures and expectations. It is a structure based on survival and thus charged with existential anxiety. This anxiety becomes embodied and forms unconscious structures or defenses.

I would argue that the true *self-quality* remains dormant throughout a person's life and can be activated or aroused at any point in time. As the true self was originally a body self, the body preserves these latent or innate qualities. An experience of wellbeing, which is primary in the experience of being oneself, can be evoked or induced through sensuous or body felt experience. Thus even when working with deeply distressed individuals, simple relaxation techniques can provide some balance and perspective.

If the true self has been deeply lost, and we are dealing with overpowering false-self dynamics, the relational wounding needs to be addressed first. The more powerfully the true self has had to be suppressed, the greater the degree of mental and emotional confusion – a disembodied sense of self which is driven by internalised misconceptions, fantasies and fears. Clients with borderline personalities or psychotic disorders, for example, are typically alienated from their own bodies. Furthermore, some people will be fearful even of closing their eyes and going within, or simply will not know what 'going within' means. Others might present a flood of images which are not really being experienced. I would argue that all those are signs that the relationship with the other has been deeply disrupted and it is particularly important here to work primarily with the relational or psychodynamic approaches that act as a catalyst for the surfacing of early experience and relational patterns.

False self dynamics can produce core images with which the person is strangely disidentified. For example, we hear clients talking about physical or emotional abuse yet feel unable to relate to it because they themselves don't seem able to hear their own story. It is as if they are deeply disconnected from their own experience.

In the following case study I want to illustrate how a client presented with such a disconnected core image. It is as if the true self offers an essential clue to their required healing but that at the same time the false self completely denies its validity. What the therapist has to do in such a case is hold the true self-image for the client and work within the transferential framework in order to relax the client's deeply-held anxiety. In my experience it is only then, when the client is ready, that they will be able to reclaim what has been lost for so long.

Vanessa, a vivacious woman in her mid 30s, came into therapy because she was suffering from anxiety attacks, which would come on without warning when she was on her own or in public places. The symptoms during these attacks included dizziness, severe breath restriction and heart palpitations. It emerged during the history taking that Vanessa's mother had suffered from postnatal depression after her birth. Vanessa was the second of three children and her mother had told her that it was because of her love for Vanessa's then 3-year-old brother that she had been able to go on living. Vanessa held the view that she was lucky because she had been 'far too little to even notice her mother's despair'. She described her childhood as otherwise being normal and happy.

During the first year of therapy Vanessa talked about her life, and the occurring anxiety attacks, in an almost entertaining, anecdotal fashion. Though during the attacks she experienced extreme terror, she was not able to connect with this in therapy. She would say that 'it is no use wallowing in it, I've come to sort it out'.

My interventions at this time were predominantly reflective, trying to help Vanessa become aware of how she was operating in her life and around the anxiety attacks. I pointed out to her that she didn't seem to take herself seriously, as if she could not believe she was suffering such distressing episodes. She agreed that she was finding it hard to believe this was happening to her and she promptly began reading psychological self-help books and reporting on the various practical steps she was taking to sort herself out. I tried to interpret this flight into action as both a familiar pattern of becoming efficient when dealing with overwhelming emotions and her need to appease me after what she might have perceived as my telling her to get on with it. None of these seemed to engage her, and I experienced an ever-increasing hopelessness and despondency. I wondered whether I was experiencing some of Vanessa's disowned feelings in the countertransference.

The image of the baby who had been left to cope on her own because her mother was too depressed to engage with her kept occupying my mind. But I had learned already that Vanessa had rigorously detached herself from this early vulnerable part of herself and whenever I had made an attempt to form a connection to this I had been met with incomprehension, cynicism or polite denial. All I could do was to remain calm and present, whilst holding on to the image of the unwanted baby for her.

This is a common feature when dealing with core images that arise spontaneously from denied or disowned parts of a client's experience. It is as if, as soon as the image has sneaked out, it has to be vehemently denied and as therapists we are left to hold and nurture the most vulnerable parts of the client whilst they deny or attack them. As Vanessa put it: 'You have this thing about me as a baby that's nothing to do with my problem. I want you to help me to get rid of my panic attacks!' Yet my silent engagement with her core image, the lonely baby, gave our relationship a background and helped me to stay empathetic and reflective. Unconsciously she must have perceived my attention and I believe that this contributed to what emerged next.

About eighteen months into the therapy something began to shift. Vanessa gradually began to lose hope that she would overcome the panic attacks. This made her feel despondent and angry with me for not helping her. She had recreated in me her unavailable mother. These were important transferential dynamics as they allowed me to interpret her feeling let down by me in the light of her emotionally unavailable mother. I believe that, as she experienced me withstanding her attacks without losing my caring attitude, her defenses began to relax, leading to the following experience. Vanessa said: 'I just don't know what else I can do to get on top of it'.

I asked her to close her eyes and to let herself stay with the image of trying to get on top of it. She saw herself trying to climb up a sand hill. It was made of very fine, slippery, grey sand and as she struggled to find some footing she became aware that she just kept on sinking deeper and deeper. She said repeatedly: 'I can't get up, the harder I try the more I get sucked in!'

Her body at this stage showed increasing signs of distress. Her breathing became erratic, her fingers seemed to try and grasp on to something, her feet moved in the attempt to find some ground. All these were signs of an unfolding spontaneous organic process which I felt sure I needed to encourage and support. I then noticed that her body was beginning to display symptoms of her panic attacks. I encouraged her to stay with these sensations and to let her body guide her.[1]

Vanessa gave way to her body's impulses and began to move with her panic. Her legs and arms moved rapidly in an uncoordinated way and I could see her stomach contract in terror. I noticed too that her energy seemed to be forcefully directed upwards and there seemed to be an accumulation of tension around her head. In response I encouraged her to stand and to push down into her feet to give her a sense of her own ground. She moved her feet and spontaneously began to stamp. Yet the stamping seemed to make her collapse around her middle; her belly contracted into what looked like silent, violent sobbing and her arms began to flail helplessly up and outward as if she was trying to grab hold of something. Responding to her hands and arms I held out a cushion, allowing her to grasp it or push it away. She just touched the surface of the cushion and her breathing and movements almost entirely stopped. She had an inward looking expression.

'What is happening?' I asked. She said: 'It's as if I am lying down, just lying, there are bars around me, blue and white, blue bars and all this white behind the bars. The white hurts my eyes. The white is huge and cold, like snow, like a vast mountain of snow. I am cold. The white hurts my eyes, I just want to go to sleep, there are colours when I sleep. I am so tired.'

Again I encouraged her to stay with what she experienced, that it was alright to give in to the tiredness. I helped her to lie down. Her hands remained on the cushion gently stroking it and she said: 'So soft, soft, the sand was soft, soft like skin . . . softness on my hands . . . lots of little dots, white dots on pink, making me sleepy . . .'.

She seemed calmer, and when after a period of silence I checked what was happening, she said: 'I feel warmer, my skin warms me'.

This imagery provided Vanessa with the first real connection of her early experiences in life. It opened the door to understanding the cold climate which she had endured during the first months of her life. She remembered that her baby blanket had been pink with white dots and it gave her the impression that she had been comforting herself by the feel and the patterns of her blanket. The process also helped her understand her panic attacks as an existential anxiety that had its roots in her infancy. The body had released its deeply-held memory and thus helped her to relate to the lonely baby and the achiever child within.

Vanessa's core image, and how it connected to her sense of true self, was both the container and the trigger for her healing process. Of course, the work didn't stop here, but her anxiety attacks started to recede from this point.

Conclusion

My aim in this chapter has been to illustrate how both our body and our imagination are powerful catalysts for change. When the unspeakable is expressed through an image, when a symptom releases its metaphor, when the pain which has lingered in the darkness of a person's unfulfilled life can finally be imagined, re-experienced and understood, then he or she can begin to make sense of who they are, not only in relation to their own life story but also in relationship to others.

The exploration and experience of imagery is always integrative and unifying. This has been understood and applied by many practitioners from diverse approaches such as cognitive-behavioural therapy, hypnosis, transpersonal psychology and of course analytical, psychodynamic and holistic psychotherapy. The role the body plays in imaging processes and in the psychotherapeutic journey has been underestimated or ignored for too long.

Note

1 It is important not to panic when we witness such a strong vegetative response. The body memory was breaking through and my calmness and trust in these functions was a vital therapeutic response, reassuring Vanessa, who was by now in a deeply regressed place, to trust her process. It felt crucial to stay engaged so that she could experience my presence in this raw state of being. I also felt certain that this was an opportunity to momentarily replace the ingrained memory of the absent mother.

References

Assagioli, R. *Psychosynthesis*, London: Mandala 1990

Damasio, A. R. *Descartes' Error*. London: Papermac 1996

Houston, J. *The Possible Human*. New York: Tarcher/Putnam 1982

Houston, J. *A Mythic Life*. Harper-Collins 1996

Jung, C. G. (1941) '*The Psychological Aspects of the Kore*'. In: Hull, R. F. C. (trans.) *The Collected Works of Carl G. Jung*. Princeton: Princeton University Press vol. 9+1

Klein, J. *Our Need for Others and Its Roots in Infancy*. London: Routledge 1997

Stern, D. *The Interpersonal World of the Infant*. London: Karnac 1997

Winnicott, D. W. *Playing and Reality*. London: Routledge 1997

Chapter 7

Psycho-spiritual body psychotherapy

Philippa Vick

'Spirit' originally meant 'breath', the breath of life; and focusing on the body's breath is one of the most universal ways to awaken the soul.

Totton 2000

Introduction

The purpose of this chapter is to introduce the underlying principles and practice of transpersonal psychology, Hakomi therapy and the work of Bob Moore through one of his principal exponents, Hilmar Schonauer.

Hakomi therapy was developed by Ron Kurtz in America during the 1970s and 1980s, drawing on the neo-Freudian work of Reich and Alexander Lowen and the Humanistic movement. As such, it values being in our bodies, in the present moment, with awareness of our experience as it is. Kurtz himself said he simply looked around and took the best. Transpersonal psychology also grew from Humanistic psychology, formally arriving in America as *The Journal of Transpersonal Psychology* in 1969. Its central belief is that healing at its most profound includes a depth relationship to that within us which is beyond the usual frame of our individual personalities. As a perspective it can be grafted onto various root stock and at present there are psychotherapists who combine psychoanalytic, existential, humanistic and also Jungian basic positions with a transpersonal perspective.

In the UK, at the Centre for Transpersonal Psychology, C.G. Jung has been foremost and this is perhaps no surprise since Ken Wilber has named Jung's analytical psychology as the most viable transpersonal psychology of the twentieth century. Transpersonal psychology, particularly in America, has also been influenced by Buddhist psychology and this is mainly represented by the emphasis placed upon the practice of mindfulness, which, as with Hakomi, involves being consciously present with our experience in each successive moment. Bob Moore's work, taught by Hilmar Schonauer in London, remains, for me, more difficult to define, even after over fourteen years of study. From his intuitive and visionary abilities Bob Moore developed a system of energy-transforming exercises or meditations that heal the person by opening blockages and making energetic connections. This work incorporates very specific descriptions of the psychophysical energetic structures of the person, sometimes collectively called the 'subtle body', which are easily misunderstood since many terms are shared with other systems. Quite simply, I have found that what is conceptually opaque becomes transparent experientially with practice (see Chapters 8 and 9 of this book).

Psychotherapy and mindfulness

I start from the belief that psychotherapy – literally, the *healing of soul* – arises from self acceptance. This is not something passive. It is not about giving up and saying, 'Well that's who I am and I can do nothing about it'. On the contrary, it has a dynamic open quality to it. This is an acceptance of self as we find ourselves right now in this present moment. Whether we are happy or sad, calm or confused, mad or sane, it leaves this experience as it is without any desire to change it in any way. What is distinctive is that this self acceptance is *self aware*. In both Hakomi and transpersonal psychology this ability to remain present with our sensations and feelings *as they are*, consciously, is linked to the practice of mindfulness. Mindfulness, the ability to be consciously present in each successive moment with whatever is happening within us and outside of us, is found in a number of spiritual practices from different traditions but it is most explicit in the teachings of Buddhism, the teaching on 'being awake'.

Transpersonally-orientated psychotherapists have called this by various names; John Welwood speaks of it as 'unconditional presence' (Welwood 2000), Mark Epstein as 'bare attention' (Epstein 1995), Wilber as 'the transpersonal witness' (Wilber 1975) while Kurtz, honouring it as one of the five principles of Hakomi therapy, stays with the term 'mindfulness' (Kurtz 1970). In all cases, what is being encouraged is the development of a state of *choiceless awareness* that is not driven by fears arising out of unconscious traumatic experiences. It is called 'unconditional presence' because we try to be present with our experience: body, feelings and mind, unconditioned by the emotions that surround them. It is called 'bare attention' because our attention is bare of the secondary reactions that cloak the vivid immediacy of experience. It is called the 'transpersonal witness' because it avoids the usual personal and defensive reactions of repression or identifying and acting out. It does this by assuming a transpersonal position of being fully in touch with experience while not identified with it; thus we have our experience but it does not have us. Larry Rosenberg, a mindfulness teacher, describes this as the ability to be intimate (Rosenberg 1998). He observes that most of us are unable to perceive and be with either ourselves or the external world without clothing ourselves or it with emotionally-laden value judgements. Thus attraction leads to the need to possess in order to continue the pleasure, while aversion leads to finding a way to remove that which offends. Either, way the internal emotionally reactive 'noise' is so loud that the simple act of communion, of being nakedly present, cannot happen.

Continuous mindfulness is, of course, an ideal. In reality any genuine experience of this is initially fleeting and will almost always be the fruit of some form of formal mindfulness meditation practice or, even more transitory, perhaps a moment's 'unintentioned being' within a therapy session. However, the modest act of remaining present or 'staying with' our experience without being driven to change it can start small and simple with a moment to pause and breathe. This takes us to a knowing of ourselves that is not only beyond the needs and wishes of others but also of ourselves as we have come to imagine ourselves to be. In that moment it heals the splits between the body, feelings and mind so that our separation from our self is progressively closed. This is important. If we understand the basic dis-ease as being divided persons who spend our lives suffering from being separated from life by our own fears, then healing, at its most profound, will be found in the state of non-dual consciousness that is no longer divided.

Psychoanalysis has frequently mistakenly depicted this as a regressive desire to return to the symbiotic union with mother, thereby confusing the prepersonal mind of the infant with the transpersonal mind of the fully-awakened state. This mistake Wilber calls the 'pre/trans fallacy' (Wilber 1998). However, those who have actually experienced it tell us that, on the contrary, this state, while empty of self, is full of clarity, wisdom and compassion. This is not transcendence as much as *intimate engagement*.

Accompanying this understanding is the more specific and technical understanding of the Bob Moore work which Hilmar Schonauer simply calls 'getting to know yourself'. As I have said, this is potentially confusing to talk about because, as well as using common words in an unusual way (for instance, 'qualities' and 'feeling'), he also uses esoteric terms such as chakra, aura and etheric and astral bodies. Perhaps what is important here is not how these terms when used in one system compare with another, nor (more difficult still) attempting to identify some common ground of meaning, but rather to question the authenticity of the experiences they hope to define.

In my experience I have found that it is extremely easy to have an idea or image about our energetic structure that is little more than fantasy. While there are many books and courses that give specific information about the appearance and qualities of the chakras and subtle body, frequently these do not correspond to the person's own energetic reality. If when this happens the person imagines that, say, the heart chakra is green and open but in fact it is not, they are in danger of alienating themselves further from their real condition. Again what is important here is not to adopt one system or another in the unconscious attempt to identify with it and so gain a more cemented sense of personal identity but rather to actually enquire and stay with our condition simply as it is. If it is going to change (as all things of nature must), then it will do so of its own accord as we remain present with it and with an authenticity that no amount of wishful thinking can create.

Seemingly more process orientated,[1] the essence of the Moore/Schonauer work is about a movement from a brittle and defended personality structure – resulting from fear generated by trauma – to a profound opening of the heart and beyond that to spiritual wholeness. The opening of the heart is recognised by both spiritual traditions and psychotherapy as an essential part of the work. In Moore's work, emotional reactions demonstrate the defence structures that under scrutiny reveal fear at their centre. These may be understood as 'energy blockages', which are reflected in both the physical and subtle bodies.

The notion of energy is complex. It is described in eastern and far eastern texts as prana and chi and, like the Greek notion of spirit, though more developed, is recognised as the life force within the individual that must be balanced and properly circulated for health. Through the exercises Moore has developed it becomes possible to identify, transform and release these blockages and so shift the locus of identity from identification with the fear structures to a more spacious and still place that he calls our 'qualities' and which are associated with the combined heart/mind. Here qualities are attributes that we seem to arrive with at birth yet are nonetheless uniquely our own. An example might be a quality of clarity, or love, or generosity. Both Wilber and Welwood shed a little more light on what precisely these qualities may be. Wilber has developed a model of a 'Spectrum of Consciousness' (Wilber 1975: 107) that describes 'transpersonal bands' as the first level of manifestation from a formless energetic ground. This transpersonal band comprises archetypes in the platonic sense and so for instance contains the 'primordial light' and the 'primordial sound' (Wilber 1998). What is interesting here is that the transpersonal band represents a level of our self that is in between the no self of the formless energetic ground and the constrictions of being identified with the contents of the individual and personal identity. As such it is still personal but in a very expanded manner. Welwood adds

> This transpersonal ground [band] is comprised of deep structures of responding and relating to reality that are intrinsic to our human makeup. Here we discover all the most universally valued qualities of human nature – compassion, generosity, humour, courage, strength, and so on.
>
> Welwood 2000: 69

Whatever the contents and origins of these qualities, making a connection with them opens us out of the emotional fear structures and connects us to the clearer and more spacious energy of the heart/mind and its feeling. Expressed so simply, this fails to emphasise a crucial point: that *this understanding proceeds from an experiential knowledge of the energy structure and its transformation rather than a generalised idea*. This is as different as talking about electric plugs to actually plugging one in. Furthermore, being empirical, it demands the same attitude as mindfulness meditation, namely that we start and stay with our experience *as we find it*, in the knowledge that this type of attention has the ability to evoke transformation naturally without any nudging from a meddling and heroic ego.

In the therapeutic setting this way of working has two principal areas of importance. First, it delineates precisely the process of opening that mindfulness engenders by revealing the places where emotional trauma, as 'stuck' energy, continues to maintain defensive closures. This is to give a level of precision to this commonly-accepted understanding, by a direct knowledge of the balance of the energies, that is not available when only a conceptual gauge is used. Second, by connecting the therapist to their own feelings and qualities, it enables a 'blending' with the client and possibly thereby enables the client to step beyond their own fear structures and gain an experiential access to their own connection with depth. Here it is important not to confuse the experience of blending with some form of symbiotic fusion in which the therapist and client enter into a collusive mutual identification. Blending, far from being a narcissistic merger, is about the ability of one person who is in touch with their own qualities and not identified with their fear structures, being able to 'sound a note' that makes it possible for the other to come into tune with. This is not an act of the therapist's will – the therapist acting from their own emotional need – but rather an act of *unintentioned possibility* which is there for the client's taking.

Furthermore, while it is obvious that our 'energy' can influence another, (for ill as well as good), it is important not to entertain some inflated notion of our own spiritual specialness. This is just something simple and ordinary that develops naturally from our work on ourselves.

Hakomi Therapy

The five principles

Let us next look at how these different perspectives may be woven into a single fabric of therapy. Hakomi proceeds from a set of basic assumptions known as the five principles. The first of these has already been mentioned: *mindfulness*. Here mindfulness specifically means an investigative attitude that is employed to research how thoughts and feelings are operating in us in each successive moment. Thus mindfulness becomes the primary Hakomi tool in therapy because it is this that the therapist tries to engender in the client, so that they may come to know themselves better through the act of mindful attention. From this position of non-judgemental observation, the client moves through a process of exploration, understanding and transformation.

Accompanying this is the second principle: *non-violence*. This emphasises the importance of simply staying with just what is – not pushing, not interpreting, but rather going with the grain, following the energy, creating an environment where all aspects of the self and its own speed and movement are accepted just as they are.

The third principle is *unity*. This speaks of the interrelatedness of all life. In psychotherapy we see this as the integration of conscious and unconscious aspects of the person, of the body and mind, of the person with the environment and, more specifically, the integration of defensive structures into the process of change. The heart of this is an acceptance of all parts of the self and a recognition that all must be included for any vision of wholeness to be real. This naturally leads to the fourth principle of *mind/body holism* which recognises that we are not split between our minds and bodies, despite what it may feel like, but, recognising the wisdom of Eastern and Far Eastern medicine, that the dynamic emptiness of the 'basic open ground' progressively concretises in manifestation and finally appears as matter. Lastly the fifth principle, *organicity*, recognises that within each person exists an innate homeostatic mechanism that always attempts to move towards the greatest potential balance and wholeness that is possible at any given time.

Character typology

Hakomi theory also values the typological characterisation of developmental wounds. This clearly shows its Reichian ancestry and the work of, amongst others, Lowen on bioenergetics. This suggests that our experience, from the intrauterine period on, conditions our attitudes towards our emotional and physical environment and ourselves within it. Kurtz calls these conditioning 'core beliefs' and it is these unconscious and profoundly pervasive and influential attitudes that not only govern the way we receive and interpret our lives but also shape our bodies, movement and energy. An example of such a core belief is 'The world is a dangerous place'. If we carry such a belief it will profoundly colour everything, distorting much of our present experience with the traumatic memory of danger from our infantile past. Inhabiting this belief will not only make the world a place of fear to withdraw from but, at its most powerful, will also make us withdraw from any parts of our self that threaten to draw us into the world. Thus we are not only estranged from the world of others but also from ourselves. Alienated from relationships and our own feelingful and instinctual nature the only place left is fantasy.

Kurtz's understanding of these psychopathological characterisations is influenced by his five principles which enable him to rename and reframe each wound. Hence a schizoid person in the earlier schema becomes a 'sensitive analytic', emphasising the positive qualities that this wound may engender. The oral person likewise gets revisioned as the 'dependent and endearing' and so on, so that each person's wounding is not only a recognition of the etiology and symptoms of its type but also of the gifts that the wound may bring (for a full description see Kurtz (1970)).[2]

This type of characterisation is fascinating and very useful when trying to understand the often complex and confusing material that our clients bring us. Many different schema exist and it is of value to compare them (see particularly the work of Stephen Johnson (1994)). Perhaps what Kurtz most gives us is a quality of kindness and appreciation for the intelligence and ingenuity of our defensive structures, thus making them easier to accept and let go of. This is a quality that is easily endangered when such characterisations are used in a detached or defensive manner.

Stages of process in Hakomi practice

In a session the character types and the five principles are translated into practice by the method of mindfulness. This creates the *Stages of Process*, which move from *making contact* in ordinary consciousness, to *accessing mindfulness*, to *processing in mindfulness*, to *working with the child* and/or *riding the rapids*, and finally to *integration and completion*. Below is a session that demonstrates these stages clearly.

Making contact

Jane brings to her session her fear of relationships. She experiences this fear as a closing down around her solar plexus which feels cold and frozen. As she talks about her partner she is entirely identified with her emotions of right-eousness and fear. The partner is entirely bad while she is good. Just preparing to see the partner she feels the attacks of the partner against her and her own fearful withdrawal. By my hearing of Jane's 'story' she feels safe enough to go deeper. Also my knowledge of her character typology (basically a 'sensitive analytic' with 'dependent/endearing' and 'expressive/clinging' overlays), slowly built up over many sessions, guides me so that I can understand the specific needs of her developmental wounding.

Accessing mindfulness

Bringing her back to her body/feelings in the present we discover she feels afraid, frozen and paralysed.

Processing in mindfulness

I invite her to be present in her body as if she is going to meet her partner now. She has already done a good deal of work like this and so when she remains present with the fearful feeling of being with the partner she also becomes aware of some partially hidden feelings of defensiveness, of wanting to shut out the partner, within the frozen feeling around her middle. Her awareness of these defensive structures enables me to suggest that we try an investigative experiment to see if we can explore these feelings on the periphery of consciousness. She agrees to this and so I take over the defence for her (in this instance by placing a piece of card in front of the abdomen where the frozen feeling is). Relieved of the burden of maintaining her own defence, energy is freed, and Jane notices that this is the feeling which accompanies a withdrawal that she has used throughout her life when she feels threatened by criticisms from others. Staying with the feeling of criticism she realises that it reminds her of the criticism she believed her father levelled at her when she was a child. This then reveals her core belief, something along the lines of 'it is not OK for me to be myself'.

Working with the child

Recognising this brings Jane some immediate relief, partially releasing the separation between the upper and lower parts of her body, and in this instance we go on to explore various remembered events when the feeling of fear of criticism was present. It is almost as if the child, the symbolic representation of repressed feelings, once relieved of the need to defend itself is released by her ability to bring consciousness to what has previously been hidden, the structure of the core belief. This is further facilitated by my acknowledgement of what she is feeling. I say very simply, 'It feels like you have to defend yourself all the time', and from this mirroring she becomes more fully conscious of the pain that the defence protects her from. (To what extent this is an actual historical truth, that the father was truly critical, or that her own anger was projected onto the father and then felt as a reflected persecutory attack or, most likely, a mixture of the two, still remains to be seen.)

Integration and completion

The essence of this is to return to the present and see whether as an adult the client has more options than when she was a child. Here Jane took from the connecting of the split parts of her body/experience a tentative knowledge of what it might feel like to be more whole. With this new position she could imagine a place from which to interact that would not be dominated by her need to defend against the perceived attack. From this position, whether it was the actual aggression of the father or her own reflected aggression became academic, the felt reality was the important realisation that it was possible to function in relationship without always picking up on the criticism issue. She found the beginning of listening to her own voice rather than that of the critical other, whether her own persecutory subpersonalities or someone external to her.

Hakomi continues to value character types understood within the five principles and worked through as in the stages of process above. However, Kurtz's thinking has continued to evolve and more recently he has come to place an increasing importance on the presence of the therapist. Hakomi has been criticised as a therapeutic method that may not be used repeatedly during an extended period of therapy because its methods are often almost overwhelmingly powerful. (*Riding the rapids* is the image Kurtz uses for the cathartic release that taking over the defences and accessing the core beliefs can frequently evoke.) Here it must be remembered that in an overall process Kurtz would use the Hakomi process for only a few sessions concurrently, evoking such powerful responses that between times much integration was necessary. Also Kurtz has described himself characterlogically as one who avoids intimacy and so it is of no surprise that the intentional therapeutic use of transference and counter-transference in Hakomi has not been central. In its place we find an emphasis of the therapist's relationship to their own unconscious, their embodiment of the five principles and the strength of their own mindfulness. The understanding is that this is unconsciously recognised by the client and thereby assists and supports their growing mindfulness of their own material (Kurtz 1988, 1994). The difference between this way of working and a therapy that places great weight on the interpretation of the transference is that in the former the therapist becomes central, whilst here the centre is the client's own mindfulness. Use of the techniques and method of Hakomi may be integrated into other psychotherapeutic models (for instance a broad transpersonal model) but because of its strong intrapsychic emphasis it is obviously more difficult to use in therapies that emphasise the interpersonal relations of therapist and client.

Transpersonal psychotherapy

Transpersonal psychotherapy is a broad church that, unlike Hakomi, does not have an established set of principles and therapeutic procedures. My own transpersonal psychotherapy training principally emphasised working with the unconscious through the Jungian vehicles of dreaming, imagination and remembering. However, in recent years transpersonal psychotherapy in the UK, at the Centre for Transpersonal Psychology, has become more influenced by its American colleagues, and particularly by the work of John Welwood (Wellings and Wilde McCormick 2000).

Focusing and unconditional presence

Welwood was a student of Eugene Gendlin, who developed the method of 'focusing' (Gendlin 1996). Welwood brings to his appreciation of focusing his experience of mindfulness meditation and extends the technique into what he calls 'unconditional presence' (Welwood 2000). Simply put, focusing asks the client to pay attention to places in their body where there is an excitation of energy that Gendlin calls a 'felt sense', that is, a mixture of a feeling and a physical sensation. The felt sense contains information beneath the level of consciousness that may be contacted by simply placing attention upon it and waiting for a word, phrase or image to emerge that exactly expresses the content of the felt sense. When this occurs a release may happen which Gendlin calls a 'felt shift'.

The advantage of this way of working is that it is *experience near*, which is to say that it connects us with the immediacy of the experience of ourselves, in the body and in the moment. Furthermore, by linking those parts of therapy where we *talk about* our experience with those parts where we simply remain *mindful within* our experience, focusing builds a bridge between *reflection* and *presence*. Welwood shares in the belief that the most profound experience of healing arises from inhabiting the awakened state of non-dual consciousness, and he recognises in focusing the ability to close the reflective gap consciously, a small but essential step towards the desired undivided state (Welwood 2000).

Welwood's extension of this method – *unconditional presence* – is principally about broadening its purpose with the principles of mindfulness. While in focusing the object is to gain access to unconscious material and facilitate its movement towards resolution, in unconditional presence the object is more simply (and much more onerously) to soften and relax around experience without any desire to change it. This is a state difficult to understand properly until it is experienced. Welwood is not suggesting that the felt shifts that Gendlin describes are without value, but rather that there are felt shifts that lead to a deeper experience of our personal selves and others, facilitated by unconditional presence, which gain access to a *trans*personal experience. The former he calls 'horizontal felt shifts' and the latter 'vertical felt shifts' (Welwood 2000). While the horizontal felt shift leads us deeper into the *understanding* of how we feel, the vertical felt shift accesses the *intimate immediacy* of experience. Here are two examples.

Horizontal felt shift   The first example is a horizontal felt shift that demonstrates 'content mutation', a movement from one feeling to another. Meg brought to her session her blanket fear that seemed to have nothing to do with the circumstances of her life as it presently was. When asked how she felt in her body right now she said she felt tense and contracted and then described feelings located in several places. Then as she continued to rest her attention upon these places in her body, the words 'shaky' and then 'unacknowledged' slowly emerged. Invited to stay with this, remaining in contact with both the body sense and the associated feelings of being unacknowledged, she began to talk about her fear of not being loved, of aloneness, of her experiences in life now and then in childhood. Continuing, I returned her attention back to her body and she found that by staying with the truth of her experience she had a new felt sense of her body warming up. With this came a small relaxation, a 'felt shift'. Meg's experience had moved, mutated, from being non-specifically fearful to becoming in contact with precise feelings of being unacknowledged, to relaxation. In essence, she was now giving herself what she felt she had not been given by others.

Vertical felt shift Ann also brought to her session concerns about acknowledgement. In her case, however, invitations to find a place of self acceptance were hindered by associating self acceptance with passivity and then, by extension, with the passivity of a mother whom she perceived as a victim. In Ann's attempt to avoid being a victim, like her mother, she had become equally enslaved to the defensive posture of armoured invulnerability. Her stance had become one who always fights in life but carries vulnerability within her shadow.

Using the focusing method I asked Ann to find if there was a place in her body where she felt this issue most strongly. Once she had identified this place we stayed with it, simply resting Ann's attention on it until a word, phrase or image spontaneously emerged from the felt sense itself. Ann found that the felt sense contained both the armouring she carried and also the hidden vulnerability and as we waited, acknowledging the coexistence of both feelings and opening fully to them just as they were, Ann felt what she described as a 'space opening inside and around her'. When we spoke of this later, it sounded to me as though she had experienced a moment where she simply stepped out of the parameters of the problem and found a place to *be with it while not identified with it*. If this was so then she had experienced a vertical felt shift that was not about content mutation but rather about a more spacious, less emotionally identified way of being with her experience; it was not concerned with either changing or understanding it. Welwood describes these transpersonal experiences in therapy as occurring in 'micro moments' and as a most powerful transformative force, creating wisdom as well as knowledge. At the next session Ann asked why no one had taught her this before, since it had had a profound and lasting effect upon her.

Of course these small vignettes exist within a much broader context within the therapeutic relationship, including the telling and listening to of stories, work with dreams, imaging and so on. While the Hakomi method of using mindfulness is similar to the focusing method, the difference is that focusing is gentler and may be used repeatedly each session. Gendlin noticed that the people who really used their therapy well used the method quite naturally, and it was by observing them that the technique was developed. We so often ask our clients how they feel; when focusing is used the answer comes not from some preestablished and concretised notion of who we have become but from the freshness of the moment, right now. Acknowledging this and opening to it fully, neither identifying with nor rejecting experience, integrates the spiritual practice of mindfulness into psychotherapy.

Moore/Shonauer work

Unfortunately this type of work cannot be learnt from the written page. It must grow from one's work on oneself using Moore's and Shonauer's meditations and exercises. Furthermore, I am aware that it is difficult to properly understand energy work if one has not experienced it first hand (yet who would have thought that placing needles in invisible energy streams known as acupuncture points would have achieved such wide acceptance?). Also there is a danger that something not commonly known will seem esoteric when in fact (at least from the inside), it is not. Having said this here is a small indication of working in this way.

Working with the subtle body

Let us return to the work with Meg, this time at an earlier stage of our work together. Sitting in the room with her, my attention is drawn to the awareness that she is disengaged from her body and feelings (this is not to say that she does not have emotions that consume her at times). Initially, informed by my Hakomi theory, I can see that her head is drawn up and that she seems to have a division between the upper and lower halves of her body. Previously, at our first meeting, we had established a contract which includes her permission to work on the table, with her body. This is important – it is inappropriate to move to body work in the middle of psychotherapy unless the contract is renegotiated.

On this occasion, once Meg is on the table, I can gain an overall impression of her physical/energetic presence, including her subtle body which penetrates and extends beyond her physical body. Within the subtle body is contained the *etheric* in which are held many of the restrictions that have grown from defences against unwanted traumatic experiences. To attune more deeply I allow a *diffuse consciousness*, which takes in what is going on in both myself and Meg – perhaps a sense of where the energy is blocked and where it wants to go. This is actually surprisingly easy to do if we remember that we all have an innate ability to sense an emotional atmosphere when it is present. Here this ability is recognised and honed. There is an objective quality to this and some practitioners can also 'see' the energy structures reflected around the client. For myself it is more a feeling or a knowledge of what is happening, frequently felt within my own body.

In the Moore/Schonauer work this is known as *blending*. Jungian psychology seemingly begins to approach this with Jung's borrowing of the Levy-Bruhl term 'participation mystique' to indicate a state of interconnectedness. Also there is Michael Fordham's notion of a *syntonic counter-transference*, meaning the therapist's ability to be in tune with the client's inner world through his own feelings and behavioural responses. However, having frequently experienced syntonic counter-transference, I believe that the form of blending that I am describing not only perceives and responds to areas of traumatic complex in the client but in addition adds the energetic dimension of the therapist's contact with her own 'qualities'.

With Meg now on the table I begin with the suggestion that, whatever emerges from the work, Meg remains consciously present with it. We continue with the rhythm of the breath, just as it is, not changing it in any way. Informed by my attunement I place my hands where I feel drawn, either on her body surface, where the inner and outer etheric meet, or above her body, within the outer etheric, making contact with points on the 'energy streams'. Meg's attention is naturally drawn to herself at these points and she then may experience a variety of things: she may find that there is no sensation whatsoever, or that her breathing stops, or that the point releases a stream of emotions, thoughts and memories. She may also experience a feeling of expansion and opening throughout her body. Whatever the result, the aim is to remain consciously in contact, allowing the experience fully while continuing to move through it. On this occasion, based upon my sensing of her energy, part of the work is bringing Meg's consciousness to points in her lower abdomen, pubic bone and hara. Here again it is important to emphasise that, while there is an intervention on my part, there is no intention to manipulate or move the energy. Merely by remaining with it unintentionally, with unconditional presence, *it moves itself*.

This type of treatment can be quite unsettling – particularly if a person has never before been touched in this way – and therefore it is important to make sure the client is properly anchored in a solid sense of self by the end of the session. One way of achieving this, once that part of the work on the body/energy is complete, is to ask the client what emerged for them. At this point the reflective dialogue, usual to therapy, begins. What Meg takes away is a sense of expansion that is not dependent on her emotions and which, as I have suggested above, may become a foundation for working from the place of her own, presently unconscious, qualities.

Working in this way has implications for the therapeutic relationship. To work collaboratively the relationship must not merely become one where the client becomes the baby who has things done to him/her by an all-powerful mother. The unconscious acting out of this type of prereflective regression is purposefully not invited by the style of the work that values an overall emphasis upon the client being mindfully responsible for work on their own material and, of course, by the therapist being aware of their own countertransferential responses. Of course in practice such regressive feelings in the client may and do occur and then it will be necessary to be present mindfully with them, using the methods described above. However, when a therapist's primary therapeutic tool is mindfulness and not the intentional use of the therapeutic relationship, issues of regression seem to take a less central place. Exceptions to this occur when the client is unable or perhaps unwilling to take responsibility for their own psychological work and uses the therapeutic vessel to unconsciously act out material. In such cases the collaborative methods I have described become almost impossible and it will be necessary to work primarily with the interpersonal aspects of the therapeutic relationship itself.

Conclusion

In conclusion, I have said that we all carry traumatic material in our bodies and that for a full reconnection to these hidden but troublesome aspects of ourselves, it is necessary to make contact at physical, emotional, mental and energy levels. Furthermore, if it is true that all suffering may be ended within the state of non-dual consciousness – the state of the fully-awakened mind – then any movement towards the realisation of this state must be of interest to psychotherapy. To this end I have identified the practice of mindfulness as an essential tool. It takes us from an unconscious identification with the contents of consciousness and leads us, via reflection, to an ability to be with ourselves, without the conflict of wanting to be other. Thus, even when used superficially in therapeutic practice it begins to close the gap that keeps us from this state. In simple terms it grounds us in our experience, body and feeling, while at the same time giving a profound understanding of our true nature. Jack Engler, a transpersonal psychotherapist, has a saying, 'You have to be a somebody before you can be a nobody' (Engler 1984: 51). Usually this is taken to mean that we must first have a strong pliable ego which is secure enough to surrender its boundaries at will before we can profitably engage in the expansion and final dissolution of spiritual practice. Spiritual practice is not a means to avoid the experience of ourselves in the world but, quite the opposite, the intimate engagement I mentioned above. To this I would add that, in addition to a 'some body', we also need an 'alive body' – one connected to consciousness, as the foundation of all spiritual work.

Notes

1 Here actually is the confluence of two mythic themes. The predominantly Eastern traditions of mindfulness necessarily value inhabiting the present moment while those traditions that have found a greater voice in the West speak more of a journey from one state to a greater other. Can they come together? The Zen adage speaks of a 'gateless gate' that, once entered, shows that there was never anywhere to go; perhaps here is our answer.
2 The full list of types is as follows: Schizoid or Sensitive/Analytic, Oral or Dependent/Endearing, Compensated Oral or Self Reliant, Psychopath 1 or Tough/Generous, Psychopath 2 or Charming/Seductive, Masochist or Burdened/Enduring, Phallic or Industrious/Over focused and Hysteric or Expressive/Clinging.

References

Engler, J. 'Therapeutic Aims in Psychotherapy and Meditation: Developmental Stages in the Representation of the Self'. *Journal of Transpersonal Psychology* 1984; 16(1): 25

Epstein, M. *Thoughts Without A Thinker*. New York: Basic Books 1995

Gendlin, E. *Focusing Orientated Psychotherapy*. New York & London: The Guilford Press 1996

Johnson, S. M. *Character Styles*. New York & London: W.W. Norton 1994

Kurtz, R. *The Hakomi Handbook*. Boulder, CO: Hakomi Institute 1970

Kurtz, R. *The Hakomi Journal*. Boulder, CO: Hakomi Institute 1988

Kurtz, R. 'Psychotherapy as Spiritual Practice'. 1994 Online: http://www. hakomi.com/spiritpractice.html

Rosenberg, L. *Breath by Breath*. Boston & London: Shambhala 1998

Totton, N. Leaflet advertising a course on 'Body and Soul' 2000

Wellings, N. and Wilde McCormick, E. (Eds) *Transpersonal Psychotherapy, Theory and Practice*. London & New York: Continuum 2000

Welwood, J. *Towards a Psychology of Awakening*. Boston & London: Shambhala 2000: Chs 5, 8 and 9

Wilber, K. 'Psychologia Perennis: The Spectrum of Consciousness'. *The Journal of Transpersonal Psychology* 1975; 7(2)

Wilber, K. (1998) *The Essential Ken Wilber*. Boston & London: Shambhala 1998

Chapter 8

Subtle bodywork

Rose Cameron

This chapter is about working with the 'subtle' or 'energy' body in psycho-therapy. The concept of the subtle body has generally been the concern of mystical rather than psychological thought, and has been hidden in the secrecy of mystical teachings. It is therefore not well understood in psycho-logical terms. It is, however, a most useful concept in psychotherapeutic work, as this chapter will demonstrate.

My focus will be on bringing energetic process – how we move and change our subtle body – into awareness. Subtle bodywork is not about feeling better quickly, though often it does have that result. It is about developing psycho-logical flexibility in order to respond more appropriately to the moment. Our subtle body changes shape as our feelings change. We become stuck in a particular emotional state when we lock our energy body into a particular shape. If we lose energetic flexibility (the ability to move our subtle body) we lose the ability to move on emotionally.

Two things make us energetically inflexible: repressed emotion and lack of awareness. Many people are simply unaware that they have a subtle body and that they can move it if they choose. Others have an awareness of their energetic process, but have difficulty integrating this awareness because they have no concepts with which to understand it. Subtle bodywork consists of helping our client become aware of a habitual way of locking their energy with a view to having more choice in whether they continue to hold that response. This may take a matter of minutes or may take years of work on past issues and on the relationship between therapist and client before the client feels able to change a habitual way of being.

I will begin by tracing the concept of the energy body in European thought to show how it has been understood as the embodiment of the psyche. (I use the word 'psyche' to encompass both the original Greek meaning of soul and our more contemporary meaning of psychological and emotional processes.) Next I will explore some of the implications of understanding the subtle body as the embodiment of the psyche and describe ways in which we change our subtle body in response to what is happening in and around us.

Understanding the concept of the subtle body involves resolving apparent contradictions. The subtle body is a semi-material thing, and 'not-thing'. It exists, and does not exist, in the region between the material and immaterial. Thinking about the subtle body may be difficult, but recognising it phenomenologically is not, as I show in the final section. When I first recognised the usefulness of subtle bodywork, I wondered what I should call the subtle body when working with clients. My clients not only understood what I was talking about when I described it in terms of self, but have often been able to change their energy body, and therefore their state of mind, very easily. The fact that they all immediately understood what I meant if I spoke of the subtle body in terms of self seems to confirm the understanding of mystics all over the world of the subtle body as the embodiment of our consciousness. We identify with it as self.

Philosophical background

Ancient philosophy

The concept of an all-pervasive vital energy that flows through us and enlivens us is fundamental to the traditional understanding of who and how we are in pretty much any part of the world. For some millennia, India and China have had particularly sophisticated maps of how vital energy, called 'prana' and 'qi' respectively, flows within the human body. In Europe, where body and spirit have long been considered separately, the concept of a 'substance' that is between the two has been marginalised, largely contained within esoteric thought.

Recently, however, various subtle energy disciplines from transcendental meditation in the 1960s to feng shui in the 1990s have enjoyed periods of being fashionable in the West and vast numbers of people have been introduced to the concept of vital energy through yoga, martial arts, t'ai chi and reiki. It seems as if the notion of subtle energy is seeping back into our worldview, despite the fact that it is not wholly sanctioned by the scientific institutions that mould so much of our view of reality. Such a notion has recently regained more widespread acceptance as the efficacy of energetic therapies such as acupuncture has become undeniable. A number of writers such as Capra (1976, 1992), and Zukav (1979, 1998) have drawn parallels between Eastern worldviews and recent developments in quantum physics.

In fact Europe has never been entirely without the idea that we are vitalised by a subtle energy. The idea has been a tenacious thread throughout European thought, and has been developed to a degree of some complexity as the number of different names and terms that follow demonstrate. Capra (1976, 1992), in his exploration of the origins of physics, reminds us that the word 'physics' comes from the Greek 'physis' which he translates as 'the essential nature of things' (1992: 24), but would translate equally well as 'being', and implies no separation between the physical and the spiritual.

'Physis' is used today by transactional analysts to describe the growthful energy inherent in our clients. The Milesian school of the first period of Greek philosophy (sixth century BC) understood *everything* to be infused with physis, and made no distinction between the animate and inanimate, the material and immaterial, or the physical and the spiritual. These early philosophers were known by later Greeks as hylozoists, or those who think everything is alive. They had no word for matter, since for them it was no different from the immaterial – everything was a manifestation of physis. Physis was supported by 'pneuma' which Capra translates as 'cosmic breath', in the same way as the body is supported by breath, and health, both physical and psychological, depended on the different proportions of pneuma.

This view of the whole universe as alive is shared by even more ancient cultures such as those of the First Peoples of Australia and the Americas. Capra also draws a parallel between the Milesian worldview and that of ancient India and China. He finds an even stronger parallel with Heraclitus of Ephesus' concept of the Logos, the unity transcending all apparent opposites.

The split between the material and immaterial, the dualism of the physical and spiritual began, Capra tells us, with the Eleatic school, which,

> . . . assumed a Divine Principal standing above all gods and men. This principal was first identified with the unity of the universe, but was later seen as an intelligent and personal God who stands above the world and directs it. Thus began a trend of thought which led, ultimately, to the separation of spirit and matter and to a dualism which became characteristic of western philosophy.
>
> Capra 1992: 25

Alchemy

The Greek concept of pneuma provided the theoretical basis for alchemy. Alchemy occupied some of Europe's most inquiring, creative minds, even that of Newton, commonly regarded as the father of scientific materialism. Westfall, Newton's biographer, tells us that alchemy offered him the 'quintessential embodiment of all that mechanical philosophy rejected. It looked upon nature as life instead of a machine, explained phenomena by the activating agency of spirit' (Westfall 1980: 112, 116–117). Europe did not quite abandon the idea of matter being infused with vital energy until the end of the seventeenth century.

Whilst European philosophy and medicine 'progressed' towards the Rationalism of the eighteenth century, alchemy kept alive the notion of a unity between the physical and the spiritual. The practice itself embraced the material and the spiritual. Some alchemists really were trying to turn lead into gold. Others read the instruction manuals as metaphors for spiritual practice, and understood that change happens in the space between the material and non-material. Pneuma, or the subtle body as they also called it, was between matter and spirit, consisting of both, binding the organic, the human and the spiritual together, permeating all things.

It was in alchemy that the European anatomy of energy really developed. Whilst the Chinese meridian system and the Indian chakra system focus on subtle energy within the body, the European model focuses on the vital energy surrounding the body. (This is something of a false distinction as the very point of all three belief systems is that the vital energy, the 'what is', is both within and without.)

By the time Paracelsus (1493–1541) became a physician the word 'physician' had lost the physical and spiritual unity of physis and become physical. However, Paracelsus was also an alchemist. He used the word 'iliaster' for both vital force and vital matter. As he understood there to be no fundamental difference between force and matter, or between different kinds of matter, he could posit a sympathetic resonance between the earthly and the cosmic, between the human body and heavenly. Our relationship with the heavens was mediated by 'archeus', subtle emanations of iliaster. And like the heavenly bodies, both stars and angels, we are surrounded by an aura of light. Paracelsus called this 'mumia', the iliaster embodied in the flesh and radiating out around us in a luminous sphere.

Since everything was essentially iliaster, everything animate or inanimate had mumia, and therefore had an individual identity or spirit. In animate things, the physical and spiritual aspects were unified by the soul. Paracelsus considered the soul *semi*-material, and having three aspects: one that is concerned with the material, another that is uniquely human and immortal, and one through which we interact with all that is around us. The material aspect of this part of the soul he called the 'sidereal' or 'astral' body, and the spiritual aspect he called the 'astral soul'. He saw the sidereal body as the ethereal counterpart of the physical body, illuminated by the spirit.

Paracelsus may well have developed such a sophisticated model under the influence of the Sufis, who had a strong influence on alchemy. It is certainly strikingly similar to the Indian concept that we are enveloped in 'koshas' or sheaths of energy, each vibrating at a different subtlety. The most dense relate to the physical body, the least dense is pure consciousness, and in between are subtle bodies that are composed of mind ('mano-maya-kosha') and awareness ('vijnana-maya-kosha'). The Chinese also have a little-known concept of energy that surrounds the body: the first two layers closest to the body are concerned with protection, and the third with consciousness. Don Juan, Carlos Castenada's Mexican sorcerer, explains Castenada's (non-chemically) altered states of consciousness as activities of his subtle body (Castenada 1994). Castenada is travelling in worlds of pure, unsymbolised energy, but otherwise it is very easy to see similarity between this idea and the European concept of astral projection.

Alchemical notions of a semi-material part of the soul, a subtle body, faded from our consciousness along with the rest of alchemical theory at the end of the seventeenth century. The idea perhaps survived in Europe's mystical schools, the Rosicrucians relying heavily on the existing European model. The Theosophists, Madam Blavatsky, Alice Bailey and Rudolph Steiner borrowed the idea from India more directly. The subtle body idea also appears in the mystical traditions of the established religions. The Kabbalah calls it 'astral light' or 'Yesod', the Christian tradition calls it the 'sidereal' or 'astral' body and Tibetan Bhuddism calls it 'bardo', and in Sanskrit it is called 'prabha-mandala' (radiant circle).

Psychotherapy

The idea of vital energy and of the subtle body survived mainly in the obscurity of the mystical schools until Jung and Reich brought the spirit and the body to analysis. Jung uncovered alchemy's subtext of psychological and spiritual transformation, showing how alchemical drawings and symbols portray archetypal psychological processes. Several (contemporary) Jungians have developed the relationship between alchemical and psychological processes. One of these, Nathan Schwartz-Salant (1998), makes the bold suggestion that Jung's 'somatic unconscious' – the unconscious as experienced by the body – is the alchemists' 'subtle body' (also called 'Mercurius' because it related to the planet Mercury). He describes the process of moving from mild dissociation, or being out of one's body, to feeling properly embodied, and continues,

> ... then one begins to feel one inhabits one's body. The condition of being embodied is an experience of a medium that exists between one's material body and mind. The alchemists called this medium *Mercurius*; others have referred to it as the *astral body*, the *subtle body*, and the *Kabalistic Yesod* (Jung 1963: 14: paragraph 635); and Jung termed it the somatic unconscious (1988: 1: 441). Alchemists and magicians from ancient times to the Renaissance believed that this medium was a substance felt within the human body but also flowing throughout space ... [italics mine]
>
> Schwartz-Salant 1998: 73

For Schwartz-Salant the very idea that one can or can not be embodied implies that we have an immaterial aspect that is not identical to our physical body. The condition of being in one's body is therefore 'an experience of a medium that exists between one's material body and mind'. Jung's concept of the somatic-unconscious and the psychic unconscious (Schwartz-Salant 1982) is very reminiscent of the alchemists' *astral body* and *astral soul*, except that the alchemists called the whole which unifies the two polarities the *soul*, and Jung calls it the *unconscious*. Later, however, in elaborating on the arche-type of the *unus mundus*, Jung proposes a transcendent level of psychic reality in which the somatic and psychic unconscious are identical, as are matter and psyche.

Schwartz-Salant also suggests contemporary field theory (Spiegelman and Mansfield 1996) as a modern representation of the alchemical idea of the subtle body. For Schwartz-Salant, the interactive field – the space in which two people influence change in one another – necessarily contains the object-ive contents of the collective unconscious, and is therefore more than the shared subjective experience of two people. He writes,

> The merger of the inner reality of the alchemist and the outer reality of the matter to be transformed exists in an area of imaginal discourse, which ancient alchemists referred to as the 'imaginatio', that was not subject to the notion of insides and outsides. The merger of inner and outer occurs in a space that alchemists called the 'subtle body', a strange area that is neither material nor spiritual, but mediating between them. Along with other imponderables of ancient science that held sway for many centuries, this 'intermediary' domain of existence has long since left our conscious awareness.
>
> Schwartz-Salant 1998: 11

The subtle body, with its lack of inner and outer, gives us a way of making sense of *how* transferential phenomena, such as projective identification, actually happen. Sadly that is outside the scope of this chapter. What con-cerns us here is where, and whether, our subtle energy is felt within our body.

Reich was, of course, exclusively concerned with energy in the body and bodily experience. He considered an examination of feeling without bodily sensation to be mysticism, which he deplored. Reich is vociferous on the subject of mysticism, dismissing that way of experiencing life as a projection of bodily sensation resulting from body armouring. However, we misunder-stand Reich if we do not appreciate the difference he makes between mysti-cism and animism. He is in sympathy with animism, the belief that everything is alive, although he also sees this as a projection of bodily sensation.

> The process of animating the surrounding world is the same as with the animistic primitive as it is with the mystic. Both animate nature by pro-jecting their body sensations. *The difference between animism and mysti-cism is that the former projects natural, undistorted organ functions, while the latter projects unnatural, perverted ones.*
>
> Reich [1951] 1973: 289

Although he does not (quite) see himself as an animist, Reich's definition of *orgone* as life energy both biological and cosmic, is unavoidably reminiscent of the Greek's physis, the alchemists' pneuma, and Paracelsus' iliaster. It is perhaps symptomatic of how split Western thinking had become by the nineteenth century that the spirit and body were brought to analysis by two different people, Jung and Reich, one of whom is commonly (and, according to Schwartz-Salant, unfairly) regarded as anti-body, and one who considered himself to be anti-spirit.

Contemporary bodywork

Many therapists strongly influenced by Reich would consider themselves to be anything but anti-spirit. John Pierrakos (1986, 1989), Barbara Brennan (1987, 1988, 1993) and Julie Henderson (1997, 1999) are three who have synchronised mystical experience of the kind so abhorred by Reich with his theory of character types, body armouring and energetic release. They all understand themselves to be working with the subtle body as well as the physical body, but their understanding of the subtle body comes from the esoteric rather than psychoanalytic thinking. Many psychotherapists are embarrassed by any association with esoteric or 'New Age' ideas like auras and chakras. I hope I have shown that these ideas are neither new nor the sole prerogative of some other culture, inappropriately tagged onto our own. Unlike Brennan and Pierrakos, Julie Henderson does not theorise in terms of Reichian character types but in terms of energetic 'habits' or processes, and it is this work that has had the greatest influence on the theory and practice that follow.

Summary of philosophical background

Whether the concept of the subtle body spread out from the East along routes of trade and commerce, was spontaneously received through grace, or surreptitiously planted by the Sufis, is probably impossible to know. We do know that it is a continuous thread running through the esoteric schools of Europe as well as the esoteric traditions of other cultures. We certainly have visual representations from all over the world and throughout history that depict something radiating out from the body. The more distant spiritual activity becomes from the living of everyday life, the more likely that images of light radiating from the body are reserved for people recognised to be in a state of grace. Christ and the saints have halos, Buddhas and Bhodisatvas are surrounded by vaporous rings of light, as are Hindu and Sikh deities. Aboriginal artists, on the other hand, not making a fundamental distinction between the material and the spiritual, the animate and inanimate, portray everything pulsating with energy.

   The world's mystics, from the alchemists to the yogis, seem to agree that our vital energy radiates out from our flesh into the world around us, and that certain rings or layers of this radiation are concerned with our state of consciousness. They are also agreed that this radiation is semi-material, existing in the domain between the material and the non-material. This is certainly not a concept likely to appeal to the rational materialism of science, though ironically Paracelsus was one of the first physicians to campaign for close observation and experimentation, and his theories arose out of this scientific approach. Although his call to the study of nature did not go down at all well with the orthodox physicians of the time, it did help to revive medical experimentation and observation at the expense of the God-given certainties and dogma of medieval medicine.

There have been consistent attempts to observe iliaster and mumia scientifically ever since, though the names have changed to magnetic fluid and electromagnetic field. Accounts of scientific attempts to measure a force field around living beings are well summarised by both Brennan (1987, 1988, 1993) and Pierrakos (1990). Concepts like *archeus*, Paracelsus' subtle emanations that define our relationship to the earth and the heavens, have been replaced by theories of magnetism. None of these experiments have found conclusive proof of mumia or auras, although convincing evidence has emerged of a force field surrounding the body.

Theory

The subtle body

The assumption that we are surrounded by a glow of subtle energy is a basic premise of subtle bodywork. Religious and mystical art across the world portrays energy surrounding the body in a radiant sphere. Kirlian photography (a technique in which photographic images are produced using an electric field, typically showing patterns of light radiating from the subject) suggests that we are surrounded by a glow of energy. Western medicine actually has no dispute with Kirlian photography as it is commonly acknowledged that we are surrounded by an electromagnetic field. My view is that Kirlian photography produces images of only the first layer of a much bigger energy field. The most detailed models of the human energy system (that are accessible), i.e. the Indian, Chinese and European, all posit a multi-layered, semi-material form around the physical body. The Chinese model of qi surrounding the body (rather than flowing within) is not well known, but the Indian and European are. Both propose a layer of the energy field which relates to our physical wellbeing, surrounded by layers that embody our consciousness. The layer that relates to the physical body, and follows its outline, is generally understood to be more material, more dense, than the progressively insubstantial layers that make up the rest of the field. Kirlian photography, I think, produces images of this first, most material, layer. The other layers (the embodiment of our consciousness) can, so far, be detected only by the far subtler instruments of our own perception.

The astral body

These other layers, the embodiment of our consciousness, are the concern of this chapter. We are particularly concerned with the layers of the subtle body that are between the densest, most physical and the most insubstantial and transcendental. The best known of these middle layers is the 'astral' or 'emotional' body. Our tradition of mystical thought holds that the emotional body can move away from the physical body, but is anchored by a cord of energy. It seems that this part of our energy field is infinitely expandable, and can enable us to visit other places without the inconvenience of physical movement. European mystics call this 'astral projection', and have possibly kept this sort of information occult, or hidden, so that it cannot be misused. The military call it 'remote viewing', and have done much research into using it for the purposes of surreptitiously acquiring information from, or about, other physical locations.

The military have found that it is relatively easy to train people to do this. Cynics have suggested that military remote viewing projects are a fiction invented to camouflage cruder espionage techniques. I have no difficulty in accepting the idea of astral projection as real, and am certain that if the military know about it, which they clearly do, then they will have had little hesitation in exploiting it. Remote viewing or astral projection is the ultimate development of something that for many people is an everyday human process. Many of us 'go somewhere else' when we are bored or daydreaming. This 'somewhere else' is usually just another space within our own mind or imagination. Remote viewers actually go somewhere else in the material world, and can draw detailed maps of where they have been. They literally project the parts of their energy body that are concerned with consciousness to a different location in space. When we daydream or are dissociated in some other way, we also loosen the attachment between our physical and emotional bodies, though to a much lesser degree. When we 'get back into our body', or 'get grounded', we return our emotional body to its usual position in relation to our physical body. Body and mind are reunited and we may be aware of a sensation of coming back into our body.

We can recognise a state of being disembodied in various degrees of dissociation, from the slight absence of mild boredom to the complete absence of somebody in a psychotic episode. Psychotherapy, unlike the spiritual disciplines, has tended to pathologise and pay scant heed to the positive aspect of altered states of consciousness. Some forms of meditation practice consist of learning to withdraw from the world as a means of spiritual development. Both dissociation and transcendental states are achieved through alteration of the energy body. At a more mundane level, the ability to disembody allows us to free ourselves from material reality – we can daydream, be inspired and creative. Freed from the constraints of what is, we can create the new. Or we can disembody in order to avoid the new by not being fully present. Like any other means we use to defend ourselves psychologically, altering the structure or shape of our subtle body, and therefore altering our state of consciousness, can certainly be useful when we really are under threat. However, like any other defence mechanism, it may become habitual and inappropriate, a problem rather than a solution. Altering the shape of our energy body is neither a good nor a bad thing in itself. Whether such a change is appropriate to our current situation will determine whether we find our altered state of consciousness useful or not.

Energetic process

In fact we alter the shape of our energy body on a pretty much continuous basis. As practitioners of yoga, qi kung, martial arts and meditation have known for centuries, our energy body as well as our physical body is nurtured by our breath. As we breathe in, we breathe in life force. As we breathe out, we rest. This produces a state of energised calm. However, our breath does not remain rhythmic as we respond to what is happening within and around us, and neither does the pulsation of our subtle body. We pull our energy body in, away from what has shocked us as we gasp in surprise. We allow it to expand out again as we breathe a sigh of relief.

Unfortunately, we do not always breathe a sigh of relief when we need to. Sometimes an unpleasant situation is ongoing, and we do not breathe out energetically. The stimulus situation may be very short-lived, and we still neglect to breathe out energetically. The contraction in our energy field is not released, and we continue to feel tense. We may hold that contraction for half a day or we may lock our energy field in a contracted state for life. If we lock our energy body into a particular shape, our emotional energy, our feelings, cannot flow and change. We trap them and become emotionally stuck. When we allow ourselves to experience an emotion – say anger – our field alters briefly. Depending on our energetic preference we may withdraw our energy body from contact by *contracting*, or else *blaze* our energy outwards by making it dense and then contracting until we can hold it no more. If we *hold* our energy field in this altered state, we continue to feel with intensity. If we *lock* our field into this state we will be in a bad mood until we finally allow it to relax. If we never unlock it, both our energy body and our physical body become permanently distorted, and grumpiness becomes part of who we are. In other words, energetic flexibility determines whether we can move on emotionally.

There is probably an infinite number of ways in which we may alter our energy field in response to the outside world. Below are some I have noticed in myself and those I work with. The names are partly Julie Henderson's and partly my own.

We may *expand* our energy field; we may allow our energy field to become *diffuse*; we may *contract* by pulling our energy field in towards our physical body; we may *become ungrounded*, allowing our energy to drift upwards; we may *disembody* by allowing our emotional or astral body to drift away from the physical altogether; we may allow our energy to become more concentrated in the lower part of our energy body, thus becoming *heavy*. We may *clench* energetically by contracting whilst simultaneously blocking our connection to what is above and below us. This usually means that we tighten particularly hard at either ends of our torso. We may do different things with different layers of our field; contracting whilst simultaneously expanding another layer into antennae seems to be a common pattern. Holding our energy in these, or other ways, for a period of time may well be very appropriate.

Expanding increases our contact with the external world. Expanding usually allows us to relax physically, and can be a very pleasant state. We expand when we want contact, and expand extensively when we feel happy, magnanimous, compassionate, in love. If we expand beyond our limit, however, our energy field will become increasingly *diffuse*. Those seeking enlightenment may well allow the further reaches of their energy field to become so diffuse that the boundary of their individuality disappears. Others may be seeking a more mundane kind of enlightenment, diffusing their energy field in order to become more sensitive to what is going on around them.

Contracting reduces the contact we have with the external world. Energetically speaking, there is no essential difference between ourselves and the external world, just changes in the density or vibration of universal energy. As we breathe in, we pull our energy body in towards the physical body, and the energy it contains becomes denser. We experience ourselves as more separate. Our boundaries become clearer. We may feel more powerful. Becoming ungrounded also reduces our contact with the external world. Allowing our energy to drift upwards allows us to be inspired and inspiring.

Disembodying can give us some psychological protection in a situation that we are physically unable to leave. Many children who are abused learn to do this, and either watch what is happening from the detachment of the ceiling, or leave the scene in which their physical body is involved altogether. We would normally call this dissociation, and indeed that is what it is. Astral projection is the mechanism by which we dissociate. Other children astral project for fun. I am often amused by the number of people in workshops who suddenly remember that as children they truly believed they could fly. The ability to become *earthed* or *grounded* again is essential as this enables us to relate effectively with the material world, and is achieved by allowing our energy field to penetrate the earth.

Becoming *heavy* is very useful if we need to come back down to earth and be grounded. This happens when we extend our energy downwards. An extension is a strong movement that reconnects our energy field back into the physical ground. This is very different from allowing our energy to collapse downwards.

Clenching allows us to cut off from the outside world even further. Our contact with the external world is reduced by clenching energetically in two ways. First we contract and in doing so form a denser, and therefore less permeable, boundary around ourselves. Second, by tightening particularly strongly at each end of our torso, we block the flow of energy that usually flows through the top of our energy field, down the body, out through our feet, into the earth, back in through our feet and up the spine. Clenching can enable us to really focus on the job in hand or help us to become detached if we don't like what is going on around us.

Altering our energy in any of these ways can, however, be unpleasant or problematic in some way if we do so inappropriately. Being overly expanded leaves us with unclear boundaries, unsure of where we end and other people begin. There is nothing inherently wrong with a large energy field. It becomes over-expanded when it stops being dense enough to afford us adequate differentiation from the external world. We become merged with whatever is around us, unobtrusive, confluent. When we are merged with our environment, we become over-sensitive to it, experiencing everything as if it is happening to us – which, at an energetic level, it is.

Being overly contracted leaves us cut off from those around us. Becoming locked in contraction has the almost inevitable potential to destroy our ability to function in relationships. Other people experience the dense perimeter of our contracted energy field as an impenetrable barrier, and so do we. When we contract our energy field to the point of it hardening into a barrier, we are less able to absorb energy from the atmosphere around us. This may be a good thing in the short term if we are in a poisonous atmosphere, but it is usually preferable to change, or leave, the atmosphere. Otherwise we may neglect to expand out again, and carry the atmosphere with us as we move on to a new situation where we will be experienced as uptight, stiff, withdrawn. We will still suffer the discomfort that initially led to our contraction as well as the discomfort of our steadily worsening social situation.

Letting go of our energetic connection to the earth leaves us ungrounded, not knowing where we stand and unable to take a firm stand. Disembodiment is the extreme end of the spectrum of ungroundedness. Not only do other people experience us as out of contact, but also we become detached from what is going on inside us. Disembodying probably has the greatest potential to adversely affect our ability to function psychologically. Taken to an extreme, we may completely lock out the layers of subtle body that relate to consciousness, and become completely dissociated from consensus reality, no longer 'with' the rest of our community.

There are different kinds of heaviness. The *gravitas* that comes with being fully present, properly grounded and solidly anchored in the real world is very different from the heaviness of an energy field that is collapsing onto, rather than into, the ground. Energetic collapse renders our energy unavailable to both ourselves and others.

Clenching probably has the greatest effect on our physical wellbeing. When we contract, we reject energy from the atmosphere around us. If we also block at the neck and pelvis, we cut ourselves off from current of vital energy that flows from the cosmos, down through us and into the earth. We leave ourselves little access to vital energy, and this can be compared to clenching so tightly physically that we leave ourselves little access to oxygen. When we stop breathing in and out properly, we stop pulsating with the rhythm of the life force. This also affects us spiritually as we effectively slam the door on the Tao.

Roger Woolger (Chapter 9) suggests that the subtle body holds the memory of physical injury from past lives like a scar. It also holds the memory of unexpressed psychological injury and this gives each different energetic response its unique emotional flavour. There is a general flavour created by what we are doing energetically; for instance, we feel isolated because we are locked into a clench and so at an energetic level we are isolated. We like or dislike this in the moment depending on how appropriate we find it to be to our current situation. And we each season the moment in our own particular way. Our range of seasonings is from our past. Unexpressed emotion does not, as we know, just go away. We hold it in both the physical body and the subtle body. As we respond by clenching or disembodying in the present, we disturb feelings from the past. These past feelings remain in our subtle body from previous occasions in which we clenched or disembodied. We once again feel as we did when we were four. If we don't disturb our feelings from the past by reawakening them with the familiar taste of clenching or disembodying, they remain in the past and don't disturb us. But if we do disturb them, they are likely to disturb us. Psychotherapy disturbs our past feelings further by looking and stirring, until the cauldron boils. The transformative alchemical process begins as we let off steam about the past; the flavour of life changes and our ability to be fully in the present becomes distilled.

Working in the relationship

Subtle bodywork, unlike some other forms of subtle energy work, such as acupuncture, supplements rather than replaces relationship work. Although moving energetically can allow us to change from one state of mind to another very quickly indeed, we may be unable to make such a movement due to the strength of repressed feeling that keeps us locked in a particular energetic shape. Unless we work through repressed feelings, they will remain in our subtle body ready to distort our perception.

Our subtle body moves in response to what we perceive. Perception, being a function of consciousness, resides in the subtle body and inhabits the domain between the internal and external, the objective and subjective, between what we see and how we see it. We respond emotionally to what we perceive, and as we respond emotionally our energy body changes shape. If, for instance, we perceive somebody as hostile we are likely to contract energetically, and if we perceive them as loving, we are likely to expand towards them. As we change psychological shape by moving our subtle energy from one place to another, we reactivate repressed feelings. These feelings then begin to determine our perception. The balance between inner and outer, between reality and experience, is tipped in favour of the inner. We no longer respond to the world as it really is but as we perceive it, and our perception is necessarily unbalanced. We adopt inappropriate defences and our relationships with others deteriorate. Unexpressed feelings lock us up energetically, and expressed feelings unlock us. We may choose to lock ourselves into an energetic cupboard in order to examine our skeletons. It is important that subtle bodywork takes place within a respectful, trustworthy, and accepting relationship. Any form of non-acceptance, perhaps in the form of judgement or hurrying the client along, is more likely to lock up than release the energy body.

There are many, many ways of working directly with subtle energy: healing, acupuncture, Reichian bodywork, Polarity therapy, Shiatsu, etc. The practitioners of such subtle body therapies can often sense, feel or see the client's subtle energy. In subtle bodywork, all the information needed is potentially available to the client's conscious awareness, and the therapist need have no special ability in perceiving energy, though such an ability is useful. The therapist helps the client first to become aware of their own energetic process and then to move their own energy with awareness, intention and choice. The next section offers some ideas as to how this can be done.

Practice

The aim of subtle bodywork is to enable our client to become aware of their energetic process. This might mean helping them to recognise how they are locking their energy in, or out, in a given moment. It may entail helping them to identify their energetic reaction to particular situations or people. It may involve helping them recognise energetic locks into which they slide habitually.

Ethics

Subtle energy can be an astonishingly powerful force. It is therefore important to observe a few basic rules of energetic safety.

1   Never suggest to anyone that they bring energy up and out though the top of their head. In through the top of the head and down is fine.
2   Never try to move another person's energy for them, unless you are trained to do so.
3   Make sure the client is grounded before they leave the session.
4   Look after yourself, and ensure that you do not become stuck in an energetic response or resonance.
5   Respect the client's individual pace of change.

Energetic self awareness

As with any means of helping our client become more self aware, the first stage must be increasing our own self awareness. Many people already have a very finely-tuned awareness of their own energetic process, and are accustomed to noticing energy move in or around their body. Others find the sensations of tingling, flowing, and moving unfamiliar. However, we can all, to some degree, perceive subtle energy, both our own and the energy transmitted or withheld by others. We perceive our own through a kind of 'subtle proprioception'.

Proprioception is the ability to experience our body in space. Some people are robbed of this ability by brain injury, and have to work out what the new position of their body will be with each movement they make. They literally have to watch, and think about, each step. Proprioception is something the rest of us take for granted. *Subtle proprioception* is the term I use to refer to our ability to experience our subtle body in space. Subtle proprioception may be a new term, but it is probably the oldest sense we have, the sense of ourselves in space. The following exercise heightens our awareness of this.

Exercise one
Think of someone you feel (or would feel) unreservedly good being with. Imagine that person in another part of the room. Just focus on them for a few moments, and take notice of any sensations (as opposed to emotions) that you experience.

Sensations of expanding, opening out, radiating energy or warmth, flowing towards the person or melting indicate that the energy body has expanded. When I use this exercise in workshops, I end it by saying, 'and now draw yourselves back in'. I then check if the 'draw yourselves back in' instruction made sense to everyone. If it did, I know they have all expanded and then contracted their subtle body, and had an awareness of their subtle body moving through space just as someone walking is aware of their legs moving through space.

Subtle proprioception is something we take as much for granted as we do ordinary proprioception. We know where we are. We know if we are in our belly, or in our head, if we are all over the place, or grounded, on cloud nine, down in the dumps, on top of the world or in a little knot inside. When we use such figures of speech, we usually say something very literal about the shape of our energy field. When we say we are all over the place, our subtle body probably is fragmented and detached from our physical body. When we are grounded properly, our energy really does extend into the ground. Our energy field is no doubt greatly expanded when we are on cloud nine or on top of the world, and collapsed towards the ground when we are down in the dumps. We probably have contracted our energy right inside our physical body when we feel small. If we listen to ourselves, and believe what we say, we will know a great deal about our energetic process.

Otherwise, it can be very difficult to recognise that we are in an energetic lock. Deliberately, and temporarily, putting our self into different locks to check out which feel familiar can be a useful thing to do, as long as we have reason to be confident that we will be able to unlock when we want to. Once we know what feels familiar, we can begin to recognise how we have reacted energetically in the past, and how we may react in the future. I, for instance, know that I am inclined to disembody by energetically jumping out of my skin. If I find that I am feeling vague, ungrounded or unable to protect myself, I check to see if I have disembodied. I do this by assuming that I have, and pulling my energy back towards my body. Because I know my tendency is to go out through the top of my head, that will be the first place I would encourage my energy to return to. I might imagine that I am pulling myself back in through the top of my head, or that I am encouraging my energy field back over the top of my head. There is no right or wrong way to do it, just what is appropriate at the time. If I have an energetic awareness of suddenly arriving back in my body, or find I suddenly feel sure of myself again, I know I was indeed disembodied.

The following exercises are designed to identify some other habitual ways of holding energy.

Exercise two
Stand in a relaxed upright position with the crown of your head facing the ceiling, and your knees soft. Check that you feel connected to the earth and grounded. Breathe easily for a few moments.

Now, gather your energy around your body (this is not the same as contract-ing – it is much softer), and then let it all sink to below your waist. Does that feel familiar? Now, let it sink to below your hips. Familiar? Below your knees. Below your ankles. Now let it drain out of your feet. Make a mental note of what you recognised, or share it with someone else.

Give yourself a shake, shake your legs particularly, and then stand in a relaxed upright position again, with the crown of your head facing the ceiling. Gather your energy again, and this time allow it to extend out through the soles of your feet and into the earth beneath you. This should feel dynamic and strong. This is the difference between being grounded and collapsing.

Exercise three
Once you feel grounded and centred again, let your energy gather above your waist. Does this feel familiar? Allow it to float up above your chest. Above your collarbone, your jaw. Above your eyes, on the top of your head. Float off.

Again, give yourself a shake, and pat yourself down with gentle little pats, all running downwards. Straighten up slowly, and make sure you feel grounded and centred again.

This exercise demonstrates how easy it is to move energy by intention, as well as indicating where we may habitually hold energy. As we saw in the theory section, we can lock our energy on an in-and-out axis as well as an up-and-down axis. You may want to experiment with pulling your energy towards your body, then letting it expand out to check what is familiar there. Be aware that deliberately locking energy in a clench – contracting whilst also pulling up and down – should only be done with great caution. Clenching is not included in any of these exercises. It is a harmful state to be locked into, and can be difficult to get out of.

Exercise four
Stand in a relaxed upright position with the crown of your head facing the ceiling, and your knees soft. Check that you feel connected to the earth and grounded. Breathe easily for a few moments. Pull your energy field in towards your body a little to find out where it is. Make a mental note and think about whether that seems like an appropriate distance, or whether you may have been holding an inappropriate over-contraction or over-extension. Now pull your energy field a little way towards your body, and hold it there. This may well feel unpleasant. Does it also feel familiar? Pull your field in a bit further, then gradually further still, pausing and holding it to check if that feels familiar. Continue with this as far into your body as you want to go.
    Now give yourself a gentle shake and move around a bit. As you breathe out, allow your field to flow out and surround your body at a comfortable distance. Make sure that energy is still extending through your legs and into the ground.
    Now allow your field to flow out further as you breathe out. Keep pausing and checking if where you are is still familiar as you extend further and further. Finish extending when you feel you want to and pull your energy field back to a comfortable distance.

Our energy field can be heavy or light, dense or insubstantial. Too thinly extended a field leaves us vulnerable, and not very grounded within our own being.

Exercise five
Sit down somewhere that you won't be disturbed, and close your eyes. Focus your energy field and allow yourself to receive an impression of its quality. Is it sparkly, compacted, soft, hard, spongy, misty, dense, heavy, etc?

If our field is compacted, very dense, hard or heavy, we may want to loosen it up by allowing our edges to soften as we relax and breathe out. If our field seems too misty, thin or wispy, we can make it more dense using the following exercise, adapted from an Aikido exercise, firstly by Julie Henderson, and then by myself. It is very useful when we find ourselves overwhelmed by the presence or feelings of others. It is also useful if we have been unsuccessfully trying to protect themselves by over-contracting, over-extending, or dis-embodying in some other way. This exercise was designed by experts in ener-getic manipulation, and is very powerful. I would not suggest practising it unless there is a clear need. It can be tiring, and a few minutes' daily practice should be sufficient.

Exercise six
Choose somewhere quiet, where you won't be disturbed. Sit in the middle of the room if possible, and allow your energy field to fill the room if it extends that far. If it doesn't, or would naturally extend out further than the confines of the room, set yourself a different boundary.
    Now gather your field in towards your body. And a bit further. Check it is surrounding you in a spherical shape.
    Now relax out and let it fill the room again.
    Now gather it in again. And a little bit further. And a little bit further still. Fill the room again.
    Gather your energy into a sphere around you. Now bounce the perimeter of your field in and out for a bit before filling the room again.
    Now gather it in again. And a little bit further. Bounce it for a while. Big bounces, little bounces, experiment.
    End by returning to a size that feels comfortable to you.

Those who find that other people often think they are angry when they are not often have rather dense energy fields that blaze out energy when con-tracted. Exercise 7 is particularly informative if done in the presence of someone who can give feedback.

Exercise seven
Stand in a relaxed upright position with the crown of your head facing the ceiling, and your knees soft. Check that you feel connected to the earth and grounded. Breathe easily for a few moments.
    Now gather your energy into a dense sphere around you, and hold it there. Breathe more and more energy into the sphere and allow the excess to blaze off around the boundary of your sphere.
    Give yourself a shake, and imagine yourself under a waterfall for a few minutes.

People who habitually hold most of their energy in the upper part of their subtle body can seem overbearing, intimidating or overpowering. Again, the following exercise is enhanced by the presence of someone giving feedback.

Exercise eight
Stand in a relaxed upright position with the crown of your head facing the ceiling, and your knees soft. Check that you feel connected to the earth and grounded. Breathe easily for a few moments.

Let your energy gather above your waist, and move it up progressively until you find a place that feels familiar. Now gather your energy into a sphere from that point up. Check if this is a familiar feeling, and then release your hold, and let your energy fill the rest of your body again. Give yourself a gentle shake and move around a bit. As you breathe out, allow your field to flow out and surround your body at a comfortable distance. Make sure that energy is extending through your legs and into the ground.

It is important to become aware of your own energetic process, not only because being able to choose to become unlocked will improve the quality of your life, but also because self awareness enables us to work more effectively with clients.

Helping the client become aware of their energetic process

Using our energetic response

I am most usually made aware that someone I am working with is holding their energy because I notice a response – either emotional, energetic, or both – in myself. I may notice that I feel slightly fearful and that I have contracted to lessen the impact of somebody who is blazing. I may notice that I feel suddenly and bizarrely huge in the presence of someone who has suddenly shrunk their energy. I may feel a sudden distance with somebody who has contracted. If I notice such a response in myself, I can offer it to my client, and we can use it as we explore our energetic process. Working in this way is particularly useful in helping both of us keep feelings and energetic movement separate, and this lessens the danger of misinterpretation. Recently, for example, I opened the door to somebody who was blazing. The force of her energy hit me immediately. I took a step back, and was aware of contracting my energy field. I felt nervous. Prior to having a clear concept of energetic interaction, I would certainly have (mis)interpreted the energetic blaze as anger. I shared this with her, and she remarked that people often think she is angry when she is not. She wasn't angry on this occasion, but sad. Using my feedback, which was free of any emotional interpretation, we worked out that because she has a dense field, her energy blazes out, especially if she tries to control an emotion by contracting. Her blaze is very easily experienced by other people who are likely to misinterpret the energetic force they feel coming from her as anger.

Working with our own response is easiest if our client happens to lock their energy whilst they are in our presence, but still possible even if the lock and response do not happen spontaneously. I was greatly puzzled by the energetic process of a client I normally work with on the phone. Despite the fact that she was petite, pretty and carrying a baby, attributes that often trigger protectiveness in others, she would experience startling outbursts of unprovoked aggression from strangers in the street. We initially dismissed these as exclusively to do with the other person, but they kept happening to her. Having checked repeatedly that there hadn't been any exchange of words or glances prior to these incidents, I began to wonder if these strangers were reacting to my client holding her energy in a particular way. She also told me that family members surprised her by saying that they were experiencing her as angry. I began to hypothesise that she was blazing, and that these other people were experiencing her blaze as aggression on her part, but this didn't seem quite to fit. I asked her to come in person for a session, and asked if she could put herself in the state she had been in when these incidents happened. She was able to do this. I felt her withdraw her energy and watched as her contraction became visible in her whole demeanour. She physically shrank away from me, her face looked pinched and disapproving, and I was a fraction of a second away from imagining that she was disgusted by my presence.

Locking her energy in contraction, and sometimes a clench, affected her as well as her family and strangers in the street. We had already noticed that the incidents of aggression from strangers seemed to coincide with when she was feeling low and vulnerable. She was revisiting a vicious cycle in which she would feel some sadness or neediness, and clench. Her sadness would be unable to move through her as a wave of energy, so she would be stuck with it. Clenching would also bring with it feelings of isolation because she was isolating herself energetically. Past experience flavoured this particular person's clench with the taste of fear. Other people would interpret her contraction as anger or disapproval and react in a hostile manner; she would feel even more frightened and isolated and contract further. This cycle would sometimes progress to the point of her being so clenched that she felt unable to breathe.

Sometimes talking and just being in relationship with me was enough for her to unlock. Sometimes it was not. At such times it was very difficult for her to recognise that she was clenched, though she would be aware that her perception of reality was vastly different than a few days previously. She knew her perception was distorted but did not remember how to return to a more balanced position. I would encourage her to put the phone down for a few minutes and dance around the room. It is very much part of the nature of a clench that she would find the thought of doing this difficult and embarrassing, despite the fact that she is a professional dancer. Her intention and the context of a good therapeutic relationship were important, and dancing in another context such as a dance class did not help her release her clench. When we first started working with her energetic process, my client would always be astonished to find that she had been in a clench. She can now recognise that a certain set of feelings, or particular reactions on the part of those around her, probably means that she is in a clench, and she can come out of it by moving her subtle body. Sometimes opening her energy field by dancing unlocks her, but sometimes it doesn't and she has to work directly with her subtle body, expanding her energy to fill her physical body, then allowing it to melt into the air around her, and extend into the air above her and the ground beneath her.

Our clients may not spontaneously go into a lock whilst they are with us, and may be unable to recreate such a state at will. It may be inadvisable to suggest they do so, especially if they are likely to go into a clench. There are a number of other ways to help your client become aware of their energetic process. Offering the experiential exercises described above ('Energetic self awareness') may be more appropriate to therapists used to using techniques in their work. It is important to offer the whole exercise, otherwise the client (or therapist) may be left in a state of energetic distortion. Other ways of helping our clients become aware of their energetic process, offering our own experience of the client for instance, are more embedded in the therapeutic relationship.

Listening and believing

Many clients tell us quite plainly what sort of energetic lock they are in. In my experience, this is particularly likely to happen at the beginning of a session, especially the first, when the client is telling us how or where they are. The trick is to listen to what they say, and then believe what they are saying. If somebody tells me that they are down in the dumps, in a heap or really low, I hear that their energy body has slumped. If they tell me they have a wall or barrier between themselves and the rest of the world, I hear that they have contracted in an attempt to protect themselves. If they say something made them feel small, or that they feel cut off from everything, I understand that they are describing a clench. If they say that something made them jump out of their skin, that they are beside themselves with worry, grief or anger, or that they are up in the air about something or all over the place, I believe them and work towards helping them get back into their bodies. I often do this by asking if they know where they have gone. Some are standing beside themselves, others are not even in the room, some know they left through the top of their head or through the front of their body. They can then, if they wish, retrieve themselves.

Watching what we are being shown

My clients may also show me what they are doing, and will most often do this with their hands. They describe contraction by waving their hands in towards their body or by making a 'stop' gesture with their palms. They tell me about disembodiment by letting their hands flutter upwards, they tell me of slumping by making downward moving gestures, and make open, outward moving gestures when describing experiences of energetic expansion. I often bring my client's awareness to what they are describing by mirroring or remarking on the gesture.

Helping the client restore themselves to a state of energetic integration

The ultimate aim of subtle bodywork is not merely that the client becomes aware of their energetic processes, but that they are able to change these processes if they are inappropriate to the present moment. For some, this will be the relatively easy matter of releasing a temporary lock, for others it may be a matter of working very slowly until they feel safe enough to risk doing without their habitual energetic defense. Such a client may need to find 'real world' ways to protect themselves as an alternative to trying to do it energetically, or may need more effective energetic protection such as that described in Exercise Six.

A client may know how to rebalance themselves energetically. It may seem obvious to them to let their energy start to fill up their body if they have shrunk to a small ball inside or to let their energy flow down their legs and extend into the earth if they have been ungrounded. And they may be able to do these things easily by just moving their energy as they would an arm or leg.

Other people do not have such a relationship of ease and familiarity with their energy body, and may appreciate initial suggestions. Some people find it easy to move their energy by using symbols (it is important that the symbols used are the client's rather than the therapist's). They may build themselves a little bridge back into their body, or pull themselves back in with a rope. They may put roots into the ground, or imagine they are standing under a waterfall. Others prefer to coax themselves back without the use of symbols or to move around physically.

Conclusion

Energetic locks are released in the usual process of any talking or body therapy as feelings are expressed, issues worked through and muscular tensions released. Sometimes, however, clients experience themselves as stuck, unable to move on. This may indeed be a necessary part of their process. Or it may be that they can move on by releasing an energetic lock or recognising an energetic process. Subtle bodywork is not something to be used to push a client on when either they or the therapist is becoming impatient, and I imagine it would not be effective in such circumstances. However, it is very useful if the 'problem' is fundamentally an energetic one.

It may be the case that our client simply hasn't worked through all the issues involved and hasn't allowed themselves to fully experience their feelings. It may be that they have held an energetic lock for so long, or so habitually, that it has become embodied in their musculature and they need the physicality of touch or movement. However, if they keep experiencing feelings of isolation, apathy, and desolation because they are clenching or slumping, for instance, awareness of that process enables them to choose to do otherwise. Both clenching and slumping cut us off from the greater source of life; we no longer allow ourselves to conduct vital energy from the cosmos to the earth, and so we lose our vitality. The energy that we are holding in when we clench becomes stuck and stale, or drains from us when we slump. We may feel the need to clench in order to endure an ordeal, but if we do not relax the energetic contraction around our body and the locks at our throat and pelvis once it is over, we will continue to experience life as an ordeal. Similarly, we may slump in exhaustion. If we remain slumped and don't return to our full height and width, both within and outwith our body, we will remain exhausted.

Our subtle body exists in the domain between the material and the immaterial, and work at this level affects both our body and our psyche. As far as I know, working through the subtle body in this way only affects deep body armouring up to a certain point, but it is an excellent means of preventing tension becoming stuck in the physical body. Awareness of our energetic process enables us to avoid becoming psychologically stuck and to access emotional energy we may have locked in or out. When we unlock our energy we unlock our vitality, our spirit. The aim of subtle bodywork is to restore psychological and energetic integration so that we once again have all our inner resources available to us.

References

Brennan, B. A. *Hands of Light: A Guide to Healing Through the Human Energy Field.* New York: Bantam 1987, 1988

Brennan, B. A. *Light Emerging: The Journey of Personal Healing.* New York: Bantam 1993

Capra, F. *The Tao of Physics.* London: Flamingo 1976, 1992

Castanada, C. *The Art of Dreaming.* London: Thorsons 1994

Feuerstein, G. *The Shambala Encyclopedia of Yoga.* Boston and London: Shambala 1997

Henderson, J. *The Lover Within.* New York: Station Hill, Barrytown Ltd 1987, 1999

Jung, C. 'Mysterium Coniunctionis'. *Collected Works*, Vol 14. Princeton: Princeton University Press 1963

Jung, C. *Nietzsche's Zarathustra.* Jarret, J. L. (Ed.). Princeton: Princeton University Press 1988

Pierrakos, J. C. *Core Energetics.* Mendocino, CA: Life Rhythm 1986, 1990

Reich, W. *Selected Writings.* New York: Farrar, Straus & Giroux 1951, 1973

Schwartz-Salant, N. *The Mystery of Human Relationships: Alchemy and the Transformation of the Self.* London: Routledge 1998

Schwartz-Salant, N. *Narcissism and Character Transformation: The Psychology of Narcissistic Character Disorders.* Toronto: Inner City Books 1982

Spiegelman, J. M. and Mansfield, V. 'Physics and Psychology of the Transference as an Interactive Field'. *Journal of Analytic Psychology* 1996; 41(2): 179–202

Westfall, R. S. *Never at Rest: A Biography of Issac Newton.* Cambridge: Cambridge University Press 1980

Zukav, G. *The Dancing Wu Li Masters.* New York: Harper Collins 1979, 1998

Chapter 9

Body psychotherapy and regression: the body remembers past lives

Roger J. Woolger

Introduction

Past life regression therapy, as described here, is a therapeutic technique that uses similar strategies and commands to hypnotic age regression (following a time line backwards, talking to the regressed persona, etc.) but which also draws strongly from Jung's waking dream technique of active imagination and the embodied re-enactments of past events called by J. L. Moreno, psychodrama (Woolger 1996). As in hypnotic regression and psychodrama, the patient is guided back to and encouraged to relive traumatic scenes or unresolved conflicts from the past that have been previously inaccessible to consciousness, but which are thought to be influencing and distorting current mental and emotional stability. But instead of being regressed solely to the patient's childhood, a strong suggestion is also given to 'go to the origin of the problem in a previous lifetime'. In other words, the notional time-line is extended backwards to assume the soul's continuity with previous existences via what some have called the soul memory or 'far memory'. In many respects the rationale of past life therapy is similar to that of post-traumatic stress therapies as well as to the cathartic or abreactive approach taken, but later abandoned, by early psychoanalysis (Herman 1992).

Past life regression and psychotherapy

The ontological status of 'past life' memories is inevitably controversial given the dogmatic adherence of western psychology and Freudian psychoanalysis to a tabula rasa view of the infant's psyche at birth, but this has long been challenged by Jung's theory of a collective unconscious that transcends historical time (Jung 1959; Assagioli 1965) and by the widely-known school that calls itself 'transpersonal psychology' (Tart 1975; Grof 1985; Rowan 1993; Boorstein 1996). Moreover, there exists the monumental work of psychiatrist Dr Ian Stevenson of the University of Virginia, an erstwhile president of the British Society for Psychical Research. For over 40 years Stevenson and his co-workers collected cases of spontaneous memories of 'past lives' from many parts of the world, mostly from among children. These cases, which he calls 'suggestive of reincarnation' – and which were meticulously verified – are published in five volumes. Their findings have never been seriously rebutted. His most recent book, *Reincarnation and Biology* (Stevenson 1997), was described by the reviewer for the *British Scientific and Medical Network* as 'one of the great classics of twentieth century psi research' (Lorimer 1997: 53). Nevertheless, Stevenson's work continues to be ignored by mainstream psychology. (For a detailed review of parapsychological, religious and metaphysical interpretations of 'past lives' see Woolger (1987).)

As for the therapeutic value of recalling 'past lives' a growing number of therapists from different countries have become persuaded of its effectiveness (Lucas 1993). Many contemporary practitioners stumbled upon 'past life' scenarios when loosely instructing clients during a hypnotic regression session to 'go back to the origin of the problem' even though neither therapist nor client believed in 'past lives'. Such was the case with eminent neuro-psychiatrist Dr Brian Weiss of the University of Miami, who staked his reputation and career on the publication of the case of a client who recovered rapidly when an an unbidden 'past life' surfaced spontaneously during a hypnosis session (Weiss 1990). As both Weiss and the present author concluded after reviewing hundreds of such cases 'it doesn't matter whether you believe in reincarnation or not, the unconscious will almost always produce a past life story when invited in the right way' (Woolger 1989: 40).

What is remarkable about this technique, first employed at the turn of the twentieth century by a hypnotist and follower of Freud, Colonel de Rochas, is that the patient does not need to believe in reincarnation or past lives for it to be effective. (By analogy, one might also say that one does need to believe in a theory of dreams for dreamwork to be effective in therapy.) He or she is simply encouraged to relive a distressing scene from some other historical time frame as if it were real and to temporarily take on the 'other life' personality as well as the body image and sensations of the 'other' personality for the duration of the 'regression'. The therapeutic effect of realistically reliving a 'past life' trauma in the imagination – whether a story of an accident, abandonment, betrayal, violent death, rape or physical abuse – is similar to the emotional releases experienced with post-traumatic stress therapies used for current life traumas (Herman 1992; Van der Kolk et al.1996). The reliving is like a fictional psychodrama that leads, as Moreno wished, to an intense cathartic release of blocked feelings, most commonly of frozen fear, grief, rage, shame or guilt.

The body in past life therapy

In line with the more physical releases sought by Wilhelm Reich, past life therapy very frequently brings about the spontaneous dissolving of bodily armouring and the recovery of blocked physical libido. Indeed, a striking aspect of much past life therapy, when seen for the first time by an observer, is the obvious physical involvement of the client in the story that is being relived. In many sessions the client doesn't just sit or lie passively, recounting an inner vision of a past life with his or her eyes closed. Instead, they may be subject to the most dramatic convulsions, contortions, heavings and thrashings imaginable. One client may clutch his chest in apparent pain as he recounts a sword wound, another may turn almost blue during a choking fit as she remembers a strangulation, while yet another may become rigidly fixed with arms above the head as he remembers being tied to a post during torture.

Many bodyworkers have reported how 'past life' images often arise during a massage or a Rolfing session when a tense, a sensitive or a scarred part of the body is touched or worked upon – in addition it is sometimes the masseur or masseuse who gets such an image, as if 'tuning in' to something in the patient's energy fields around the body. For example, a male patient, during a session when his wrists were being deeply massaged, saw himself in a different body, that of a slave pulling painfully on a huge oar in a Roman galley; in the same session, the therapist also got images of the body rowing while working on the client's legs. In another case, when a female patient was asked to explore chronic neck and shoulder pain by moving her arms and head in different directions, suddenly her hands froze at ear level, her head hung forward and she screamed in pain: 'I'm in the stocks; they're throwing things at me!' She had momentarily experienced the persona of a seventeenth-century adultress who was being punished by an angry New England Puritan community.

Occasionally invasive medical or dental treatment will trigger extreme fear responses and what seem to be flashbacks of 'past life' torture or abuse. During oral surgery a woman reacted with terror when a cloth surgical cover was put over her face for a procedure. In a subsequent regression she felt herself having a hood put over her head and then being guillotined during the French Revolution; once she had relived the death and seemingly gone out of her body to see her decapitated 'past life' self 'down there' all the fear went away.

In another very striking case, a woman client sought therapy because her sexual responsiveness had always been so blocked that she resisted penetration of any kind. During a session she was regressed to a childhood scene from this life where she had been given a urethral probe in hospital. This in itself had been extremely traumatising, but during the reliving an even more horrible and painful image came when she said, 'it's burning!' She saw herself as a woman in a medieval village who had become pregnant out of wedlock; she is cruelly punished by having a red-hot iron inserted in her to cauterise her uterus. When these and similar visions and sensations of physical trauma emerge in regression, psychodrama or bodywork they can be successfully cleared by past life therapy and released energetically from the body with very marked remission of pain and other chronic physical symptoms.

To the inexperienced observer this may appear distressing, if not dangerous. Even trained therapists (more often those using Freudian, cognitive, or purely verbal techniques) will come up to me after a particularly violent demonstration of the past life technique and warn me of the dangers of provoking a psychotic breakdown. Yet for many therapists now practising past life therapy strong physical as well as emotional release is not just a commonplace of our work but in many cases an essential part of it. More and more therapists are finding that all kinds of behavioural problems and complexes have traumatic underlays from past lives which are plainly physical as well as emotional. As a result, we are naturally finding ourselves using cathartic methods to release the old trauma. Seen from a historical perspective this kind of emphasis on the reliving of traumatic events and their treatment through abreactive or cathartic methods marks a return to the very approaches Freud abandoned 90 years ago in favour of his later psychology of the ego and its defense mechanisms.

As Stanislav Grof has observed in his overview of the history of psychotherapy in *Beyond the Brain* (1985), many of the more recent therapies – Gestalt, Primal Rebirthing, LSD therapy, for example – are currently emphasising the experiential component in reaction to the purely cognitive and interpretive emphasis of much neo-Freudian psychotherapy. In other words, from Grof's point of view – with which I am fully in agreement – much of the post-Freudian enterprise, and even the Jungian, has been an ineffective intellectual detour in the evolution of practical methods of psychotherapy.

I raise the issue of these fundamentally different therapeutic strategies – let us call them the cathartic vs the cognitive – not for polemical reasons but because they radically affect how we proceed with regard to both therapy in general and past life therapy in particular. One obvious consequence of these differing views is that when we aim for cognitive understanding we tend to neglect the body. By contrast, when as therapists we emphasize catharsis, we must inevitably remain focused in the body for the simple reason that it is in the body that both physical violence and emotion are most vividly experienced. This has recently been underlined by the ground-breaking work on trauma therapy by the Harvard group of psychiatric researchers headed by Bessel van der Kolk and Judith Herman. They emphasise that it is the limbic system of the brain and sensorimotor pathways that are responsible for storing traumatic memories and not the verbal regions of the cortex as in normal memory. A key paper by Van der Kolk is entitled *The Body Keeps the Score* (Van der Kolk 1996). The implications for trauma therapy are clearly that effective remembering and release of traumatic residues must involve the body.

The body as experiencing subject

From the viewpoint of cathartic or experiential therapy the body itself becomes what, for want of a better term, I will call an experiencing subject or, more strictly, a multiplicity of experiencing subjects. My head may think this, my heart may feel that, my guts may feel something else and so on. Every part of the body has something to say or express. This is what Fritz Perls, inspired both by Wilhelm Reich and by J. L. Moreno's psychodrama, saw so clearly: that there are all kinds of unfinished monologues, dialogues and conversations going on in different and often opposing segments or parts of our bodies. The complexes, to switch to Jungian terminology, speak in and through our bodies if we are prepared to give them ear; we are the embodiment of the totality of our complexes.

We are particularly in debt to Wilhelm Reich for grappling in a practical way with the most pervasive problem of western, westernised and 'civilised' men and women, namely the so-called Cartesian split of head and body, mind and matter, spirit and nature. At the very time that Freud was moving away from the physiological implications of his theory of sexual repression and the damming up of libido, Reich was exploring the issue of rigid character structures and how they are expressed by the body. Reich coined the term 'character armour' to describe those rigid patterns of unconscious muscular holding we find in the head, jaw, neck, shoulder, thorax, diaphragm, pelvis, legs, arms, hands and feet (Reich 1949; Dychtwald 1977). What he showed us was that these rigid structures were not the result of physical or somatic stress but direct expressions of psychic trauma, deeply repressed emotions, and a basic unconscious denial of life. All the libido that should be flowing out of the organism and into life, however conflictual that might be, remains locked beneath the musculature. This in turn depresses the autonomic function, affects organic functioning adversely, and often distorts the whole skeletal posture (Reich 1949; Alexander 1971).

To give some examples: if a child lives in fear that he will be hit by a brutal parent he learns to cringe and raise his shoulders to protect his head. If there is no deliverance from that fear, the defensive shoulder armouring is never relaxed, and neither, correspondingly, is his tight 'nervous' stomach and apprehensive shallow breathing. After a while the child adapts to being permanently 'on the alert' so that the fear remains locked in his organism in the form of chronically raised shoulders, bent back, tight chest and stomach. Over the years such holding patterns may degenerate further into a certain characteristic fixed posture (Kurtz 1976).

Or suppose that a young girl has been subject to regular sexual molestation by her father. In this case it is her genitals that will be held tightly, her pelvis gripped in a frozen posture, and her thighs and legs kept rigid by a mixture of fear and rage. In addition, there may be revulsion held in her stomach and shallow breathing. In later years she may well experience urogenital tract infections, deeply inhibited sexual responsiveness and gynaecological difficulties, all due to deep-seated psychic armouring that has now become chronic.

These examples are typical of the way that Reich (1949) and his contemporary followers (notably Keleman 1975; Kurtz 1976; Lowen 1977; Boadella 1985; Pierrakos 1987) have all followed the traditional psychoanalytic route of looking for the causal origins of later organic complaints and character armouring in the bodily deformations and traumas of early childhood. Certainly there is no shortage of parental neglect, brutality or sexual abuse in the modern world. Much of the time, therefore, it is not necessary for therapists to look any further for the cause and the release of the embodied symptoms we have described. But as more and more therapists are discovering, there are all kinds of neurotic complaints of both an emotional and a physical nature that simply refuse to be resolved through exploring infantile stories, no matter how early we trace them back. Many children, it is now being admitted, are obviously born fearful, depressed, rage-filled, withdrawn, unable to eat (i.e. starving), desensitised, and so on. It is precisely in such cases that past life exploration is proving particularly effective, now that we are free to ask the very questions that Freudianism and the tabula rasa doctrine of development have proscribed for so long.[1]

Physical residues from past lives

Let me refer to a case mentioned briefly in my book *Other Lives, Other Selves* (Woolger 1987). A young woman, whom I will call Heather, suffered since early adolescence from ulcerative colitis. Naturally, every kind of dietary therapy had been tried and, in more recent years, psychotherapy. Her psychotherapist referred her to me, admitting that she could find no cause of anxiety to account for the ulcers in Heather's present life, despite many months of probing. So we agreed to try a past life session.

The story that immediately surfaced took us to Holland during World War II at the time of the Nazi invasion, Heather found herself as an eight-year-old girl in a Jewish family living in the Jewish neighbourhood of a small Dutch town. In the first scene to surface she finds herself happily helping her mother bake bread when the sounds of explosions first reach their ears. The Nazis are systematically blowing up and setting fire to the terraced houses to 'flush out' the inhabitants onto the streets. The mother, panicking, pushes the children onto the street, telling them to run. The street is full of townspeople running in all directions. There are armoured cars and jeeps following them and the sound of gunfire. The little girl runs down an alleyway, thinking it to be safer, and watches for a time from behind a wall, seeing some neighbours and friends shot, but mostly rounded up by the Nazis. Fleeing farther from the smoke and explosions, she turns a corner and almost runs into a van commandeered by the soldiers. They catch her and shove her into the back of the van with other captives.

Shortly, she and the others are herded out and lined up in front of trenches that have been dug as mass graves. Standing watching lines of people being machine gunned as she awaits her turn, she reports that her stomach is totally knotted in terror. Eventually her turn comes and she falls back, shot, onto a pile of dead and dying victims. She doesn't die immediately; other bodies fall on top of her and she finally dies of suffocation and loss of blood. Her stomach remains knotted in terror throughout this appalling ordeal.

My approach during our session was to direct her to breathe deeply and to let go of all the fear and anguish as much as possible. Given this permission she broke into convulsive sobbing, screaming and keening. As the young Jewish girl, she had died, so it seemed, unable to express both the terrible shocks of losing her parents, seeing mass slaughter, and facing her own premature death. Phrases such as, 'I'll never see them again', 'Help me!', 'I can't get away', 'It's too late', surfaced spontaneously and her body went through violent convulsions and dry vomiting for a while.

When it was all over Heather was exhausted and depleted, yet she felt unburdened of a fear she had always dimly sensed and which she now understood. Her stomach condition improved radically after this and a couple of follow-up sessions.

In many cases, once we shift our focus away from supposed early childhood traumas in this life and give the deeper unconscious permission to express itself, we find that the presenting symptom seems to be derived from a past life memory. There had been no event in Heather's current life experience remotely severe enough to induce fear symptoms as heavily somaticised as ulcers; in fact, her complaint was quite out of proportion to the relatively untroubled course of her current life. Yet immediately the past life story of the Dutch Jewish girl emerged, we found traumatic images which were entirely consonant with her symptoms. In Heather's case, as in many others, I was led to conclude that the unconscious fear, which manifested in her stomach as ulcers, was not a residue from this life but from another.

Every part of the body, it would seem, has in one person or another revealed some old accident or wound. But past life traumas always have a specific and not a general relationship to the current physical problem. Not all migraines derive from head wounds or all throat problems from strangling. A similar throat complaint in several people may carry quite different stories: in one it may be a death from a beheading, in another a choking death, while someone else may remember having been hanged. In different people a painful chest or pains in the heart region will bring up memory traces of all kinds of stabbings, gun wounds, lances, arrows, shrapnel, etc. Sore legs and arms remember being broken in accidents or war, crushed by fallen trees, shattered by torture, crucifixion or the rack, or else ripped off by wild animals. A weak or sensitive belly area may recall cuts, slashings and disembowelings, or else starvation or poisoning. Sensitive feet and hands have in past lives been subjected to every kind of accident and mutilation, to say nothing of performing horrible acts on others.

How can this be? The sceptic unfamiliar with past life regression might ask, how can memory traces and somatic reactions be caused by experiences felt and sensed by an entirely different body?

The problems of non-physical transmission

Some theories have attempted to answer this question – sometimes called 'the problem of extra-cerebral memory' – by recourse to genetic inheritance. Yet my own finding is that out of many hundreds of cases involving past lives, only in a handful could the particular affliction possibly have been passed on genetically. The huge majority of stories I have recorded can in no way be accounted for by genetics, that is to say by ancestral transmission. The cultural discrepancies and discontinuities are for the most part too extreme.

I have proposed elsewhere (Woolger 1987) that we talk about inherited psychic contents as 'past life complexes', an extension of Jung's description of the complex (Jung 1934), since it is now abundantly clear that the psychic, emotional and physical impressions laid down in one lifetime are in some way transmitted to future lives.

Yet regardless of what we call them, how exactly are complexes from past lives transmitted? Is there some psychic substrate or vehicle for this transmission from life to life, from body to body? Jung's own theory of the collective unconscious, which is a repository of the residues of all of human history, would seem an attractive proposal, yet, in this formulation, its contents – the archetypes – have no personal memories, only impersonal forms.

Here again, I believe we must turn to the East for ideas more compatible with our data, to theories that have taken root in cultures which have always been open to the idea of transmigration, unlike the West with its dogmas and priestly persecutions. Yoga teaching, in fact, offers highly sophisticated concepts of both a universal psychic substrate called the *akasha*, which records impressions of all events mental and physical, as well as a vehicle, the *subtle body*, which transmits individual psychic residues.

It is beyond the scope of this chapter to go into the traditional doctrine of akasha (translated as psychic or cosmic 'space' or 'ether'), a doctrine that goes far beyond the image of 'the akashic records' popularised by the Edgar Cayce readings and Theosophy. Suffice to say that if we in the West truly understood it, the concept of akasha could radically alter fixed ideas about matter, transformation and healing that are only recently being challenged in the West.[2] More useful, from the practical perspective of past life therapy, is the concept of the subtle body. Here is how it is summarised by an authority on Indian religion:

Within the gross body, which suffers dissolution after death, every living being possesses an inner subtle body, which is formed of the sense-faculties, vital breaths, and inner organs. This is the body that goes on and on, from birth to birth, as the basis and vehicle of the reincarnated personality. It departs from the sheath of the gross body at the time of death, and then determines the nature of the new existence; for within it are left the traces – like scars or furrows – of all the perceptions, acts, desires and movements of will of the past, all the propensities and trends, the heritage of habits and inclinations, and the peculiar readiness to react this way or that, or not to react at all.

Zimmer 1952: 324

The subtle body in theory and practice

Scientific investigation of energy fields around the human body has up until now been very limited in the West. Since parapsychology is still held in disrepute by mainstream academic psychology – the American Psychological Association has consistently rejected the formation of a Parapsychology Division, for example – we still have very little to turn to. Nevertheless, Krippner and Rubin have reported on Russian research into the Kirlian phenomenon of energy discharges around plants and animal organisms and humans in their *Galaxies of Life* (Krippner 1973). These energy emanations, which it is hard not to describe as auras, can be recorded by a quasi-photographic process.

In this collection of papers, Moss and Johnson report on the little-known but revolutionary theory of 'bioplasma', which the Soviet researcher V.M. Inyushin has characterised as 'the fifth state of matter.'[3] Here is their summary of these findings:

> V. M. Inyushin . . . has opted for the term 'bioplasma body' as descriptive of the emanations and internal structure of the objects photographed, quoting from such authorities on bio-energetics and bio-electronics as Szent-Gyorgy and Presman. In conversation with Inyushin, Moss learned that he conceives of the 'bioplasma body' as similar, if not identical, to the 'aura' or 'astral body' as defined in Yogic literature.
>
> Moss and Johnson, in Krippner and Rubin 1973: 29

Unfortunately, the Russian term is obviously a physical metaphor derived from 'plasm' which tends to make it a reduction of the psychic realm to the physical. This fits very well within the Soviet philosophy of dialectical materialism but is rather clumsy for those not so committed. On the other hand, we in the West are ourselves still caught in our body/mind, nature/spirit dualisms generated by Christian theology and the predominant philosophical tradition that follows Descartes.[4] G.R.S. Mead surveyed alternatives such as 'soul' and 'spirit' in his valuable book, *The Doctrine of the Subtle Body in the*

Western Tradition (1919), but he makes no attempt to encompass modern psychology.

A major problem with many terms like 'bioplasm', and other even more general terms such as 'energy field', as far as psychotherapy is concerned, is that they fail to pinpoint the crucial interface between 'energy' and specific feelings and thought patterns. Possibly Reich's 'orgone' theory is the only Western attempt to date to do this. By stressing the idea that repressed emotional energy is also repressed life or orgone energy, he was able to show how fixed neurotic patterns lead to the degeneration of organic systems. Certain followers of Reich who have attempted to extend his radical perspective have, like Inyushin, been struck by the resemblance to yoga and subtle body phenomena such as perceivable 'auras'. John Pierrakos' method of 'core energetics' (1987) works with the auric field in psychotherapy, as does David Tansley's healing system called 'radionics' (1977). The work of Barbara Brennan (1988) with subtle body healing should also be mentioned. All three of these researchers draw upon yogic concepts of the chakras and subtle layers of energy surrounding the body. Brennan admits to clairvoyantly 'seeing' past lives in the aura.

Tansley's use of Alice Bailey's version of the yogic subtle body theory (1953) is one I have found especially valuable, particularly since it defines very clearly three distinct levels of subtle energy and shows how they interpenetrate. Bailey used the yogic terms for these subtle bodies but in an approachable fashion. In summary and in descending order, containing each other like Russian eggs, they are:

1   *The Mental Body*: this very broad energy field is the most subtle of the three and is the locus of all powerful mental contents or fixed thoughts. These thoughts may be conscious or unconscious and can radically influence an individual's overall life patterns or self-image (e.g. 'I'll never make it', 'Don't trust people', etc.). Such thoughts can be the residues of negative past life experiences. They do not necessarily affect the lower bodies but, if they do, their influence is extremely strong.

2   *The Emotional Body* (sometimes called the astral body): this energy field adheres closely to the physical body by a radius of about two to four feet and is the locus of the feeling residues from past events, including past lives. These may be sadness, rage, disappointment, apathy, etc. This energy level may be strongly affected by negative thoughts from the mental body. Physically it is denser than the mental body. When its feeling contents become highly charged and not released, it will affect the lower etheric energy body adversely.

3   *The Etheric Body* could be called 'the physical memory field' because in it reside all the painful subtle memory traces of physical trauma, whether lesions, fractures, tumours, amputations, wounds or diseases – traces that Patanjali, in the Yoga Sutras, calls the *klesas* or 'sufferings' carried by the

subtle body. The 'phantom limb' phenomenon experienced by amputees is a well-known example of how a residual memory of trauma can be held in the etheric body.

The etheric body is strictly the equivalent of Inyushin's 'bioplasma body' (not the astral body as mistakenly reported to Moss and Johnson) and the energy systems of chi in Chinese medicine and prana in yoga. It is also close to Reich's orgone energy. The etheric body or energy field is the denser of the three subtle bodies and is physically perceptible to many people as heat emanating from parts of the body. It radiates out from the physical body about one to two inches and is the field worked with in such practices as acupuncture, shiatsu, therapeutic touch and hands-on healing.

This field can be affected electrolytically by cold water, mineral baths, sunlight and certain coloured filters. In it are many of the residues from physical traumas such as accidents and surgery, as well as past life traumas. Repressed feelings from the emotional body will lodge at the etheric level to produce organic problems.

The important principle that may be gleaned from this highly condensed description is that there is a descending order of influence from higher to lower among these three bodies. In Heather's case, which we looked at earlier, the following pattern can be discerned:

1   The unconscious *thought*: 'I am in danger' (mental level) makes Heather feel perpetually anxious (emotional level).
2   Heather's perpetual *anxiety* (emotional level) creates constant tension in her abdominal region (etheric level).
3   The constant *tension* in Heather's abdomen (etheric level) affects the gastrointestinal system to produce ulcers (physical level).

Since the subtle causation of these symptoms is descending, it is broadly true (though there are many variations) that healing follows the opposite direction, a movement upwards from the etheric to the mental. So, for example, in the case of someone with a past life trauma associated with the legs, we may observe the following pattern:

1   *Physical* massage or manipulation releases etheric energy (experienced as heat, tingling, etc.) in the legs.
2   The *etheric* energy flow brings up incoherent *feelings* of fear.
3   The *feelings* of fear lead to images of being chased as a child, then of being hounded in a past life story, and finally the *thought*, 'I've got to get away'.

It may help to conceive of how the three levels of subtle body energy relate to one another if we take the analogy of the different states of water or H_2O.

When it is frozen, water is dense, solid and hard to manipulate without smashing it or cutting it up. When water is fluid it can be moved around easily but still has substantiality and it can still penetrate and erode. When water is evaporated, as cloud or steam, it is at its lightest, most subtle, and most pervasive. By analogy with water, then, the psychic contents of the subtle body which are the hardest to work with are those that are 'frozen' in the physical body as postural patterns, organ weaknesses and disease. These conditions may be easier to influence when they are more 'fluid', that is to say, when they are experienced as feelings and emotions that can be undammed. But even more subtly it may be possible to perceive pervasive thoughts underlying these feelings which, once identified, can now be totally evaporated.

Bodywork, then, may be imagined as a way of 'melting' residual psychic conflicts from this life or a previous life that have become fixed and rigid in the total psycho-somatic being of the individual. Morris Netherton (1978) was the first psychotherapist to document a series of cases where past life traumas underlay severe chronic illnesses such as ulcers, migraines, epilepsy and more. (Earlier, Alice Bailey (1953) had outlined the principles governing the karmic inheritance of severe illnesses such as cancer and heart disease, but she had offered no suggestions for therapy.) Meanwhile, Stanislav Grof has emphasised, from findings during LSD and experiential therapy (Grof 1985), that we all carry major unconscious imprints where we have suffered a physical accident or trauma from this life.

It would appear then, that all operations, sicknesses, broken limbs, deprivations, or minor hurts leave some degree of residue in the etheric body. Physically these may be perceived as 'cold' spots or blocked energy meridians, or else as poorly functioning chakras (the yogic term for the subtle energy centres). But at the same time, because these energy fields are multi-dimensional or holonomic[5] frequently there will be past life imprints of physical trauma also present, often directly co-extensive with the same region of the body. While using deep breathing work to help a woman client to release trauma buried in the region of her uterus from a recent hysterectomy, we found ourselves suddenly in a primitive past life sacrifice where her belly was being ripped open. Similarly, in working with a young man who had had several difficult knee operations following a skiing accident, we found no fewer than three past life traumas involving a shattered knee; on two occasions he had lost a leg beneath that same knee in battle. Again the principle holds that subtle body imprints at the etheric or bioplasma level are multiply determined or layered.

It seems quite apparent that certain areas of the body will be inherently weak and prone to further accident, disease or malfunction because of these old imprints in the etheric body. It is a useful practice in an initial psychotherapy interview to ask about recurrent illnesses, damaged parts of the body, typical physical fears or weaknesses, hospitalisations and so on. Often chronic headaches, backaches, a weak bladder, low blood sugar, indigestion, bad eyesight, and so on, are major clues to etheric or bioplasma scars and hence to the residue of past life traumas to that area of the body (Dethlefsen 1990).

When a past life complex lodged in the etheric or bioplasma body is mostly the residue of a physical trauma, it will often be enough to rerun the trauma. In other cases some kind of etheric rebalancing, therapeutic massage, therapeutic touch, acupuncture or reflexology can be very effective adjuncts to treatment. In a case described in *Other Lives, Other Selves* (Woolger 1986), a woman suffering from lupus and attendant arthritic-like pain in her joints experienced a dramatic cathartic release of pain when she relived being dismembered in a bomb explosion in a seeming past life. In the past life replay the shock of the bombing had clearly driven the victim out of (his) body. When the past life secondary personality, a Russian anarchist, was able to see his body mutilated on the ground he also briefly, but agonisingly, recapitulated the phantom pain. But as a result of this highly intense psychodrama the woman experienced a huge release, tantamount to letting go of a frozen death trauma and the negative dying thought, 'I'll never use my legs and arms again!'

The post-traumatic dissociation from the heavily wounded dying 'past life' body in this dramatic replay in effect healed the subtle body by re-associating consciousness with the body – albeit painfully. In our work with severe trauma from both past and present lives, we have found that core post-traumatic shock symptoms invariably entail a leaving of the body in some way. This inevitably means that the physical and emotional components of the trauma remain frozen and unconscious in the energy field of the subtle body. And to all intents and purposes all the traumatic residues remain fixated imaginally in the frozen moment in time of the accident or catastrophe. Like a nightmare from which a dreamer awakes just before a deathly onslaught, ego consciousness escapes the crucial moment but leaves the unresolved fear continuing to re-cycle like a needle stuck in the groove of an old gramophone record (Patanjali's *Yoga Sutras* actually call the karmic imprints 'ruts' or 'grooves' in the subtle body; Woods 1927). Playing out a full past or present life death trauma such that the replay stimulates full release of the horror, trembling, panic, screaming and tears can fully clear quite severe post-traumatic symptoms in a relatively few sessions. In this respect past life therapy closely resembles the early forms of 'shell shock' therapies developed in the wake of the wars of the twentieth century.

Not all physically held etheric or bioplasma imprints disappear as quickly as the example of the woman carrying the residues of a dismemberment trauma. Some traumas may represent the accumulation of a number of past life catastrophes carrying an overall karmic meaning that may require long periods of therapy and also meditation to be relinquished. As he lay dying of tuberculosis, D. H. Lawrence recognised in his disease the need for 'long difficult repentance, realisation of life's mistake'. From the greater perspective of karma, that is to say our spiritually inherited patterns of fate, it may seem that sometimes the soul has chosen for us to be crippled, deformed or subject to an irreversible disease because of what we have inflicted previously on others. Here our etheric imprints are forms of karmic penitence and have a symbolic or spiritual meaning. In cases like the following we must be clear that it is not the ego personality that 'chooses' but rather a transcendent or 'higher self' – 'not my, but Thy will be done.' (Jung proposed the term 'Self' for this function, regarding it as the centre of the soul (Jung 1969; also Bailey 1953).)

Another woman patient, who suffered from severe arthritis in her legs and arms, saw a past life in which she had been a Roman commander who cruelly crucified whole villages of rebellious Gauls, but died remorseful and seemingly taking into his own subtle body the impressions of the pain of his victims. Bodywork and psychodrama were ineffective before the deep remorse had been fully expressed. Finally, a prayerful entreaty for forgiveness seemed to invoke spiritual forces to mobilise the patient's healing. Yet many clients, despite all kinds of physical and emotional catharsis, still do not relinquish their pains. I speculate that it is as though, deep within, they feel they deserve to suffer; that their pain is a kind of dimly-understood karmic punishment. Here we verge on philosophical questions about the meaning of suffering and evil, for which there are no simple answers.

But when we are ready to let go of old pains and what may be ancient self-inflicted punishments, the etheric or bioplasma body can begin to cleanse itself over a short or long period of time, depending on various individual factors. Often when a crucial story is released from the etheric or bioplasma body, there will be extraordinary discharges of subtle energy in the form of shaking, vomiting, tingling, hot and cold flushes, vibrating, and even the release of strange odours from the body. Such movements of energy, called 'kriyas' in yoga and 'streaming' in Reichian work, are little understood by Western science but are all part of the rebalancing of the subtle energy system at the etheric level.

Much more complex, and therefore somewhat harder to work with, are cases where the past life residues in the emotional body penetrate and deform the etheric system or the bioplasma, and with it, the physical body. These are the clients who somaticise their emotional problems, carrying them, as it were, in different parts of the body.

Figure 11 is a composite representation drawn from many typical cases. It shows how the etheric/bioplasma and the physical systems may be afflicted by past life complexes when these manifest in the emotional body as feelings or deeply-felt thoughts. The unconscious thoughts that crystallise in past life stories as complexes are shown outside the circle, since they belong to the more subtle mental body. (Perhaps it should be emphasised that none of these

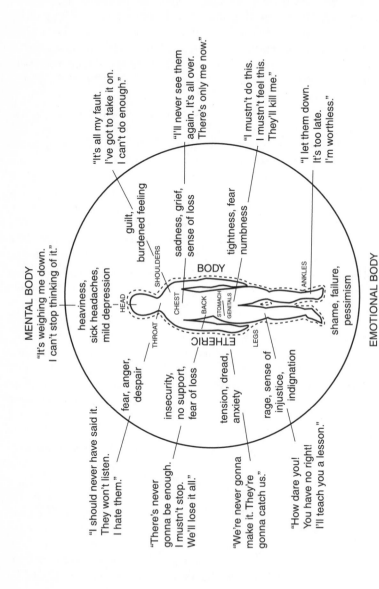

Figure 11 Mental body/emotional body.

complexes belong specifically to any one part of the body; a depressing thought can as easily be held in the back as in the head.)

To take some of the examples in the diagram opposite. A person may experience recurrent sick headaches combined, when carefully interviewed, with a general feeling of heaviness, especially around the head. Exploration of these feelings may reveal a predominant metaphor or image of 'heaviness' that, when exaggerated, might produce the thought: 'It's weighing me down, it's always oppressing me'. Such a thought may easily prove to be the point of entry or somatic bridge into a past life story fraught with guilt, such as 'I ran away from the massacre and never returned. I should have helped my brothers, my family. I can never stop thinking about it. It's always with me, weighing me down'.

Another person may have extremely tight hamstrings in his legs, with accompanying stiffness in the joints and difficulty walking. When explored, the tightness may reveal that tension and anger are held in the legs. A simple bioenergetic exercise (Lowen 1977), or an opportunity to kick freely in a psychodrama, may reveal images of being dragged away to be thrown in a dungeon as well as the desperate thoughts, 'How dare you do this to me! You have no right. Get off me.' Here, rage at some unjust incarceration is still being held in the legs.

Yet another person may experience extreme stiffness in the ankles, combined with actual memories of breaking his ankles on different occasions in the current life. But deeper probing may reveal gloomy thoughts of failing, of not trying hard enough and of shame somehow associated both with the accidents and with the ankle region in general. In pursuing these thoughts while focused on the ankles we may find a somatic bridge, for example to a young man who fell in battle as a young, untried warrior and who was pierced ignominiously through the ankles when half dead.

When further examples are reconstructed from the composite diagram it will be noticed that the different feelings pictured as belonging to specific parts of the body are by no means fixed. The young warrior just mentioned might just as well have died from blows to the head and chest, leaving the ankles unscathed; in which case his sense of gloom and failure would be lodged in these regions instead. Every body story, as well as every wound, is very specific and individual and needs to be treated as such. Also, since the afflicted areas of the etheric or bioplasma body are multiply determined at the past life level, there may be several stories, each with different shades of emotions and other post-traumatic reactions to be unlocked. In addition, there may be interfaces with accidents or illness from the current childhood on, all seemingly revolving around certain core feelings that characterise the issue as a past life complex (see Woolger 1987).

Clearing the subtle bodies of present and past lives

Earlier we noted how the three subtle bodies or energy fields affected each other. Using this perspective it is often quite simple to see how a thought belonging to the mental field can influence feelings within the emotional field. For example, the residual unconscious thought that 'I'm a failure' can easily generate persistent feelings of depression in a person. Further, we saw how feelings can exert a negative influence upon the energy or vitality of the physical system by depressing the etheric field; such a person may literally experience low energy, which can manifest physically as poor appetite, shallow or constricted breathing, heart pains, or other forms of depletion.

These principles have, in one form or another, been known for a long time to bodyworking psychotherapists of certain schools, especially those associated with biofeedback techniques (themselves inspired by yoga) and those influenced by Wilhelm Reich. Since Reich's psychological perspective was basically Freudian when it came to searching for the origins of the negative thought or the emotional trauma, his followers usually assume that the obvious place to look is early childhood. From my perspective, the limitation of Reich's work, far reaching as it is, is that it focuses too strongly on the body, organicity and energy, and far too little on imagery and human experience (Jung, by contrast paid too much attention to imagination and too little to the body!).

Reich and his followers have all tended to assume – Boadella is an exception – that the majority of cases of rage, fear or shame and so on are due to parental abuse and childhood traumas of one kind or another. From my own experience in several years of Reichian therapies I rarely remember being encouraged to release rage or other feelings towards or around anyone other than my mother or my father; the implicit or explicit suggestion was that these feelings belong to parental situations and nowhere else. Yet my finding in past life therapy is that if a client is encouraged, during the strong release of, say, anger or tears, to just follow any images that arise with these emotions, then all kinds of fragmentary scenes will emerge spontaneously from past lives to which the emotion seems to belong far more appropriately.

To take an example: during a therapy group a woman expressed extreme rage towards her tyrannical and harsh father and said that she 'saw red' while doing it. Rather than interpreting this phrase as just a metaphor – a sure way to kill imagery – and rather than assuming it still applied to the father I asked her: 'How does it appear red?'. She replied that it was as if he was wearing a long red robe and a red hat. Encouraged to stay with the image she realised she was seeing a Roman Catholic Cardinal condemning a group of heretics to the stake and that she was in the body of a young monk who was outraged at the cruelty.

Another example: during a therapy session a man was expressing his grief at the death of a beloved sister in childhood, and the strong phrase, 'I'll never see her again' recurred. I encouraged him to free associate the feelings of loss to any other strong event, using this highly-charged phrase. Almost imperceptibly the phrase became 'I'll never see them again', and this time elicited a much more agonising round of crying. 'They're taking my family – my mother, my father, my sister!' he screamed, seeing himself as a young Jewish boy being herded by Nazi soldiers onto a cattle truck en route for a concentration camp where he died never knowing their fate. In ways such as these, using what hypnotherapists have called 'the affect bridge', it is often possible, using spontaneously arising imagery, to broaden and deepen the application of Reich's techniques of physical and emotional catharsis by extending situations from the personal to the collective unconscious (Jung's useful term).

We know then, from copious reports of past life regression sessions, that trauma or negative thoughts or attitudes can just as easily arise from a previous lifetime and that this can leave its residues in the unconscious mind. Indian yoga doctrine has always held that psychic and physical dispositions to negativity, to reiterated trauma, and to emotional patterning are passed from one life to another via the entity called the subtle body. The closest we have in the West to this idea is the astrological chart, which posits that we are born with all our psychic and physical dispositions laid down at birth in seed form like a blueprint. The past life perspective, as more and more therapists are realising, can often open up places where conventional therapy – which only probes early experience in this life – has reached a dead end. Cases entailing past lives may be complex, but the interrelationship of the three levels – the mental, the emotional and the etheric – can be shown to operate equally across lifetimes. In other words, Reichian principles can be used to dramatise and physicalise past life stories as effectively as they can be applied to current life issues in therapy – and sometimes more so. To give a short example:

A woman in her fifties, whom I shall call Veronica, had suffered since late adolescence from severe sinusitis. She had undergone all kinds of medical treatment, which had proven ineffective. Conventional psychotherapy revealed a connection between the onset of her chronic sinusitis and a certain residual sense of loneliness and mild depression but, failing to find any loss or obvious emotional upheaval around adolescence, therapy basically failed to change her condition. During a weekend introduction to past life therapy, Veronica had the following experience. She found herself reliving the past life of a young Englishman, who had grown up in an orphanage and who was conscripted into the army at the outbreak of the Great War in 1914. Like so many raw recruits, his combat experience was tragically short. He died within weeks of arriving in the trenches when a mustard gas assault wiped out his whole unit.

The short period of boot camp and the camaraderie of the trenches had been one of intense emotional opening for this young man. As Veronica relived his death, she fell into paroxysms of intense weeping, which were clearly mixed with painful choking. When the lengthy catharsis was over, she reported that she had realised that the young man's untimely death by asphyxiation had prevented him from grieving for his lost comrades in arms.

She also reported that her sinuses had fully cleared for the first time in 30 years. The unfinished grief from the adolescent period of the past life had apparently been unconsciously reactivated when she was in adolescence, but because of the choking trauma the tears of the past life had remained lodged, as it were, in her sinuses. All her problems with loneliness in this life and her fears about committing to relationships for fear that they would not last, immediately became clear to her.

In this case, which is typical of many, the release clearly begins on both the etheric and the emotional levels when both the sense of loss and the choking memory, now made conscious from the other life, surface spontaneously. The possibility of releasing the original feelings of grief had been blocked by the gassing trauma, so they had become imprinted, along with the choking, at an etheric level of subtle body transmission. To release one was, therefore, to release the other. Hence the unblocking of Veronica's sinuses, which had been mimicking the fatal gas attack with all its unexpressed sadness all those years.

It was also extremely important for Veronica to realise why she felt so bereft in the past life and to make the connection to her present life. This completed the clearing of the mental level of the past life scar, without which she could easily have fallen back into old emotional patterns. She was now able, with the help of verbal affirmations, to reverse negative thoughts like, 'I'm all alone, friendships never last', into 'I'm never alone: my friendships are growing and getting deeper all the time'.

When all three levels of clearing are not taken into account, there is often reversion to the earlier pattern. For example, certain bodyworkers whose sole focus is the body, as in Rolfing and chiropractic, will sometimes admit privately that often with the most skilled work of realignment and rebalancing at a postural or energy level, their clients will often revert to old patterns. This is due, I believe, to the fact that when the emotional and mental levels of the posture or organic complaint have not been allowed to surface, they continue to exert negative influence on the etheric body to the detriment of the physical organism. A woman who chronically holds deeply in her pelvis because she feels unconsciously that 'I mustn't let go of it' when 'it' means a baby she once miscarried in a trauma, will only experience temporary relief from deep tissue work until she is also able to relinquish the mental injunction to 'hold on tight'.

Equally, certain types of therapy that only stress emotional cathartic release can often get stuck. In my practice I have often found clients who cannot get out of certain so-called 'primal' emotions from early childhood, because the meaning of the trauma had not been raised in their previous therapy. Early childhood abandonment is so often a re-run of a past life trauma of a similar, but often more severe, nature that it frequently requires only a minimum of further probing into a past life background to arrive at insight and the beginning of healing. In such a way, for example, a client of mine reported: 'I see now why being separated from my mother at three, when she went to hospital, was so agonising: I had lost my mother at three in a past life, when she was killed by soldiers, and I myself died shortly afterwards.'

Therapeutic strategies in past life bodywork

When working with clients who either have presenting complaints that are somatic as well as psychological or who have a history of recurrent illness or accidents, I have arrived at a number of rules of thumb:

1   When taking a case history, I always make sure the client tells me all his or her physical illnesses, accidents or impairments (deafness, needing glasses, high blood pressure, etc.). When noting them, I ask if any emotional upheaval occurred shortly before or around the same period of their life.
2   When the client is describing the particular presenting problem or symptom, I ask them to describe what they are experiencing in their body as they talk to me.
3   During the actual regression I ensure that the person reports the entire story from within the body, not from some disembodied vantage point (see also Woolger 1986).
4   During the session, I note all physical movements – tightening up, contortions, shallow breathing, etc. – especially when a trauma is being relived but little emotion is being released.
5   I encourage those parts of the body that are reacting to the story (as in 3) to express themselves, either physically or in words, or both. For example, with tight legs I might say, 'Let yourself kick. Good! Now let your legs do what they want to do to this person. Let them kick!' The client then shouts, 'Get away from me, you pig!' kicking a mattress representing the brutalising figure imagined from the past life story.
6   Whenever there is a specific pain reported or an organic problem, have the client focus in on the pain or the afflicted area, taking their consciousness right into its core and allowing images and feelings to emerge spontaneously. It is helpful to use guiding phrases such as 'What is the pain like? Is it sharp or dull? Does it come from inside your body or outside? What might be causing it? What does your body feel like doing?'

Essentially we are encouraging an image to unfold via the analogy implicit in the highly-potent little phrase 'as if': 'It's as if my back were being beaten; it's as if my head is being crushed; it's as if my belly has been cut open' etc.

The last technique, of taking consciousness into the pain or afflicted area, is one well-known to practitioners of Buddhist Vipassana meditation. Steven Levine makes extremely valuable use of it in counselling individuals who are terminally ill (Levine 1984). Here is a short example of how I have used it in past life therapy.

Charlene was a career woman who had assiduously avoided any relationships that might lead to marriage. She had had a series of relationships where men left her for someone else, severely damaging her self-esteem. She was troubled by the discovery of cysts in both her breasts but wished to avoid surgery if at all possible. I had her focus in on the hardened areas in her breasts and let any feelings and words surface. 'They're quite hard and useless. It's so sad. I'm so tired. It's as though they've dried up. I've nothing to give.' With hardly any direction, she found herself in an industrial city in the north of England in the early 1800s. She was a young woman sitting against a wall slowly dying of starvation, with a baby futilely trying to suckle from her. The full extent of her bitterness and despair dawned upon her: 'I don't have anything to give. I'm disgusted with myself and my breasts'. Charlene was soon able to see that at a deep emotional level she had rejected herself as a nurturing mother and was carrying this old memory of failure in her breasts. The negative thoughts that went with this also contributed to her being rejected by men; she was really rejecting herself and the maternal function of her body. Her therapy consisted in forgiving the past life body, dialoguing with the lost child, and reaffirming her potential as a mother and a woman.

The case of Mike: public speaking anxiety

Mike was a social worker who consulted me because he had panic attacks every time he had to make any kind of presentation to his colleagues at meetings. About an hour before the appointed time of a meeting, he reported, he would get uncontrollably nervous. His chest would get very tight, his breathing became constricted, and he would experience severe heart palpitations. In Mike's case I did not need to encourage him to be aware of his body since he described his state so vividly: 'My palms are starting to sweat as I talk about it,' he said. He also described a tight chest and stomach.

Were these reactions new? By no means. Mike recognised them from childhood, where he remembered a painful experience at a talent show he had been forced to perform in. The overriding feelings then as now were of fear and shame. And yet, neither as a child nor as an adult could he find any memory of anyone actually doing anything to humiliate or shame him. Here is a condensed extract of how our exploration of these feelings and somatic reactions proceeded.

Th: So what does it feel like every time you go into one of your staff meetings?

Mike: Terrible panic. I feel like I'm gonna die. (*Touches his chest.*)

Everything feels like it's gonna shut down. I can feel my heart beating like crazy when I talk about it now.

Th: So what thoughts go with this? You're clearly in a huge conflict.

Mike: I've got to do it, but I don't wanna do it. Oh, my God! No! How do I get out of it? (*His stomach seems to be tensing up and his arms are becoming rigid.*)

Th: What does your stomach want to say?

Mike: I don't want to do it. How do I get out of this? Oh God! It's this terrible sinking feeling. My chest is all tight and my stomach feels like it's gonna drop out.

Th: Stay with the feelings and what your stomach wants to say and just follow it.

Mike: I don't want to. I want to be left alone. Please don't make me! No, not in front of them all! I'm trapped. I can't get out of it. (*He is noticeably writhing from side to side now.*)

Th: Let yourself go into any other life story these words apply to.

Mike: I get a church. And a crowd. Yes, lots of people . . . Oh no! I don't want to. Don't make me!

Th: Say that to them, not to me. Stay with the images and your body.

Mike: It's terrible, I'm afraid. I'm not gonna show my fear. They're making me go there. Oh help! My hands and neck! They're really hurting.

Th: What seems to be happening to you?

Mike: They've got my wrists bound behind me. Something touching my face. I can't see. Now it's my neck. Oh help! They're gonna hang me!

Th: I want you to go all the way through it until it's over. The pain will pass, but it needs to be released. Keep saying exactly what you feel as it happens.

Mike's breathing now became intense as he lay writhing on my mattress. He reported tingling in his hands and feet and increasing panic fear in his stomach. His struggle increased until the end. He was obviously fighting the execution all the way. I encouraged him to do so, since this was where all his tension was locked up.

Mike: I can't get out of it. I'm really stuck now. I don't wanna be part of this, but there's no way out. (*There are clearly elements of birth trauma in this part of the story.*)

Mike continued his death struggle as the hanged man for some while. He experienced huge electrical tingling in his hands, face, neck, chest and stomach. He kicked violently, reproducing the desperate attempts to touch the earth his former self has been deprived of. A huge etheric release happened as the parts of the body that had held the subtle body imprint of the trauma relived the event. Finally, his body went limp, as he reached the moment of the past life death. He wept, his chest heaving: 'There was nothing I could do.' There was more release and opening in his chest. His breathing expanded considerably when the trauma was past.

We took as long as he needed for the energy release to be complete and for all the feelings to be expressed and verbalised. Then we went back to the events that led up to the hanging. Mike remembered himself as an adolescent boy who had robbed a man and then, in a tussle, knifed him. He was caught by the villagers and brought to trial, where he was condemned to death by hanging. Mike remembered the jail cell, his huge public humiliation and, above all, the sense of doom and powerlessness that sat in his chest and stomach in the last hours before he was taken to the scaffold. Needless to say, as an adolescent in this story, his life force was very strong, which was mirrored in his physical resistance to dying. This is why I encouraged him physically to express all aspects of the struggle, to maximise the etheric release, aspects of which were clearly locked into his chest and stomach today.

The remainder of our work consisted in helping him disassociate the old trauma from its current life parallels. I suggested affirmations such as: 'I am on the earth. I am fully in charge (for his stomach). I am proud of my work. There is nothing to be ashamed of any longer.' One interesting corollary to his experience was that Mike then remembered that he had several times stolen unimportant things as a child, always feeling deeply ashamed and unworthy when he was caught. He realised how he had been unconsciously replaying the old story, testing to see if stealing would be as fatal as in the past life. He did not, until now, connect it to his public speaking anxiety.

In later sessions Mike reported almost total absence of panic feelings at meetings and a sense of greatly increased vitality and power in his life in general. The trapped and humiliated adolescent in him had been freed and was now contributing energy to his life instead of draining it.

The place of regression work in psychotherapy

The remission of Mike's symptoms in therapy was relatively fast; the presenting complaint was specific and situational, not deriving from any deep-seated character disorder. Phobic issues will often clear up very swiftly with this approach once images of a violent or sudden death are worked through imaginally, provided that there are no compounding elements such as deep guilt, remorse or shame to be faced. When the latter occur there will be a need for longer work that may require a kind of penitence and self-acceptance; often we are dealing with personality fragments Jung called the 'Shadow', images of the self incompatible with our conscious self-image. In these cases, as Jung put it, 'the whole personality is challenged'. One woman unable to accept sadistic impulses in herself finally saw a male past life self as a witch persecutor ordering the torture and burning of women. Not only was this hard to own but it required much remorse and inner revaluation before it was integrated.

Past life traumas that have involved long-term abuse from oppression, slavery, imprisonment and so on may also take considerably longer to work through since they often leave deep psychic scars of despair, depression and anaesthetisation. All that the Harvard School has found about post-traumatic therapy with current life survivors of torture and totalitarianism applies here and the therapy may be quite lengthy (Herman 1992; Van der Kolk et al. 1996). Painstaking and careful work with a primary therapist embracing transference issues of trust, shame, disclosure and alienation may be required. This therapist might decide to intersperse experiential sessions with the client as needed, but only within the framework of longer periods of conventional therapy which maintain a safe container to integrate split-off parts of the self, allow mourning, create good ego-boundaries, establish self-esteem and generally nurture healthy emotional responsiveness (see Herman 1992: Part II).

The case of Dorothy: blocked sexual response

Dorothy was a married woman in her thirties whose major presenting problem, as presented in a large public workshop, was that she had absolutely no sex drive with her husband. In fact she loathed being penetrated by him and, from her description, was in many respects genitally frigid. Many years of conventional therapy had failed to deliver her from the complaint. Dorothy had the courage to share her very painful problem with the large number of people present. (Her session was recorded, and has helped many people, both therapists and others who have heard it, so I am presenting here an abbreviated version of the essence of our work.)

As Dorothy sat down to work with me she admitted to tremendous fear as she confronted the problem. I encouraged her to close her eyes and stay in touch with the fear, which, as is so often the case, had nothing to do with the workshop, but was part of the story that wanted to surface.

Th: So what's happening for you right now?
Dorothy: My body's shaking and not as much, you know, but . . .
Th: What's making you cry?
D: I don't know.
Th: Okay, just stay with it. Take a little breath. Just say in your own words, anyway, what is troubling you deeply in your life right now.
D: I really love my husband but I just don't have a sex drive. It's like I feel that I really like holding and snuggling and just touching and spooning but when it comes to having intercourse, it's like it just stops, I just stop.

Th: Stay with that feeling, 'I just stop'. How do you just stop?

D: I don't know.

Th: You do know. What happens in your body when you stop?

D: It becomes rigid.

Th: Can you show me that? (*She draws her legs together and pulls her arms in.*) And where exactly is it rigid? Is it all the way down, all the way up?

D: Yes, it just feels like it is rigid.

Th: Just stay with that rigidity right now. You can exaggerate it if you like. What words or thoughts come? Something like 'I don't want to?'

D: Just don't touch me. I don't want to.

Th: Stay with 'Don't touch me'. Remember this may become some-one else other than your husband, so just let anything come. I just want you to go with those words 'don't touch me'. (*I encourage her to repeat these words several times and any others that come.*)

D: Don't touch me. I don't want it . . . I just don't want it. I don't have to do this. I just don't have to do this. (*She speaks angrily now.*)

Th: What are your legs doing?

D: Tight. My dress is being pushed up. It's long . . . I'm trying to push it down.

Th: You're trying to push it down, and your legs are trying to do what?

D: Just be tight.

Th: What are your legs saying?

D: I don't know, but there's a sword, I see a sword. I see some legs. (*She is very tense now.*)

Th: Breathe! And your body is still tight? Just let the images come.

D: I see this green on his legs . . . He's trying to have sex with me and I don't want it.

Th: Tell him that.

D: I don't want it. I don't have to, I don't want it . . .

Th: Go on. Loud as you like!

D: I DON'T WANT IT! You don't have to do this. You do not have any right. He's saying it's his right. He's my husband and it's his right. I'm saying no . . . I have to stop him . . . I just want to hit him. . . .

Th: Feel it in your body . . . Just say all the words that come.

D: You bastard! . . . I don't have to do this. I'll never do this again. Never going to do this again . . . It's not right.

I helped point Dorothy's awareness to how this phrase 'I'm never going to do this again' underlay her sexual resistance to her husband. Almost immediately she reported that she was not feeling it any more, that it was gone.

I had her look back to see what happened and a gruesome scene emerged. The husband had killed her, apparently thrusting his sword into her genitals. There was blood everywhere. She did not recognise the woman. It was clearly a past-life self.

On my further questioning Dorothy was still aware of tension in her genitals. This alerted me to the fact that the trauma was by no means cleared. There was still a lot of emotional hurt and anger locked in there, so I encouraged her to express these feelings from her wounded genitals.

D: He used his sword. Damn him. Damn you! . . .
Th: Loud as you like!
D: DAMN YOU!
Th: Any other words in there to say to him?
D: You'll never do this again! (*Having her address these words directly to the past-life husband is important; they belong to this man, not her present husband.*)

I helped Dorothy see and remember the whole of this bloody death, checking out whether there were still any feelings being held in the body. I asked her to breathe to any parts of her body where she felt pain, since the breath facilitates etheric release. It seemed that we had already reached the core of the wounded area, for very shortly she said:

D: It doesn't hurt any more . . .
Th: Are you in the body still? What are you getting?
D: This blue-green light, really beautiful.
Th: Yes, stay with that light. I want you to be in the blue and green light; but also look back and see that body on the ground with all the blood . . .
D: She's not on the ground, she's on a chaise or something.
Th: I just want you to be aware that you're not in that body now.

At this point, we reached an important opportunity for detaching from the trauma completely. The etheric release seemed complete since there was no more pain and her legs were quite relaxed now. In addition, the emotional release had been accomplished by expressing the buried hurt and rage at her cruel past-life husband. To help consolidate all this I suggested some affirmations.

D: I'm not in that body now. I let go of all the pain that woman felt. I let go of the trauma in my genitals. I let go of trauma all over my body.

And because of the very negative thought, 'I'll never do this again', I had her repeat at the end of the session, an important affirmation to re-own her body and her sexuality:

D: It's OK to do it again. It won't kill me this time.

What this case demonstrates is that it is possible to work through quite severe trauma very effectively provided that the whole body is engaged. When fully encouraged, etheric and emotional release can be accomplished very swiftly. Painful as it looks to the observer, it is actually a huge relief for the experiencer, as everyone in the workshop could attest from the way Dorothy looked after our work.

Many psychotherapists whom I have watched work with severe death memories like this order the client out of the body when trauma arises, invoking healing guides, white light or colour, often instructing them 'just to watch.'[6] This may seem to work, but I have found more often than not, that such strategies are merely temporary, only driving the trauma further into hiding, that is to say deeper into the body. Essentially they serve to dissociate the client, reinforcing rather than breaking down a hitherto necessary schizoid or dissociative defense whereby the client early on gave themself the message 'I'm not feeling this'. The late Californian therapist Alice Givens, who specialised in cathartic regression to childhood as well as past life scenes of abuse, claimed that the dissociative phenomena so common in such scenes – 'I'm watching him doing things to me from up on the ceiling,' for example – displayed a form of defensive auto-hypnosis.

'The victim is in complete hypnosis,' she wrote, 'because the fear and pain paralyze the critical factors of the conscious mind' (Givens 1991: 156). Another well known American therapist, Jack Schwarz, who became an expert at working with severe physical pain, used to graphically demonstrate how it is possible to self-anaesthetise specific areas of the body, maintaining that we can do this in times of extreme stress (Schwarz 1980). Himself a survivor of a Nazi camp where he had learned to do this under torture, he often publically demonstrated pain control by hypnotising his own arm and then piercing it fully with a long knitting needle. As R.D. Laing also put it: 'I consider many adults are or have been in a hypnotic trance: we remain in this state until we dead awake and find that we have never lived.' (Laing 1971, cited in Givens 1991: 156).

We saw with Dorothy that when genuine, as opposed to temporary release, occurred she experienced peace, the dispersal of her genital pain, the spontaneous (unguided) appearance of a blue-green healing light, and full insight into her symptoms. In subtle body language, she had cleared old traumatic imprints lodged in her body at the etheric, the emotional, and the mental levels, leaving her free to pursue a happy and fulfilled sex-life with her husband.

Conclusion

Where the past life based approach to trauma and somaticised complexes differs from most conventional therapies – including the Reichian schools – is that it takes the position that the soul is much greater than the ego-personality; a position to be found strongly in Jung, James Hillman (1977) and in the work of recent transpersonal psychologists. Thus the traumas that may surface during the therapeutic exploration of the current life may have other levels or deeper resonances to them. Often the releasing of trauma with this approach is like peeling skins from an onion. In other words, not only must we posit that the psyche is multidimensional but that the sufferings of the soul exist in a variety of subtle forms not restricted to the gross body or the immediate constraints of time and space. Such awareness, difficult as it is for the materialist to grasp, may take us into surprising depths and heights within the psyche.[7] Compared to the great psycho-spiritual disciplines of the East, Western psychotherapy is still in its infancy and is still learning to work with other dimensions of the soul such as residues of previous lives, ancestral memories or the influence of spiritual healing from other realms. And, like much uncharted territory, we would be wise to regard most maps and reports – like this one – as purely provisional, and remain open to making constant revisions as new vistas open up.

Notes

1 It is my belief that we could all do with looking at our 'karmic' issues, both physical and psychic, and stop the perpetual scapegoating of our parents. And we would all benefit from practising something like meditation and integrating our psychological work with our spiritual lives. I recommend all my clients bodywork, meditation and dreamwork as adjuncts to what I do.

2 'Modern science with the atomic theory admits that all matter is composed of the same prime material – electricity. But where this oriental theory differs with Western science is when the Hindus claim that this prime material – Akasha – can be changed by means of the mind, not by mechanical methods' (Shah 1973: 127).

3 The four states of matter are: solids, liquids, gases and matter. Inyushin's classic statement is his paper *Bioplasma: the Fifth State of Matter?* (n.d.), which can be found in White and Krippner's *Future Science* (1977).

4 For a unique and learned examination of the Western philosophical problem of mind-body dualism in terms of both the subtle body and modern psychology, see Avens (1982).

5 See Grof's valuable exposition of the application of the holonomic principle in psychology in his *Beyond the Brain* (1985). See also the present author's chapter 'The Multi-dimensional Psyche' in *Other Lives, Other Selves* (Woolger 1987).

6 There are major schools of hypnotherapy as well as therapists using techniques like 'colour therapy', 'guided visualisation therapy', etc. – all calling themselves *psychotherapists* – who believe physical traumas like rape can be healed by dissociating from the body, by altering body images, by loving forgiveness and by totally by-passing catharsis. This population represents, in my experience of talking at conferences to hundreds of US therapists over the years, maybe 40–50 per cent of the

professional population. Perhaps in Britain there is some consensus about what a psychotherapist does, but this is by no means the case in the US. Certainly I have met hypnotherapists in Britain who are against all catharsis as a matter of principle. It is, alas, an ongoing controversy.

7 I have argued for the multidimensional nature of the soul and the spiritual interface in psychotherapy in *The Presence of Other Worlds in Psychotherapy and Healing* (Woolger 2002).

References

Alexander, F. M. *The Resurrection of the Body*. New York: Dell 1971

Assagioli, R. *Psychosynthesis*. New York: Viking Press 1965

Avens, R. *Imaginal Body: Para-Jungian Reflections on Soul, Imagination and Death*. Washington: University of America Press 1982

Bailey, A. *Esoteric Healing*. New York: Lucis Trust 1953

Boadella, D. *Wilhem Reich: The Evolution of his Work*. London: Arkana 1985

Brennan, B. *Hands of Light*. New York: Bantam 1988

Boorstein, S. (Ed.) *Transpersonal Psychotherapy*. New York: SUNY Press 1996

Dethlefsen, T. and Dahlke, R. *The Healing Power of Illness*. Shaftsbury, UK: Element 1990

Dychtwald, K. *Body-Mind*. New York: Pantheon 1977

Fiore, E. *You Have Been Here Before*. New York: Ballantine 1979

Gerber, R. *Vibrational Medicine*. Boulder, CO: Bear 1988

Givens, Alice M. *The Process of Healing*. San Diego, CA: Libra Books 1991

Grof, S. *Beyond the Brain*. New York: SUNY Press 1985

Hillman, J. *Re-Visioning Psychology*. New York: Harper 1977

Herman, J. *Trauma and Recovery*. New York: Harper 1992

Jung, C. G. 'The Archetypes and the Collective Unconscious'. In *Collected works*, Vol. 9, Part 1. Princeton: Princeton University Press 1959

Jung. C. G. 'Psychology and Religion'. In *Psychology and Religion, Collected Works*, Vol. 11. Princeton: Princeton University Press 1969

Jung, C. G. 'A Review of the Complex Theory' In *The Structure and Dynamics of the Psyche, Collected Works*, Vol. 8. Princeton: Princeton University Press 1969 [1934]

Keleman, S. *Your Body Speaks its Mind*. New York: Simon and Schuster 1975

Krippner, S. and Rubin, D. *Galaxies of Life: The Human Aura in Acupuncture and Kirlian Photography*. New York: Gordon and Beach 1973

Krippner, S. and Villoldo, A. *The Realms of Healing*. California: Celestial Arts, Millbrae 1976

Krippner, S. and Villoldo, A. *Healing States*. New York: Simon and Schuster 1986

Kurtz, R. and Prestera, H. *The Body Reveals*. New York: Harper 1976

Levine, S. *Meetings at the Edge*. New York: Doubleday Anchor 1984

Locke, S. and Colligen, D. *The Healer Within: the New Medicine of Mind and Body*. New York: Dutton 1986

Lorimer, D. (Ed.) *Network: The Scientific and Medical Network Review*, No. 65. Fife, Scotland 1997

Lowen, A. *Bioenergetics*. New York: Penguin Books 1977

Lucas, W. (Ed.) *Regression Therapy: A Handbook for Professionals*, 2 vols. CA: Crest Park 1993

Mead, G. R. S. *The Doctrine of the Subtle Body in Western Tradition*. London: Watkins 1919

Moss, T. and Johnson, K. 'Bioplasma or corona discharge'. In S. Krippner and D. Rubin (Eds) *Galaxies of Life: The Human Aura in Acupuncture and Kirlian Photography*. New York: Gordon and Breach 1973

Netherton, M. and Shiffren, N. *Past Lives Therapy*. New York: Morrow 1978

Pierrakos, J. C. *Core Energetics*. Mendocino, CA: Life Rhythm 1978

Regush, N. M. (Ed.) *The Human Aura*. New York: Berkeley Medallion 1974

Regush, N. M. (Ed.) *Frontiers of Healing*. New York: Avon Books 1977

Reich, W. *Character Analysis*. New York: Farrar, Straus & Giroux 1949

Rowan, J. *The Transpersonal: Psychotherapy and Counselling*. London: Routlege 1993

Schwarz, J. *Human Energy Systems*. New York: Dutton 1980

Shah, I. *Oriental Magic*. New York: Dutton 1973

Stevenson, I. *Reincarnation and Biology: A Contribution to the Biology of Birthmarks and Birth Defects*, 2 vols. VA: Praeger 1997

Tansley, D. *Subtle Body, Essence and Shadow*. New York: Thames and Hudson 1977

Tart, C. *States of Consciousness*. New York: Dutton 1975

Van der Kolk, B, McFarlane, A.C. and Weisaeth, L. (Eds) *Traumatic Stress*. New York: Guilford Press 1966

Weiss, B. *Many Lives, Many Masters*. New York: Simon and Schuster 1990

White, J. (Ed) *Kundalini, Evolution and Enlightenment*. New York: Doubleday 1979

White, J. and Krippner, S. *Future Science*. New York: Doubleday 1977

Woods, J. H. (trans.) *The Yoga Sutras of Patanjali*. Cambridge, MA: Harvard 1927

Woolger, R. J. 'Imaginal Techniques in Past Life Therapy', *Journal of Regression Therapy* 1986 1(1)

Woolger, R. J. *Other Lives, Other Selves*. New York: Doubleday 1987

Woolger, R. J. 'Past-Life Regression Therapy'. In Boorstein, S. (Ed.) *Transpersonal Psychotherapy*, New York: SUNY Press 1996

Woolger, R. J. *'The Presence of Other Worlds in Psychotherapy and Healing'* in Lorimer, D. (Ed.) *Beyond the Brain*. Edinburgh: Floris Books 2002

Zimmer, H. *Philosophies of India*. Princeton: Princeton University Press 1952

Chapter 10

The future for body psychotherapy

Nick Totton

Introduction

There seems little doubt – and the publication of this volume supports the view – that body psychotherapy now has a secure place within the range of therapeutic styles and approaches. Certainly it is vulnerable to some types of criticism, which portray it as 'wild', dangerous, unboundaried, potentially exploitative. Certainly it is never likely to become the dominant therapeutic modality – at any rate, not until huge social and cultural changes take place! But neither, it seems, is it going to disappear nor become wholly marginalised. There are enough strong and eloquent voices speaking from within the body psychotherapy community, enough skilled and sensitive practitioners, and enough satisfied clients, to ensure a future. So the next question is: What is body psychotherapy's appropriate agenda for that future?

In this chapter I propose to explore the thesis that the core project should now be for body psychotherapy to become a coherent discipline, in which training and supervisory practice inform and are informed by clinical practice, and all these likewise inform and are informed by metapsychological theory. This thesis seems to me a strong one; but in what follows I want to 'rattle and shake' it, to test it against several other strong ideas which seem to pull in other directions. At the end of the chapter I will consider whether or not the original thesis has survived. Entwined with this is the exploration of another idea: that body psychotherapy, by its nature and by its history, has an inescapable involvement with certain political and cultural, not to mention professional, controversies.

One or many body psychotherapies?

I should make it clear immediately that I am not suggesting the many distinct traditions and approaches of body psychotherapy should amalgamate into some lumpy and implausible whole. The current tendency to ecumenicism in psychotherapy has its good and bad aspects; but it seems to me wholly unhelpful to pretend that there is a single, generic activity of psychotherapy, to which the range of existing approaches and disciplines are relatively minor variations – wrinkles and local colour applied to an activity which is fundamentally the same throughout. Nothing could be further from the truth; the term 'psychotherapy' is an umbrella covering activities which have very little of significance in common with each other. The label is still useful – after all, how much do whales and giraffes, both mammals, have in common? – but it is perhaps not useful in some of the ways in which centralisers try to use it. In other words, there is perhaps no single, central, generic activity of psychotherapy to be identified.

Projects of professionalisation will eventually have to reckon with this indigestible truth; so far, however, it is generally blandly ignored and, like every other broad grouping, body psychotherapy is being encouraged to affiliate, federate, and iron out differences in the interests of both self-protection and 'scientific validation'. I shall try to show in this chapter that such a homogenising project produces confusion rather than coherence and that, in fact, a greater degree of pluralism and outright difference is to be encouraged. 'Coherence' does not mean 'homogeneity' – far from it; what it does mean is that gradations and thresholds of difference are clearly articulated and placed within some overarching, sense-making context. I shall be trying to do some of this in what follows.

Does body psychotherapy exist?

Beyond the question of homogeneity, however, there is a real and basic question as to whether 'body psychotherapy' actually constitutes a meaningful category; a 'mainstream', as the European Association for Body Psychotherapy (EABP) calls it. Might it not rather be the case that very different forms of work have come together to circle the wagons because of hostile external pressures – uniting not around a central commonality but around the shared factor in our work that causes us to attract other people's criticism and suspicion? Perhaps 'body psychotherapy' is as much a defensive tactical alliance as it is an authentic identity.

The emphasis on 'body' as our most significant shared characteristic in a sense reinforces the Cartesian split of 'body' from 'mind' which many of us wish to put into question. A more confrontational approach might argue that we are in fact psychotherapists in the full sense, relating to body, mind and (hopefully) spirit, while others are restricted to verbal psychotherapy alone. Over the past decade or so organisations in this field have tended to move from self-descriptions such as 'holistic psychotherapy' to 'body psycho-therapy' – not (one trusts) because their work suddenly ceased to be holistic but to conform with the terminology taken up by the EABP. Why is 'body psychotherapy' to be preferred over 'holistic' or 'bodymind'? I suggest that the reasons are political – ultimately, a question of 'spin'. Like the developing child, our practice and terminology do not exist in a vacuum, but are conditioned by the surrounding environment; in many aspects they constitute defences – more or less creative – against that environment. Accepting the 'body psychotherapy' label has certain resemblances to Native Americans accepting the reservation: a homeland which is secure in some limited ways but also is marginal and restricted.

Body psychotherapy as a science

Defence and defensiveness are important issues here, because body psychotherapy (as I will continue to call it) very easily feels itself vulnerable to attack or dismissal. It can be marginalised – or fears that it can be marginalised – as freakish, new age, eccentric, dangerous and generally 'unprofessional'. Hence the decision of the EABP to accede to the bizarre requirements of the European Association for Psychotherapy (EAP), and seek to justify body psychotherapy as a scientifically evidential undertaking. Again, the effect of this is the opposite of coherence: much of the theory and practice of body psychotherapy militates against such a positioning, and an attempt to achieve it involves amputating, ignoring or camouflaging aspects of our work.

This issue of scientific validity demonstrates very clearly the political dimension of theory, in psychotherapy as in other fields. The EAP adopted its interpretation of psychotherapy – that it is 'an independent scientific discipline', training in which 'takes place at an advanced, qualified and scientific level' – primarily under pressure from its Austrian members: in Austria, only 'scientific' forms of psychotherapy are legal. The EABP, in turn, has decided that it needs to accede to this view in order to safeguard the careers of its members not only in Austria (where body psychotherapy is not currently accepted as scientific), but across Europe, since the EAP proposes to award European Certificates of Psychotherapy conferring the right to work as a psychotherapist in any European country.

Thus the theoretical base of body psychotherapy – its identification as a science rather than, say, a craft, an art, a spiritual or educational practice, or a form of folk-healing – derives not from an intellectual conclusion but from a political constraint, a perceived need to act defensively in the face of external power. One should acknowledge that the document produced by the EABP to satisfy the EAP's requirements (50 pages long with 145 pages of appendices) is a remarkable achievement, plainly exhilarating to create, and a valuable summary of the evidential base and scientific linkages of body psychotherapy (the document can be found on the EABP website at http://www.eabp.org).

However, it does not address the fundamental question of whether or not body psychotherapy, or psychotherapy in general, should be conceived of as a scientific enterprise (nor, indeed, on which bit of science it should base itself; science is not a monolithic entity). More than one body psychotherapist has argued in print against this identification, including two of those centrally involved in drafting the EABP response (Young and Heller 2000; cf.

Totton 2000). Richard Grossinger, in his towering work *Planet Medicine* (Grossinger 1995), has argued at length that body psychotherapy should be considered, along with techniques like herbalism and homeopathy, as one of humanity's primal systems of healing, originating in Palaeolithic shamanism.

Energy

Any serious attempt to position Body Psychotherapy as scientific – or indeed, to give it theoretical coherence at all – would need to address the concept of 'body energy' or its variants, which is widely used by Reichians, post-Reichians and neo-Reichians of all stripes, as well as by several other varieties of bodyworkers. For the more orthodox Reichians, this simply means orgone, which they regard as a scientifically demonstrable cosmic energy fundamental to living and non-living processes. There is no point in trying to fudge this issue, or to pretend that believing in an unrecognised cosmic energy is a minor matter! The cold truth is that, rightly or wrongly, it places you firmly on the intellectual fringes, at any rate until science catches up with you.

Many other body psychotherapists, though, speak of 'energy' in a much looser and vaguer way but as a concept that is often actually fairly central to their practice: they decide how to approach a client by their assessment of the state of the client's energy, and the perceived movement and variation in body energy gives them crucial feedback on the effect of their interventions. For example, the Chiron Training web page says that

> Even when a session might look to an observer similar to any other form of psychotherapy – two people sitting together talking – a Chiron therapist would be using their perception of the client's energetic presence to gain a sense of all levels of the client's communication. The client would experience this mainly as a sense of being really listened to, and fully responded to. In using the word 'energetic' we are referring to the body/mind as a dynamic system, so that any look, gesture, phrase, etc. contains the essence (the energy) of an individual's life story.
>
> http://www.chironcentre.freeserve.co.uk/training.htm

Many body psychotherapists would probably feel that they understand what is being quite eloquently described here. Most other people, however, would be baffled – especially any sort of physical scientist, who would conclude that the word 'energy' is being used here in a very unusual sense and certainly not with its conventional thermodynamic meaning. And even body psychotherapists might find it very difficult to justify this sort of language. How, exactly, is the 'essence' of someone's life story a sort of 'energy'? How metaphorical or how literal is one being in talking like this? Is 'energy' – here and in other bodywork usages – a description of emotional tone, what Daniel Stern calls 'vitality affect' (Stern 1985: 53–60; cf. Totton 1998: 166–169); or is it referring to the equivalent of an aura, or chi, or prana? (Orgone, aura, chi and prana, although very broadly parallel, are distinct and precise concepts that cannot be loosely thrown together: they have separate and specific qualities. For example, orgone is bluish, and has an affinity to water; the aura is a multi-layered, multi-coloured field, rather than a flow; chi flows up the back of the body and down the front, and is focused in the hara below the solar plexus; prana is a fiery energy which follows a specific network of channels in the body known as the 'nadis'. One cannot do acupuncture with orgone, or Reichian therapy with chi.) What sort of evidential status is being claimed when bodyworkers speak of 'energy', and what sort of research has been or should be done? Talking about 'energetics' instead of energy may sound impressive, but makes little real difference.

Most body psychotherapists do not have clear answers to these questions, and there can be very different views on whether this matters. Certainly it does matter, though, if we are trying to stake a claim to a niche in the mainstream. If issues such as body energy are played down, then effectively we are performing a masquerade, an attempt to pass for something we are not. This seems to me an ongoing issue for body psychotherapists: how honest are we being in our public presentations as to how we really think about our own work?

Theory

Whether considered as a science or otherwise, it is plain that body psychotherapy does not rest upon a single theoretical base. Historically speaking, body psychotherapy in the Reichian tradition derives from one very specific theoretical model: psychoanalytic drive theory. I argue in an earlier chapter of this volume – and indeed have written an entire book (Totton 1998) to argue – that Wilhelm Reich's work is deeply committed to drive theory, and makes sense of it in ways which Freud failed to do. Drive theory is, so far, the sole psychoanalytic approach that addresses body-mind unity.

However, drive theory has gone out of fashion; also, Reich was expelled from the psychoanalytic movement, and most of his heirs have identified more with the Humanistic or growth movement in psychotherapy. As a result, many forms of body psychotherapy try to marry a body-oriented practice with some theoretical model other than drive theory – either Humanistic (Gestalt, co-counselling, person-centred) or psychoanalytic (object relations, ego psychology, attachment theory) – or to 'integrate' more than one of these. These marriages are not easy; frequently, they have not been properly worked through, and can amount to simply adding ' . . . and the body' to each proposition of the theory concerned.

One may intuitively agree – as I do – that an object-relational body psychotherapy or a person-centred body psychotherapy are viable undertakings (or, more properly, that holistic psychotherapy in these and other modes is viable); but still point out that the necessary work has not yet been done to understand and articulate what this would entail – for example, how the relationship between the psychic and somatic aspects of experience is to be conceived within these approaches. (The best claim to being an exception here is that of Gestalt therapy, which has a thoroughly worked-out body-mind theory; however, the research on which this theory was originally based is now very outdated.)

Another way of putting this is to ask whether what is needed is a theory of body psychotherapy (i.e. holistic psychotherapy), or a theory of psychotherapy which can be extended to body-oriented techniques. The latter is much easier to provide than the former, because most existing forms of psychotherapy are still enmeshed in the prevailing mind-body dualism of our culture. So far, only psychoanalytic drive theory comes close to providing an intelligible picture of how the actual unity of psyche and soma can give rise to an experience of mind alienated from body. (D.W. Winnicott sketched some very important and suggestive ideas on this from an object relations point of view (e.g. Winnicott 1949: 243–254), but they have yet to be developed.) A model is almost certainly possible which will go beyond and improve upon drive theory; no doubt this will incorporate insights from neuroscience (e.g. Taylor 1992: 464–488; Schore 1994; Damasio 1996, 2000), from developmental research (e.g. Stern 1985; Bermudez et al. 1995) and from philosophy (e.g. Cataldi 1993; Lakoff and Johnson 1999), as well as from many areas of psychotherapy. We should, however, face the fact that, despite much exciting work, this model does not yet exist.

It may be felt that this lack is not crucial since integration of different therapeutic approaches really happens on an experiential rather than a theoretical level. Most forms of psychotherapy are to some extent effective in the hands of their better practitioners (Mair 1992; Seligman 1995); and perhaps our theoretical orientation, insofar as it develops beyond what we inherit in our training, is more truly a reflection of unconscious process than of conscious cogitation (Samuels 1989: 5, 217). Integration, then, becomes – as Tree Staunton described it in response to an earlier draft of this chapter – 'a process of a therapist attempting to bring together different aspects of themselves which they have projected' into various forms of psychotherapy.

This is certainly a crucial aspect of integration, to which we will return. But is it enough? Doesn't a core theoretical model need to be intellectual as well as experiential? One might say that 'experience' is unconscious theory (just as 'theory' is unconscious experience); and as therapists should know, theorisation, the testing of experience against conceptual models, is a vital way to safeguard creative integration against unconscious distortion and acting-out. Thus the relationship between conscious and unconscious aspects of our core theories can be maintained as a constructive dialogue.

A strong argument has however been made that no core theoretical model is required, or indeed perhaps is possible, in psychotherapy. This has been well put by Colin Feltham:

> It is difficult to defend the position that any one model ... can adequately prepare therapists to help most clients referred to them. ... Insistence on a core model perpetuates a tradition-driven model of psychotherapy rather than one based on empiricism.
>
> Feltham 1997: 119–120; cf. Feltham 1999

Arnold Mindell, the founder of Process Oriented Psychology, proposes further that

> Work with clients shows clearly that specific psychotherapies ... are spontaneous creations which arise by amplifying events in given channels of the 'therapist-client' interaction even when the two are unfamiliar with these therapies. For instance, if the process worker ... amplifies a client's repeated tendency to stretch, yawn and groan, specific postures from ancient yoga and modern bioenergetics appear as part of a fluid flow of events.
>
> Mindell 1989: 8

In other words, for both authors from their very different perspectives, a truly adequate psychotherapy would not contain specialists in body-oriented work or verbal-oriented work, but generalists who were willing and competent to approach the uniqueness of each client from a unified body-mind perspective. Many body psychotherapists would agree with this, and strive towards that ideal in their own practice.

Mindell's work, however, does rest on a core theoretical model that, while generalist and pluralist, is also very precise and coherent; while Feltham's position seems finally to be that no adequate core model exists as yet, and that we need to become empiricists in order to generate the data from which such a model can be formed. Rejecting specialism does not have to mean rejecting theoretical coherence. Any empiricism must rest upon a notion of desired outcome, which constitutes, however minimally, a theory of human nature: in order to decide what empirically 'works', we need to decide what 'working' means, which involves knowing what we think human life should be like – or else concluding, like several Humanistic but few psychodynamic practitioners, that the client's conscious ego is the final arbiter of whether therapy has 'worked'. And even this position, of course, rests on a view of human nature! An explicitly-held theory is probably more helpful than an unowned and implicit one.

Three models for body psychotherapy

Assuming, then, that we are in search of a theory, and leaving aside numerous variants and sub-variants, we can identify three core models presently at work in body psychotherapy. In practice these are often not clearly described or distinguished from each other, and are often used in combination or in succession, despite the real intellectual contradictions between them. The models I have in mind can be called the Adjustment model, the Trauma/Discharge model, and the Process model. They do not operate solely in body psychotherapy, but are also found in a number of verbal modalities. Each of the models, though, as we shall see, has a particular importance and relevance for body psychotherapy. We cannot simply list which schools of therapy use which model because they cut across the boundaries between schools; generally all three are present, though with varying emphasis, in each system.

The first, Adjustment model, is now widely agreed to be inappropriate for a fully psychotherapeutic bodywork: it views therapy as a corrective treatment which realigns the body – physically, energetically, or both – and thus indirectly brings the mind back into a correct and desirable condition, of which the practitioner claims to have a privileged understanding. This view is clearly expressed in a passage from Lowen's classic work, *Bioenergetics*:

> A person's emotional life depends on the motility of his [sic] body, which in turn is a function of the flow of excitation throughout it. Disturbances of this flow occur as blocks ... Generally one can infer a block from seeing an area of deadness and sensing or palpating the muscular contraction that maintains it.
>
> Lowen 1976: 53

Hence, by removing these blocks and increasing the flow of energy one restores the patient to their healthy 'first nature', as opposed to the 'second nature' of neurosis (Lowen 1976: 107). The biggest limitations of this model – which Lowen inherits from one side of Reich's thinking – are first, that it crudely privileges the bodily over the psychological; second, that it has no room for an appreciation of the complex protective and expressive functions of bodily 'disfunctions', or for phenomena like ambivalence; and third, of course, that it assumes the therapist's right and ability to decide what is best for the client.

The Adjustment model is operating every time we use words like 'healthy', 'normal' or 'proper'. However hard we try to move away from this simple view, it is deeply embedded in the traditions of body therapy, and is not so easy to dispose of. For example, in David Boadella's well-received speech to the First Congress of the World Council of Psychotherapy, one finds this:

> As motility is freed, one of the key physiological anchorings of character

is loosened, with the result that outer movement expression becomes deeply connected to inner states of feeling; instead of flaccid or spastic states of armouring, the client connects with the gracefulness of movement.

Boadella 1997: 33

This is directly Reichian in tone and content and – as the case vignette to which Boadella moves on clearly shows – it is combined in Boadella's practice with both of the other two models I identify. However, it is worth insisting that this very familiar style of thinking about and looking at clients clearly privileges some particular concept of health and normality; and that, certainly in less skilled hands than Boadella's, such a style of thinking can set up a potentially stultifying transference/counter-transference clash, where the therapist struggles to impose 'cure' (here, 'gracefulness of movement') on a client whose unconscious is deeply invested in their so-called 'disfunction'. I shall return to this issue when I discuss supervision and ethics.

The second model is the powerful theory of traumatic shock and reparative emotional discharge first formulated in modern terms by Freud and Breuer, who identified the origins of hysteria as 'psychical traumas which have not been disposed of by abreaction' (Freud and Breuer 1991 [1893]: 66), and specifically related this to bodily symptoms and experiences. This continues to be a central model for many body psychotherapists. If the ruling metaphor of the Adjustment model is straightening a crooked limb, that of the Trauma/ Discharge model is expelling a splinter which has created painful swelling and inflammation around itself. We should note that usually the body itself expels the splinter; generally, the Trauma/Discharge model suggests that the practitioner's role is to support and encourage a natural healing.

Currently there is a strong movement in body psychotherapy towards a more gentle and gradual approach to working with trauma, which avoids 'retraumatising' the client and focuses on supporting their strength and competence, on managing the traumatic memory rather than reliving it. But the same basic model is still in play: that 'post-traumatic symptoms are, fundamentally, incomplete physiological responses suspended in fear,' which 'will not go away until the responses are discharged and completed' (Levine 1997: 34; cf. Rothschild 2000, which shifts the emphasis even further from 'discharge' to 'completion').

Modern trauma theory is an excellent tool for approaching specific psychological wounds in given individuals – the whole area currently conceptualised as 'post-traumatic stress disorder'. Again, though, I would identify several limitations to this approach (the concept of PTSD itself is usefully critiqued in Bracken and Petty 1998, and in Leys 2000). First, as generally employed the Trauma/Discharge model does not fully incorporate transference and counter-transference issues in the way that I advocate in my earlier chapter – in other words, it does not identify the therapeutic contact itself as a replication of trauma. In fact, it specifically tends to position the therapist as friend and ally.

As an extension of this, the model (especially in its more contemporary forms) often focuses on specifically and grossly traumatic events, and not sufficiently on the universal, sub-critical trauma of socialisation. And third, perhaps most importantly, the model may not address the profound questions about fantasy and external reality which trauma work raises, tending to assume a simple one-to-one relationship between what the client experiences in their bodymind, and what has historically occurred. Anyone who works with birthing experiences, for instance, knows that clients can have deep experiences of birth, both positive and negative, which are very different from their historical delivery. The more sophisticated contemporary trauma therapists certainly acknowledge that 'memories' are not always factual; but they offer few tools for working with the non-factual element.

Lastly, the Process model takes even further the idea of supporting a natural healing process; in fact, it drops the idea of 'healing' entirely, along with the idea of anything being wrong.

> If you want to help someone . . . turn the person inward towards experience. Don't turn them inward for explanations. Don't ask them why they feel that way – you're wrecking the process right there. You are taking the ship ashore. Don't ask for explanations. You don't need them. You don't need anything. It's not your problem. If you're being a therapist, just turn them inwards towards their experience. You don't need to understand a thing.
>
> Kurtz 1985: ii–iii

Working with the Process model, a therapist will allow the client's bodymind to guide the therapeutic journey, to act rather than be acted on, and to generate imagery and motifs freely and playfully. Hence the ruling metaphor here, rather than straightening a limb or expelling a splinter, is more like an improvised dance where the therapist follows the client.

The modern tradition of process-centred body psychotherapy originates with Reich's analysand Fritz Perls, and its most prominent current expressions are Process Oriented Psychology (e.g. Mindell 1985) and Hakomi (Kurtz 1985, 1990). Hakomi can in fact provide a useful example of the interaction of the three models I am describing. The Process model exists alongside a strong and systematic Trauma model, a system of 'sensitivity barriers' that responds to deficits or traumas in the childhood environment and gives rise to character structure. There is even a vestigial Adjustment model present here, as the following passage indicates:

> For example, the ability of the masochist to bear up under difficult conditions has left the same person with a slowness and seriousness that

interferes with . . . the capacity to feel any *normal* sense of joy and lightness . . . the overdeveloped strengths of patience and bearing up lead to *malfunctions* in responsibility and the capacity to take action.

Kurtz 1985: 18/1–18/2; my italics

This sort of entwining of the three models is the norm rather than the exception in contemporary body psychotherapy. It is also to be seen in the work of Wilhelm Reich, whom most body psychotherapists regard as the founder of the discipline. Reich frequently talks in terms of adjustment and correction, a 'concentrated attack' upon muscular and psychological rigidities (Reich 1983: 269); but he also draws very deeply on the Trauma/Discharge model. Reich seldom uses the actual term 'trauma'; but the theory of psychic/somatic defence as a means of 'holding' old pain is central to his thinking, as appears in the same passage from which I have just quoted: 'Affects had broken through somatically after the patient had relinquished his attitude of psychic defense', embodied in a stiff neck (Reich *ibid.*). For Reich, undischarged feeling is literally held in muscular tension, of which psychological tension is the functional equivalent. As well as his investment in both the Adjustment and the Trauma/Discharge models, however, Reich also struggles towards (as we might retrospectively see it) a process-centred view of body psychotherapy (see Totton 1998: 107–112 for a detailed analysis along these lines of one of Reich's case histories).

Clinical practice

I originally intended a very brief discussion of theory, mainly as a basis for talking about practice-oriented matters like training, supervision and ethics. However, I found it impossible to shortcut an exploration of theoretical issues. Naturally this reflects my own character structure; but I believe that it also represents the reality of the current state of body psychotherapy, where half-conscious and incompatible theories often underlie inconsistencies of practice.

We need to maintain a delicate balance here. It should be clear that, although there are arguments for some sort of cross-fertilisation between the three models I have just outlined, and although they often coexist in practice, as they did for Reich, they are in very straightforward ways incompatible or antipathetic. For example, if we work in terms of Adjustment, from the Process point of view we are interrupting the free unfolding of the client's themes and imposing a blueprint of our own. We may therefore also be retraumatising the client, in the terms of the Trauma/Discharge model, by repeating the sort of interference with their self-determination which they experienced in childhood. If we work from a Process viewpoint, on the other hand, both the Adjustment and the Trauma/Discharge models argue that we may be skating over deep problems and merely doodling around on the surface by following the client where they find it relatively easy to go. A Trauma/Discharge approach, in turn, can be seen from a Process point of view as backward-looking and static, and from an Adjustment point of view as failing to restore healthy functioning.

On the other hand, the existence of these clashes needs to be reconciled with the experiential fact that many or most body psychotherapists find that in practice, to a greater or lesser extent (and not always consciously), they can work creatively with all three models, moving between them from session to session or moment to moment as different qualities of material emerge. On the basis of this one might argue it is wrong to demand that clients be consistent, that they conform at all times to any one theory! This experienced usefulness of all three models suggests that there may be grounds for a new synthesis, for what one might call, in Einsteinian terms, a General Theory of Body Psychotherapy, within which the three models will fall into place as three facets of a whole.

In the absence of such a synthesis, though – and there are several ambitious people working on it at the moment, contributors to this volume among them – there is a noticeable tendency for body psychotherapists to look outside their own tradition for clinical guidance. Again, this tendency can take us away from, rather than towards, a genuine coherence. It is certainly valuable to draw on other forms of therapy for cross-fertilisation; but it is less helpful, and can even be destructive, to transplant external theories and models wholesale, as substitutes for the development of authentically body-psychotherapeutic models – that is, models which start out from a concept of functional bodymind unity.

I am thinking of the way in which, as I have already mentioned, a number of contemporary body psychotherapy approaches draw on object relations theory, attachment theory or ego psychology for their model of the therapeutic relationship. These models need, at the very least, to be deeply rethought in a body psychotherapy context: as I have argued above and elsewhere, Reich's work is founded on drive theory, from which he develops his own very specific version of object relations:

> There is but one desire which issues from the biopsychic unity of the person, namely the desire to discharge inner tensions, whether they pertain to the sphere of hunger or of sexuality. Hence, the first impulse of every creature must be a desire to establish contact with the outer world
>
> Reich 1972 [1945]: 271

What model we use makes a difference to clinical practice in several ways. For instance, object relations very strongly privileges the therapeutic relationship, since the 'drive to relate' is conceived of as fundamental; a similar statement can be made about attachment theory. In both cases, bodywork tends to become a means to an end of relating; rather than understanding relationship, as Reich does, as a consequence of libido (see Totton 1999: 180), libido virtually becomes a consequence of relationship. An ego-psychology model (see for example Johnson 1985; but Lowen is also strongly influenced by this approach) equally takes the emphasis away from libido and from the unconscious, privileging ego structure as the primary realm of therapy and encouraging qualities of independence and coping rather than surrender and relaxation. It is not that Reich is automatically to be taken as right on these matters; but the issues need to be argued through.

More generally, the introjection of conventional psychoanalytic values by body psychotherapists tends to inculcate a withdrawal from hands-on body-work. More than one body psychotherapist has set out to deepen their work through psychodynamic training or supervision, and ended up bowing to the conventional psychodynamic 'hands-off' approach – that 'physical touch disrupts neutrality' (Rosenberg 1995). It takes both strength of will and a clear grasp of the tenets of 'body psychoanalysis' to withstand the pressure of decades of anti-touch tradition.

However, to import a Humanistic model can impose on a Reichian foundation an equally foreign stratum of concepts. Although Reich's theories are a good deal more optimistic than more conventional psychoanalysis, they remain clearly psychoanalytic, and retain the analytic emphasis on infancy, repression, the unconscious, resistance and transference, for example. Genuinely Humanistic body psychotherapies are from a different tradition altogether; generally they base themselves on Rogers' belief in an innate organismic tendency to self-actualisation:

> Therapy is not a matter of doing something to the individual, or of inducing him to do something about himself [sic]. It is instead a matter of freeing him for normal growth and development.
>
> Rogers 1942: 29

They also tend to ignore or minimise questions of regression and transference, using some equivalent of Richard Mowbray's concept of SAFAA – Sufficient Available Functioning Adult Autonomy (Mowbray 1995) – to claim that body psychotherapy is a transaction not only between equals, as it certainly is, but between effective equals, which in my view it often is not. This is both a technical and an ethical issue.

Training

I have been trying to show how much body psychotherapy theory and clinical practice is unthought-out, a mixture of 'whatever works' improvisation, emergency fixes which become permanent fixtures, and deeply embedded tradition which has come adrift from its *raison d'etre*. This is even more the case for training, not just for body-oriented work, but throughout the psychotherapy field. Practices that originated in a quite different environment can be found fossilised within most contemporary trainings. Every trainer knows that there is never quite enough time to properly reconsider the training programme: the next batch of students is already at the door. This is as true in body psychotherapy as in any other branch of therapy; and perhaps there is little to be done about it. Recent pressures of professionalisation and regulation have superimposed a whole new layer of required topics of study onto the programmes of each training body.

Is there a specifically body-psychotherapeutic approach to training? One thing we can certainly say is that a body psychotherapy training *must be experientially grounded*. Despite everything I have written above about the role of theory in establishing coherent practice, in a training context theory and supervision will not do as central modalities: it is not primarily our heads that have to learn body psychotherapy, but our hearts, our guts and our hands. In many ways our heads have to learn to get out of the way, at least for the first couple of years of training; after that, they play a vital role in helping us make sense of all the new experiences we have had. Personally, I believe that many body psychotherapy trainings – partly for the usual reasons of defensiveness and 'professional credibility' – are over-intellectualised, sometimes in ways that create theoretical confusion rather than clarity.

A quick trawl of the Internet confirms that body psychotherapy trainings vary enormously. Some teach a self-contained system developed by their founder – for example Bodynamics, where the content of the first year basic training is: 'The seven developmental stages from in utero through age 12 . . . Characterological issues from each developmental stage that are commonly seen in therapy . . . Somatic techniques for working with these characterological themes . . . How to unblock natural developmental resources from childhood . . . Beginning body reading to assess character structure' (http://www.bodynamicusa.com/). The later years of training basically deepen and extend these themes.

In other words, the Bodynamics training teaches Bodynamics! And this 'exactly what it says on the tin' approach has a lot in its favour. Other trainings, however, aim to be integrative, often seeking to synthesise huge amounts and ranges of material for which a real theoretical integration does not yet exist. For example, Chiron tries to unify in its training not only a wide range of Reichian and post-Reichian approaches – Reich, Boadella, Boyesen, Lowen, Pierrakos, Rosenberg – but also Gestalt therapy, and both Freudian and Jungian analytic theory. Certainly no one has yet published an adequate synthesis of these systems; there must be a certain scepticism as to how far such a synthesis can be taught.

Even more ambitiously, and almost certainly unrealistically, the Australian College of Contemporary Somatic Psychotherapy aims to cover 'Freudian, Object Relations, Self Psychology, Intersubjectivity, Existential Phenomenology, Humanistic, Somatic (including contemporary approaches) &

Narrative . . . the philosophical bases of psychotherapy theory and practice . . . post-modern and post-structural analyses of psychotherapy theory and practice . . . human neurophysiology and neuroendocrinology and their relationship to personality development, stress states, trauma and illness . . . the integration of somatic and verbal skills in the therapeutic relationship using an integrated theoretical framework' (http://www.somaticpsychotherapy.com.au/prospectus.htm). Not infrequently, body-work trainings offer more random and bizarre 'integrations'; for example, the Hendricks Foundation Breathwork and Movement Training incorporates a slimmed-down version of Pilates.

Integration can be a response to external pressures from professional organisations or state requirements. It can also be a work in progress, repre-senting the personal voyage of the lead trainer(s); or, at worst, simply a ragbag summation of the various skills available from the training faculty. The most important thing is surely that at some point those responsible sit down and consider whether they can genuinely articulate the theoretical and practical relationship between the various components of their training. It is perfectly reasonable to teach, for example, a psychodynamic version and a Humanistic version of body psychotherapy on the same training; but one would need to state explicitly that each trainee must draw their own conclusions as to how or whether the two fit together.

Supervision

Supervision is an example of the embedded traditions of psychotherapy which I mentioned above: one that is certainly experienced as useful by a large majority of practitioners, but which – although much work has been done on improving supervision practice – has perhaps not been rethought from the ground up for many decades.

> The importance of supervision in order to ensure the efficacy of – par-ticularly novice – psychotherapists seems to be an article of faith for most counsellor and therapist educators. . . . However, there is absolutely no sound evidence that this is the case.
>
> McLennan 1999: 169

Lack of evidence notwithstanding, most practitioners experience supervision as a valuable – if sometimes challenging – support, bodyworkers as much as anyone else. But are there specific features of body-oriented supervision that need to be identified and thought through?

Most body psychotherapy supervision seems to focus primarily on the therapeutic relationship rather than on techniques of bodywork. This is the norm across the range of psychotherapies, and not surprisingly: the relation-ship, however we conceptualise it, is where all practitioners are most likely to lose their perspective and to need the external viewpoint of their supervisor. This is why many body psychotherapists can successfully receive supervision from someone outside their own training background – often from someone who does not themselves work with the body. Although many verbal psychotherapists are uncomfortable supervising bodywork, it is generally not too hard to find someone sympathetic, or at least neutral.

In a general way, therefore, body psychotherapy supervision can appropriately use the frameworks and conceptualisations of verbal psychotherapy. Having said this, though, there are some special features of body psychotherapy that could be thought of as making a difference. For example, much supervision works with the concept of parallel process, i.e. that important aspects of the therapeutic relationship will be reproduced in the supervisory relationship. How might this operate in a bodywork context? Certainly it will be helpful to have a supervisor who is alert to their own bodily process, and willing to bring it into the work.

Are there specific qualities to the therapeutic relationship in body psychotherapy – unique aspects to the transference and counter-transference situation? Certainly the use of touch, and even the explicit acknowledgement that there are two bodies in the room, tends to 'heat up' the transference relationship, whether in an oral, a masochistic, or whatever other developmental style. Beyond this, though, I have argued in another chapter of this volume that bodywork transference is always hysteric in nature; always, that is, involves experiencing the therapist as an invasive, abusive, and/or seductive external force onto which is also projected the threat of both pleasure and death from the client's own bodily impulses.

It is partly this primal, hysteric intensity of feeling, I suggest, which makes many verbal psychotherapists shy away from bodywork; and supervision needs to offer containment and support for these feelings. I have also argued in my earlier chapter that body psychotherapists themselves tend to cover up this intensity with false and simplistic notions of cure, adjustment, and adult-to-adult relationship. Supervision needs to be a place where these comforting falsehoods can be challenged.

For someone starting out as a body-oriented therapist, supervision also needs to offer continuous strong support for moving to the body. Our anti-touch social context combines with all the (quite appropriate) technical warnings of training to inhibit the fledgling therapist from touching too soon/too much/in the wrong way/in the wrong place – even from touching at all. Just as the analytic therapist has to surmount the threshold of 'couching' the client, the body therapist has to make the move from two people sitting and talking to two bodies interacting; and this can prove so difficult, anxious and awkward that they gradually withdraw from active bodywork altogether. The supervisor can play a very important role here in continuously keeping the option of bodywork in play.

For the more experienced practitioner, though, there is less need for a body psychotherapist as supervisor. My own experience of supervision is mainly with two non-body-oriented practitioners: an analytic psychotherapist and a Jungian analyst. The first of these had no personal experience of bodywork, but her position was that she trusted my clinical judgement and was prepared to accept that this was a part of what I did; however, she emphasised that she could not comment on that aspect of my work. This perhaps sounds more awkward than it proved in practice; our work together went very well over a period of some years. There were points at which a degree of uneasiness emerged on her part over some of the bodywork I did; but overall, I experienced this as a useful challenge rather than as undermining. If I had been a fledgling practitioner, though (although I don't think the supervisor would have taken me on in those circumstances), I could imagine being discouraged from doing much hands-on work, or even abandoning it entirely. The second supervisor, although not using bodywork himself, had been in body psychotherapy as a client; I felt that he was open to pretty much anything I might want to do, and in fact – as a supervisor rather than as a practitioner – was rather a daring bodyworker!

The other major function of supervision is to monitor the practitioner's ethical practice; and here also there are some issues specific to bodywork – enough to require a separate section.

Ethics

The ethical issue which is obviously specific to body psychotherapy is that of touch: the majority of verbal psychotherapists identify touch between therapist and client as either unethical or ethically dangerous *per se*. Some analytic therapists will not even shake hands with a client; rumour has it that certain analytic traditions specify the minimum distance which should be maintained between client and practitioner. Even when touch is acknowledged in mainstream therapy as ethically acceptable (e.g. Hunter and Struve 1997), it is comforting, hug-style touch which is being considered, not the skilled touch that we use therapeutically. Clearly, body psychotherapy has to hold the line on this, insisting that touch is in itself ethically neutral, and a wholly acceptable part of the therapeutic process. This means that there are specific ethical (and technical) issues that are not covered by the generally-agreed ethics of psychotherapy, and which we need to work out for ourselves.

I suggest that we can only do this successfully through acknowledging the real difficulty of working with touch. Certain body psychotherapists, operating out of both Humanistic and object relations perspectives, claim that non-sexual, nurturant touch (good) can quite simply be identified and separated out from erotic touch (bad). This is a profoundly non-Reichian reading of the human condition: the Freudian tradition in which he worked understands nurturance itself as an inescapably erotic act. To claim otherwise, I suggest, drastically over-simplifies the reality of the body psychotherapy situation, where an erotic charge always exists, consciously or unconsciously, and is simultaneously intensely 'good' and intensely 'bad', each on any number of levels. The body psychotherapist certainly needs to maintain a clarity around the charge of touch – and nurturance itself is as charged in its own way as eros! – but a real involvement and contactful presence is equally required. Simple pieties about refraining from sexual involvement do not really address the depth of the issue.

As Stanley Keleman says,

> . . . the deprivation of actual physical contact is so enormous in our culture that anything that touches us has such an enormous impact, and anyone practicing touch becomes a guru.
>
> Keleman 1992: 25

This necessarily places an enormous responsibility on body psychotherapists; a responsibility, for example, to resist every attempt by the client or anyone else to recode therapeutic touch in more familiar terms: as (simply) sexual, as parental or as medical. We also have a linked responsibility to resist and interrupt the gravitational pull of the cure. Cure as performance is a model that frequently tries to impose itself on the therapeutic encounter; and most particularly so in body psychotherapy, as part of the hystericisation I discuss in my earlier chapter – in line with Keleman's description, touch becomes a laying on of hands which commands the client (or in this context, patient) to rise up and walk. There is a tremendous emotional pay-off in this transaction for both therapist and client; but it is, of course, wholly untherapeutic, enacting rather than exploring positive transference/counter-transference, or, even worse, imposing a counter-transferential need for cure on an unwilling client. This point is, again, both technical and ethical; in neither context is it simple.

Culture and politics

I said at the beginning of this chapter that it would take major cultural and social shifts for body psychotherapy to become the dominant modality. We can also put this the other way around, and suggest that body psychotherapy could and should be aiming to contribute to such shifts – to helping our society move beyond the mind-body dichotomy. This entails a political role for psychotherapy, which for some people these days is anathema. Historically, however, it has been a commonplace (Totton 2000). Reich's own work was, of course, crusading; it would be fair to say, in fact, that actual psychotherapy was only one element, and at some points not the central one, in his project for social and cultural change (e.g. Reich 1983).

So do we believe that the issues over which Reich fought have been superseded, that the battles have been won? This position can hardly be sustained: although certain specific causes that he supported, like freely-available contraception and abortion, have to an extent been achieved in many Western countries, one cannot maintain that sexuality occupies a healthy and central place in our culture; or that women have achieved parity with men in all spheres; or that childbirth has become a positive and nontraumatic experience; or that society is organised through work democracy; or, of course, that the functional unity of body and mind is taught in every elementary school. Do we no longer consider that these goals are appropriate? Do we think that body psychotherapy can be separated cleanly from its socio-political context? Or have we simply given up?

Part of the current socio-political context, of course, is the more-or-less universal defeat of those progressive forces with which, in the 1960s and 1970s, many psychotherapists and body psychotherapists in particular strongly identified. Posthumously, Reich became an honorary member of the Growth Movement and an inspiration for many activists and revolutionaries. Many of those who are now well-established body psychotherapists were radicals in the 1970s, and we naturally share the sense of failure and hopelessness which the survivors of that project have had to absorb. Some of us, in fact, moved into the field of therapy in an attempt to grasp why revolution appeared to be impossible, to understand the social aspects of character that produce conformity and apathy, as in Thatcher and Reagan, Blair and Bush (Reich 1975). We took up with some relief the idea that working as body psychotherapists was in fact itself a form of radical political activity – that we were helping people change into freer, more creative, less conformist and less easily-manipulated characters.

There is certainly some truth in this comforting picture but does it let us off the hook as regards direct political involvement? Reich's own view was that psychological freedom in one individual is much like socialism in one country: in other words, impossible. Material social forces impinge inescapably on our personal experience: traumatic birth and childhood events, disturbances of nurturing, independence and creativity, sexual frustration and mislearning, conditioning to conform and obey, all deeply distort our capacity for 'love, work and knowledge' (Reich 1983: epigraph). Thus, psychotherapists who encounter the results of social repression are in the position of the two Zen monks walking by the river who encounter many drowning people being swept downstream. One wades in and starts trying to rescue them; but she sees her companion running upstream along the bank. 'Why don't you help me? Where are you off to?' 'I'm going to find the b-*-* who's throwing them in!'

Apart from his important and incisive work on the social origins and underpinning of fascism, Reich also set in motion a particular analysis of violence and alienation in human culture which identifies the motor force of this phenomena, very concretely, as the suppression of emotional and organismic spontaneity in infancy and childhood. Reich predicted – and considerable supporting evidence has since been amassed (Prescott 1975; DeMeo

1998) – some simple linear relationships: the degree of physical affection given to infants will correlate negatively with the degree of adult violence in the society, as will the freedom of sexual expression and satisfaction. If there is any truth in this theory then surely body therapists, and their organisations, have a responsibility to campaign loudly and clearly for the social changes which the theory implies.

Reich proposed that self-regulating cooperative anarchism was essentially inherent in human beings; he found it, so to speak, in the body and body psychotherapy was his tool for uncovering it. I tend to agree with him but then anarchism is my own political position. Looking objectively at the bodywork field, there seem to be representatives of most political positions; right-wing libertarianism is possibly as common as anything else. There is also a tendency still within body psychotherapy – regrettably inherited from Reich – to pathologise homosexuality and other 'deviant' sexual behaviour. So one must be cautious as to what politics one projects onto body psychotherapy! However, what I would insist on is the appropriateness, even the necessity, of discussing the political and social context and implications of our work, both with each other, and also not infrequently with our clients (Samuels 1993).

Professional organisation

We must each come to our own decisions about the relationship between our position as bodyworkers and our place in the broader culture. But as body psychotherapists perhaps we have an unavoidable responsibility in one specific political arena: that of professional organisation. This is a space where we encounter issues of hierarchy, control, authenticity and self-regulation: issues that would have meant a great deal to Reich, who went to prison rather than allow his work to be controlled by the state.

One would like to imagine that body psychotherapists have a position to take here. As Bob Dylan might have said, even the Chair of the United Kingdom Council for Psychotherapy sometimes must have to stand naked; and body psychotherapy heightens and sustains our awareness of our naked existence as embodied and emotional beings, an awareness which should perhaps in theory lessen our susceptibility to the hypnosis of formalism and hierarchy. Unfortunately there is little evidence that this is in fact the case.

Reich claimed from early in his career to have found that, as the therapy progressed, his clients became less obedient to authority, less willing to work according to dictated rhythms and structures, less willing to conform to stereotypes. Looking at the relationship of most body psychotherapists to the regulation of psychotherapy, one wonders whether Reich was mistaken – or whether some aspects of character are no longer being challenged in clinical practice, including training therapy. Veterans in various schools of psychotherapy have repeatedly complained over the years that the new trainees are more conventional and 'normalised' than in their day, as the practice of each form of therapy becomes a more normal career path. Can this finally have happened even to body psychotherapy?

Whether or not this is the case, there are specific dangers to body psychotherapists from the current drive to regulation; dangers even beyond those which in my view are entailed for the entire psychotherapy community (Totton 1999). As I have suggested above, in order to appear sufficiently mainstream and respectable, body psychotherapy engages in a subtle, only partly-conscious distortion and concealment of its real, radical approach to therapy and to life, in order to 'pass' as registrable and regulatable. A registered body psychotherapy, it is arguable, may be no body psychotherapy at all.

Conclusion

> Somatics as a recognised field of research may presently be in a disordered state, but fortunately the result is creativity rather than confusion.
>
> Grossinger 1995: 205

As I said at the outset of this chapter, my intention has been to 'rattle and shake' an initial thesis that body psychotherapy needs to strengthen its coherence as a therapeutic approach, testing that thesis against a number of alternative positions. As part of that process, I may appear to have been constantly shifting my ground in a mischievous and unhelpful way – at one moment claiming that body psychotherapy needs to be more coherent, at another that it should recognise its significant internal differences and contradictions, at yet another that it does not really exist. I also maintain at one point that body psychotherapy is not primarily an intellectual activity, and at other points that it is essential for us to grasp our underlying theory and its implications for practice. Can these diverse statements be reconciled?

Well, not entirely. I believe that the contradictions and ambivalences are not just my own but are inherent in the current situation of body psychotherapy; that they need to be taken on and worked through in order to achieve fruitful future development. We do not all need to agree in order to move forward; in fact, the opposite may well be the case – that a number of dissenting voices represent a healthier state of affairs than a false monotheism. What is not helpful, I suggest, is to fudge, to make do, to adapt to external pressures, to dissemble for the sake of respectability. I have been trying to bring out into the open our existing incoherences in the belief that any authentic coherence will follow from recognising and understanding them.

References

Bermudez, J. L., Marcel, A. and Eilan, N. (Eds) *The Body and the Self*. London: MIT Press 1995

Boadella, D. 'Embodiment in the Therapeutic Relationship'. *International Journal of Psychotherapy* 1997; 2(1): 31–44

Bracken, P. J. and Petty, C. (Eds) *Re-thinking the Trauma of War*. London: Free Association Books 1998

Cataldi, S. L. *Emotion, Depth and Flesh: A Study of Sensitive Space. Reflections on Merleau-Ponty's Philosophy of Embodiment*. Albany, NY: State University of New York Press 1993

Damasio, A. *Descartes' Error: Emotion, Reason and the Human Brain*. London: Papermac 1996

Damasio, A. *The Feeling of What Happens: Body, Emotion and the Making of Consciousness*. London: Heinemann 2000

DeMeo, J. *Saharasia: The 4000 BCE Origins of Child Abuse, Sex-Repression, Warfare and Social Violence in the Deserts of the Old World*. Ashland, OR: Natural Energy Works 1998

Feltham, C. 'Challenging the Core Theoretical Model'. In House, R. and Totton, N. (Eds) *Implausible Professions: Arguments for Pluralism and Autonomy in Psychotherapy and Counselling*. Manchester: PCCS 1997: 117–128

Feltham, C. 'Against and Beyond Core Theoretical Models'. In Feltham, C. (Ed.) *Controversies in Psychotherapy and Counselling*. London: Sage 1999: 182–193

Freud, S. and Breuer, J. *Studies on Hysteria*. London: Penguin Freud Library 1991 [1893–1895]

Grossinger, R. *Planet Medicine: Modalities*. Berkeley, CA: North Atlantic Books 1995

Hunter, M. and Struve, J. *The Ethical Use of Touch in Psychotherapy*. London: Sage 1997

Johnson, S. M. *Characterological Transformation*. New York: W. W. Norton 1985

Keleman, S. 'Professional Colloquium'. In Grossinger, R. (Ed.) *Ecology and Consciousness*. Richmond, CA: North Atlantic Books 1992: 16–23

Kurtz, R. *Hakomi Therapy*. Self-published 1985.

Kurtz, R. *Body-Centered Psychotherapy: The Hakomi Method*. Mendocino, CA: Life Rhythm 1990

Lakoff, G. and Johnson, M. *Philosophy in the Flesh: Embodied Mind and its Challenges to Western Thought*. New York: Basic Books 1999

Levine, P. A. *Waking the Tiger. Healing Trauma*. Berkeley, CA: North Atlantic Books 1997.

Leys, R. *Trauma: A Genealogy*. Chicago: University of Chicago Press, 2000

Lowen, A. *Bioenergetics*. Harmondsworth: Penguin 1976.

McLennan, J. 'Becoming an Effective Psychotherapist or Counsellor: Are Training and Supervision Necessary?' In Feltham, C. (Ed.) *Controversies in Psychotherapy and Counselling*. London: Sage 1999: 164–73.

Mair, K. 'The Myth of Therapist Expertise'. In Dryden, W. and Feltham, C. (Eds.) *Psychotherapy and Its Discontents*. Buckingham: Open University Press 1992: 135–168

Mindell, A. *Working with the Dreaming Body*. London: Arkana 1985

Mindell, A. *River's Way: The Process Science of the Dreambody*. London: Arkana 1989

Mowbray, R. *The Case Against Psychotherapy Registration*. London: Trans Marginal Press 1995

Prescott, J. 'Body Pleasure and the Origins of Violence'. *Bulletin of Atomic Scientists* 1975; November, 10–20.

Reich, W. *Character Analysis*. New York: Touchstone 1972 [1945]

Reich, W. *The Mass Psychology of Fascism*. London: Pelican 1975 [1944]

Reich, W. *Children of the Future: On the Prevention of Sexual Pathology*. New York: Farrar, Straus & Giroux 1983

Rogers, C. *Counselling and Psychotherapy*. Boston: Houghton-Mifflin 1942

Rosenberg, V. 'On Touching a Patient'. *British Journal of Psychotherapy* 1995; 12 (1): 29–36.

Rothschild, B. *The Body Remembers: The Psychophysiology of Trauma and Trauma Treatment*. New York: W. W. Norton 2000

Samuels, A. *The Plural Psyche: Personality, Morality and the Father*. London: Routledge 1989

Samuels, A. *The Political Psyche*, London: Routledge 1993

Seligman, M. E. P. 'The Effectiveness of Psychotherapy: The Consumer Reports Study'. *American Psychologist* 1995; 50(12): 965–974

Schore, A. N. *Affect Regulation and the Origin of the Self: The Neurobiology of Emotional Development*. Mahwah, NJ: Lawrence Erlbaum Associates Inc 1994.

Stern, D. *The Interpersonal World of the Infant*. New York: Basic Books 1985

Taylor, G. J. 'Psychosomatics and Self-regulation' In Barron, J. W., Eagle, M. N. and Wolitzky, D. L. (Eds) *Interface of Psychoanalysis and Psychology*. Washington, DC: American Psychological Association 1992: 464–488

Totton, N. *The Water in the Glass: Body and Mind in Psychoanalysis*. London: Rebus 1998

Totton, N. 'The Baby and the Bathwater: "Professionalisation" in Psychotherapy and Counselling'. *British Journal of Guidance and Counselling* 1999; 27(3): 313–324

Totton, N. *Psychotherapy and Politics*. London: Sage 2000

Winnicott, D. W. 'Mind and its Relation to Psyche-Soma' In *Through Paediatrics to Psychoanalysis: Collected Papers*. London: Karnac 1987 [1949]: 243–254

Young, C. and Heller, M. 'The Scientific "What!" of Psychotherapy: Psychotherapy is a Craft, Not a Science'. *International Journal of Psychotherapy* 2000; 5(2): 113–131

Afterword

Tree Staunton

One of the major 'splits' in both theory and clinical application that has dogged body psychotherapy – namely the interplay between *body* and *relationship* – is well-represented in this book. As has been argued here, this should be a concern of all psychotherapies; the aim of all of our endeavours can be seen as bringing these two into a workable relationship with each other.

In a recent article (*Energy & Character*, Vol 31, 2) David Boadella argues that the recent developments in 'Body–Analytic' psychotherapy are raising false dichotomies between *relationship* – traditionally seen as the analytic domain – and *energy* – the foundation of body-oriented psychotherapies.[1] However, this 'split' has been present since Reich; we have seen how neo-Reichians such as Pierrakos, Kurtz and Boyesen privileged the internal body–mind connection over the unconscious relationship dynamics; whilst Lowen attempted to retain the psychoanalytic aspect of Reich's work,[1] (*'There is no analysis in Bioenergetic analysis'*), the strongest part of the teaching and experience carried forward in Bioenergetics remains the body analysis and exercises: the 'Adjustment' model in Nick Totton's formulation.

This 'splitting of energy and contact' is being consciously addressed by many in the field of body psychotherapy today. Post-Boyesen biodynamic methods attempt to synthesise Boyesen's depth and commitment to the organic process with a conscious working through of the relationship dynamics; the Chiron centre training now has an intentional focus on the integration of 'energy and contact'; all the contributors to this volume have shown how their relationship to and through the body informs their work; whilst my own work, for example, appears to have strong Jungian and psychodynamic influences, in practice 'energetics' always forms the underlying basis. Whether we conceive of the body as the carrier of a personal mythology or as the broken container which needs to be repaired, once trained in 'somatic resonance' and 'energetic perception' it is hard for body-oriented psychotherapists to relinquish these aspects of the process, regardless of other frames of reference they may use.

In a sense we have become part of the problem; we have played into a polarisation – Reich's principle of functional identity of body and mind versus dualistic thinking in which body and mind are dichotomised – and perhaps we should rather be insisting that *all* psychotherapies need to be body psychotherapy. It seems that the integration of object relations and psychodynamic principles, as well as the recent surge of interest in neuroscience, begin to open up this third way: *the body and mind are interrelated*; sometimes they mirror each other, sometimes they polarise; sometimes the body occupies the Shadow, forming a particular 'negative object' for the mind; different aspects of the self are expressed in different parts of the body, and a further dimension is added when we think in terms of the body 'housing' the soul. We must all, as mature therapists, turn towards other traditions and models to see what they can offer to our practice.

Nick Totton's final chapter raises the question whether, in fact, we are 'taught' to be psychotherapists by undergoing a training, or if the synthesis of theory and practice occurs over time within the therapist themselves. Perhaps it is a process of becoming. We *are* all those therapists, clients, teachers and students with whom we have worked. Advancing theory and practice necessitates integration. There is no going back; we owe our practice today to all those teachers, healers and therapists in every tradition who have gone before us.

If you have not lived through something it is not true.

Kabir

Note

1 'There is no analysis in bioenergetic analysis' Sandor Kirsch – unpublished manuscript

Appendix: Training in body psychotherapy

The training institutes listed below are contacts for Body Psychotherapy in the various countries; the list is not exhaustive and the trainings on it are not necessarily recommended or endorsed by the authors of this book. Some of them are accredited by various organisations using different systems. The United Kingdom Council for Psychotherapy (UKCP) in Britain accredits all psychotherapists and the European Association for Body Psychotherapy (EABP) is primarily an accrediting organisation for European Body Psychotherapists. A strong debate is continuing both in Britain and abroad on the subject of accreditation, with arguments for and against. It is not the focus to discuss this here, but rather to provide contacts for further exploration of this approach.

Australia

The Australian College of Contemporary Somatic Psychotherapy (ACCSP)
Zoeros Melbourne, 201 Fitzroy Street, St Kilda 3182. Tel: +61-3–9537–2111
Zoeros Sydney, 223A Glebe Point Road, Glebe 2037. Tel: +61-2–9552–1633
Email: ACCSP@somaticpsychotherapy.com.au
Training Director: Jeff Barlow, PO Box 1240, Healesville, Vic 3777, Australia
Email: Jeff_Barlow@SomaticPsychotherapy.com.au

Austria

Arbeitskreis für Emotionale Reintegration (Accredited)
Praterstraße 9, Vienna, A-1020
Dr Peter Bolen: +43-1-810-8558

Verein für Integrative Biodynamik
Matznergasse 8/34, Vienna, A-1140
Wolfgang Hutter: +43-1-98-898234

Canada

Bodynamic Institute Inc.
3026 Arbutus St. (2nd Floor), Vancouver, British Columbia V6J 4P7
Tel: (604) 878 7660; Fax: (604) 734 3938
Email: bodynamcan@telus.net
Website: www.bodynamiccanada.com

Denmark

Bodynamic International (EABP Accredited)
Struenseegade 13A, Copenhagen, DK-2200 N
Lennart Ollars: +45-9854-6160
Website: www.bodynamic.dk/

Finland

Finnish Institute of Character Analytic Vegetotherapy
Kalevankatu 33 B 8, F1-00100 Helsinki
Markku Välimäki: +358-9-22430095

France

Ecole Européanne de Psychotherapie Socio- et Somato-Analytique
Place de Halles 20, Strasbourg, F-67000
Richard Meyer: +33-388-224692

Ecole de Psychologie Biodynamic (EABP Accredited)
Evolutive 999 Ave Pont Trinquat, Montpelier, F-34000
Christiane Lewin: +33-467-22-4050

Germany

European School of Biodynamic Psychology (Accredited)
Hüxterdamm 22, Lübeck, D-23552
Hanskim Voet: +49-451-70041

Arbeitsgemeinschaft Funktionelle Entspannung
Killingerstrasse 66, Erlangen, D-91056
Ursula Günther: +49-030-793-3391

Aus- und Fortbildungszentrum Transformative Körperpsychotherapie
  (EABP Accredited)
NassanischeStraße 59, Berlin, D-10717
Bettina Schroeter: +49-30-211-9862

Core Energetic Institute
Postfach 143206, Essen, D-45262
Siegrmar Gerken: +1-707-937-2673

Hakomi Institute of Europe
Friedrich-Eber-Anlage 9, Heidelberg, D-69121
Martin Schuhmeister: +49-6221-166560

Institut für Körper-psychotherapie Berlin
Cosimaplatz 2, Berlin, D-12159
Manfred Thielen: +49-30-851-9906

Institut für Somatische Psychotherapie
Igelstr. 1, Iserlohn, D-58644
Peter Anders-Hoepgen: +49-2374-850-800

Körpertherapie Integrativ Training
Hermannstr. 48, Berlin, D-12049
Volker Knapp-Diederichs: +49-30-436-73089

Zentrum für Integrative Körper- und Psychotherapie (EABP Accredited)
Paulinallee 32, Hamburg, D-20259
Michael Meiffert: +49-40-435-077

Zentrum för Integrative Körpertherapie und Humanistische Psychologie
   (EABP Accredited)
Bachmannstr. 2–4, Frankfurt D-60488
Gustl Marlock: +49-69-789-5701

Greece

E.I.N.A. – Greek School of Training in Vegetotherapy and Character
   Analysis (EABP Accredited)
3 Megalou Spiloeu Street, Ambelokipi, Athens, GR-11522
Clorinda Lubrano: +30-1-641-0160

Italy

European School of Functional Psychotherapy (SIF) (EABP Accredited)
Salia San Filippo 1/c, Napoli, I-80122
Luciano Rispoli: +39-081-66-0284

Italian School of Biosystemic Psychotherapy (EABP Accredited)
Pzza S.M. Liberatrice, 18, Rome I-00153
Jerome Liss: +39-06-574-4903

Ireland

The Centre for Biodynamic and Integrative Psychotherapy
Tracht Beach
Kinvara
County Galway
(+35-3-9637-192)
Email: cbip@eircom.net

Netherlands

International Academy for Bodytherapy (IAB) (EABP Accredited)
Stationsstraat 48, Molenhoek, NL-6584 AW
Hans Krens: +31-24-358-2934

Nederlands Instituut voor Biorelease & Biodynamische Psychologie
Brouwersgracht 266, Amsterdam, NL-1013 HG
Cora Slieker: +31-20-625-4084

Vereniging voor Unitieve Psychotherapie (EABP Accredited)
Hugo de Grootkade 86W, Amsterdam NL-1052 LX
Bregyta Rooney: +31-20-6810-596

Spain

Escuela Española de Terepia Reichiana (ES.TE.R.)
c/ Republica de Guinea Ecuatorial 4 1:c Valencia, E-46022
Xavier Serrano: +34-6-372-7310

Associació Catalana Teràpia d'Integratió Psico-corporal
A Sant Elies 31-33, Esc B 4t, 3a, Barcelona, E-08006
Marc Costa: +34-3-209-5540

Switzerland

International Institute for Biosynthesis
Benzenrüti 6, Heiden, Switzerland CH-9410
Sylvia Boadella: +41-71-891-6855

Institut für Körpercentrierte Psychotherapie
Kanzleistrasse 17, Zürich, CH-8004
Yvonne Maurer: +41-1-242-2930

United Kingdom

Cambridge Body Psychotherapy Training
Training Office: 8 Wetenhall Road, Cambridge CB1 3AG
Tel: 01223 214658
Email: gillwestland@cbpc.org.uk
Website: www.cbpc.org.uk

Chiron Centre for Body Psychotherapy (UKCP Accredited)
26 Eaton Rise, Ealing, London W5 2ER
Tel and fax: 020 8997 5219
Email: chiron@chiron.org
Website: www.chiron.org

Embodied-Relational Therapy (one year training)
Contact: Nick Totton, 86 Burley Wood Crescent, Leeds,
   West Yorks LS4 2QL
Tel: 0845 345 8597
Email: nick@erthworks.co.uk
Website: www.erthworks.co.uk

Karuna Institute (UKCP Accredited)
Natsworthy Manor, Natsworthy, Widecombe in the Moor, Devon, TQ13 7TR
Tel: 01647 221 457
Email: office@karuna-institute.co.uk
Website: www.karuna-institute.co.uk

London School of Biodynamic Psychotherapy (UKCP Accredited)
Willow Cottage, off Wokingham Road, Hurst, Berkshire RG10 0RU
Tel: 07000 794 725
Email: enquiries@lsbp.org.uk
Website: www.lsbp.org.uk

USA

Arny and Amy Mindell
2305 NW Kearney number 320
Portland, OR 97210
Tel: (503) 796-0779

Bodynamic Institute USA
P.O. Box 1708, Novato, CA 94948
Tel: (415) 258-4805
Website: www.bodynamicusa.com

California Institute for Integral Studies
Somatic Psychology Department, Box Cb, 765 Ashbury Street,
   San Francisco, CA 94117
Founded by Don Johnson

Hakomi Integrated Somatics
The Hakomi Somatics Institute: Sensorimotor Psychotherapy
P.O. Box 19438, Boulder, CO 80308
Tel: (303) 447-3290/(800) 860-9258; Fax: (303)-402-0862
Email: robin@hakomisomatics.com
Website: www.hakomisomatics.com
Founder and Director: Pat Ogden, MA

The Braddock Body Process
P.O. Box 260123, Lakewood, CO 80226-0123
Tel: (303) 985-7310; Fax: (303) 989-9813
Founded and directed by Carolyn Braddock

The Hendricks Institute
1187 Coast Village Road, Suite 109, Santa Barbara, CA 93108-2794
Tel: (805) 565-1870/(800) 688-0772
Founded and directed by Kathlyn and Gay Hendricks

The Moving Cycle Institute (formerly the Moving Centre)
P.O. Box 19892, Boulder, CO 80308
Tel: (303) 415-3774; Fax: (303) 413-9003
Founded and directed by Christine Caldwell, PHD, LPC, ADTR

The Naropa Institute
Somatic Psychology Department, 2130 Arapahoe Ave., Boulder, CO 80302
Tel: (303) 444-0202/(303) 546-5284
Founded by Christine Caldwell

The Pesso-Boyden Institute
Lake Shore Drive, Franklin, N.H.
Tel: (603) 934-5548
Founded and directed by Al and Diana Pesso

The Rancho-Strozzi Institute
4101 Middle Two Rock Road, Peraluma, CA 94952
Tel: (707) 778-6505; Fax: (707) 778-0306
Founded and directed by Richard Strozzi Heckler

The Rosenberg-Rand Institute, Inc.
1551 Ocean Avenue, Suite 230, Santa Monica, CA 90401
Tel: (310) 394-0147

The Rubenfeld Centre
115 Waverley Place, New York, NY 10011
Tel: (212) 254-5100
Email: rubenfeld@aol.com
Founded and directed by Llana Rubenfeld

Yugoslavia

TePsynthesis (YU Training School of BodySynthesis)
Joce Jovanovica 7, Belgrade, YU-11040
Ljiljana Klisic: +38-111-667357

Index

Note: page numbers in *italics* refer to diagrams.